MUSTANG PERFORMANCE 2
HANDBOOK

Chassis and suspension modifications for street, drag and road racing use. Includes suspension geometry, chassis setup, brakes, tires and wheels, testing and tuning. Covers all Models of the Ford Mustang, 1979 to Present.

WILLIAM R. MATHIS

HPBooks

HPBooks
Published by
The Berkley Publishing Group
A division of Penguin Putnam Inc.
375 Hudson Street
New York, New York 10014

© 1995 William Mathis
19 18 17 16 15 14 13 12 11 10
Printed in the U.S.A.
First edition January 1995

Visit our website at www.penguinputnam.com

Library of Congress Cataloging-in-Publication Data

Mathis, William R.
    Mustang performance handbook 2: chassis and suspension
modifications for street, strip, and road racing use for all models
of the Ford Mustang, 1979 to present / William R. Mathis.
          p.   cm.
    Includes index.
    ISBN 1-55788-202-9 (pbk.)
    1. Mustang automobile—Motors—Modification. 2. Mustang
automobile—Performance.   I. Title. II. Title: Mustang performance
handbook two.
TL215.M8M313   1995   94-24719
629.222′2—dc20   CIP

Book Design & Production by Bird Studios
Front cover photo courtesy *Mustang & Fords* magazine.
Interior photos by William Mathis unless otherwise noted

CONTENTS

INTRODUCTION

The third-generation Mustang is arguably the most popular high–performance car on the road today. It is the darling of the enthusiast press, and a great deal of ink (including several entire magazines) has been devoted to the 5.0 liter Mustang. Many a former "Brand X" driver has transferred his loyalty to the Blue Oval because of the Mustang's low cost and performance potential. I say "potential," because although a street-stock Mustang has okay handling and V8 power, it still requires quite a few modifications to realize its full potential, especially where the chassis and suspension are concerned. The Mustang is also easily modified for competitive racing use, such as for autocrossing, drag racing and road racing, which makes it even more popular.

There are plenty of shops that will build a trick Mustang for any of these applications. All you have to do is bring money—usually several suitcases' worth. The modifications presented in this book are provided to give the average racer with average means sufficient information to build a competitive race car without having to pledge his first-born. It is also intended for performance buffs with better-than-average mechanical skills who want to build the ultimate street machine without getting a divorce first.

There is an enormous selection of aftermarket parts available to modify the Mustang for these uses, and most of them are excellent. Many of the modifications presented in the following pages utilize these off-the-shelf parts. However, the cost of the parts to achieve a high level of success at the drag strip or on a road course is beyond the reach of most amateur racers. When you add on the cost to assemble or modify the car so that the parts actually work, the price generally becomes prohibitive.

With this in mind, I've included detailed drawings that allow you to fabricate most of the suspension and chassis parts required for specific types of handling. Although the fabrication drawings are referred to in the text, they are located at the end of each chapter, in sequence. Also, please note that the dimensions in the drawings are either in degrees or inches. Many of these parts, as well as most of the other modifications, have been thoroughly tested on a prototype Mustang I built

called the *Slot Car Mustang*. Some of the parts are difficult to make and require above-average skills and tools, but at least you'll have a choice. You could purchase a G-load brace, for example, or fabricate one yourself for half the price. If you are inclined to make the parts yourself, take your time. It's better to finish 30 minutes later than to hit the bank account for the purchase of the parts you screwed up.

This book is devoted to modifying and/or building a Mustang chassis and suspension for high performance. There are complete sections for building a chassis and suspension for street/autocross, drag racing or road racing. To avoid duplication, steps that are identical in different chapters are referenced to the preceding chapter where the procedures were first defined. It is very important to read the entire chapter and the referenced steps in other chapters before attempting to make the modifications. Be sure you understand the procedures and you have the correct tools and parts before you start. This is extremely important! Many of the modifications shown in this book are beyond the ability of a casual armchair mechanic. Any procedures beyond your mechanical abilities should be either avoided or farmed out to a competent professional. For example, if you are not a proficient welder, then please don't attempt to weld up a roll cage designed to protect you during a high-speed crash. Chances are it won't.

Be sure you understand the dangers and safety procedures associated with performing these modifications. If you don't understand the need to use jackstands to support your car when working underneath or the dangers of dealing with a compressed coil spring, then leave the modifications to a competent mechanic and enjoy the driving part.

For those of you who have limited mechanical skills and handling needs, you can significantly improve the ride and handling performance of your Mustang by using any of the recommended bolt-on suspension kits I list in Chapter 7. As the installation of these components is pretty straightforward, and most come with good instructions from the manufacturer, I've limited my discussion of these kits to just listing what they are all about. ∎

GETTING STARTED

Blasting around an SCCA road course, tripping the lights with yet another record E.T. or running down your favorite mountain road with supreme handling and control, requires significant changes to a Mustang. Unfortunately, these changes can radically alter the streetability and ride quality of a daily-driven car. You must know what you intend to use the car for, and what it is you are willing to put up with if you drive your Mustang to work every day. The intended use will greatly affect the level of modifications you can perform. There are also a variety of other factors and considerations.

Collector Value

If you have a rare car such as an SVO, ASC McLaren, '84 1/2 Anniversary Mustang, Saleen, SAAC, '93 Cobra or the '79 Indy Pace Car, then be aware modifications will generally have a significant negative impact on their value. I know it may be hard to imagine how anyone could find a stock Mustang more appealing than your 11-second doorslammer. However, a Sunday's outing to one of the many car shows will set you straight. Some original-equipment rare Mustangs with anemic stock engines fetch premiums that one could almost retire on. A car with a supercharged 800 hp engine and the trick four–link Pro Stock suspension will probably only sell for a small portion of the original price. Think about it before you begin.

The 1994 Cobra Mustang is the latest hot rod from the Ford SVT group. It continues the performance heritage of the Mustang, with improved chassis, brakes and overall handling, but there's still room for improvement.

The SVO was the finest-handling Mustang ever mass produced by Ford. Large four-wheel disc brakes, Koni shocks and a turbocharged 2.3L inline four make this a unique and valuable collector car. If you own one of these, you probably should think long and hard before making modifications that could affect its value.

Cost

Every hot rodder has read the testimonials in various high–performance magazines boasting about the 11-second racer with only "$814.27" invested in it. If you believe this then you probably also own several acres of beautiful dry swamp land in the Florida everglades.

You probably will never recover what you spend on your machine. Although this book is written for the average person with average means, somehow we always end up spending more than we expect to. Anyone who believes they will be able to sell their car and recover all the bucks spent on those neat go–fast modifications is probably half a bubble off. Unless you have plans to become someone famous, you should recognize that the modifications you do to your car are largely for your own enjoyment.

Streetability

Most of the modifications in this book will have a significant impact on the performance of your daily-driven Mustang. You must carefully weigh the

Sandra Rumney stands proudly next to her rare 1988 ASC McLaren convertible Mustang. Built in very limited quantities, the ASC McLaren was popular as the only convertible Mustang available when it was first introduced.

To celebrate the 20th anniversary of the Mustang, Ford built approximately 5,000 of these cars with a unique red interior, white paint and some very costly GT-350 stripes.

consequences before you invest the time and money into a car you hate to drive. One of the many lessons I learned the hard way was racing the same car I needed to drive to work everyday. The ride quality of your car may suffer. To the hard-core autocrosser (Conehead), this is not a consideration. However, if this is your only means of transportation

or you have trouble with rough, bumpy rides, then limit your modifications to those areas that don't affect ride quality. This means no short, stiff springs or race-only shocks. Many of the basic chassis modifications in Chapter 3 and elsewhere can be made to your car to produce a major improvement in handling without a bone-jarring ride. Unfortunately, for

drag racers, the inherent limitations of the Mustang's suspension will require modifications that cause a noticeable reduction in ride quality, so you do not have much choice.

Local Laws—Know the laws of your state and city concerning vehicle modifications. Many states have ride height requirements and tread depth

The Saleen Mustang, first introduced in 1984 by Steve Saleen, featured improved aerodynamics, four-wheel disc brakes, and a bone-jarring suspension. These cars are all numbered and considered to be good investments.

specifications. The ride height requirements are generally not going to be affected by the modifications presented in this book. However, some unnamed state on the left coast has been known to harass hot rodders for this, so be aware.

Lack of tread depth and D.O.T. approval are two of the most common items your friendly policeman will want to talk to you about. For the road racers and autocrossers, the selection of D.O.T.-approved sticky tires is only limited by one's bank account. For the straight-line group the M&H street slicks or Hoosier "Quicktimes" are the only choice. Unfortunately, the price one pays for the sticky rubber is repaid in its typically short tread life.

Drag Racing—Changes to your chassis for the best quarter-mile launch will make your car considerably less stable in ordinary driving. The drag racing modifications presented in this book require removal or substitution of certain suspension components. Don't kid yourself about this. Changes to your chassis so that it will go in a straight line, work the opposite effect on your car's ability to negotiate a turn, especially a sudden turn in a panic situation. If you're setting your car up for serious drag

This collection of Auburn differential pieces is the result of rushing a project. Brain failure when installing a new assembly (forgot to insert the spider gear pin) can be an expensive lesson. Take your time!

racing, then it would probably be safer to keep it on the trailer between passes down the drag strip. It is very important that you remember this limitation.

SELECTING PARTS

There are multiple levels of modifications for the suspension and chassis. Each modification requires you to make choices about the extent of changes you are willing to commit to. If money is not a factor, then buy the new stuff when available; however, you can build the same car with parts from the salvage yard. Some of the parts are no longer serviced by Ford and must be purchased from salvage anyway. With few exceptions, most of the factory-backed cars have used salvage parts on their race cars.

Getting Prepared

Before you start work on your car, give it a thorough bath. This means outside, under the hood, underneath, inside the wheelwells, and all chassis components—especially chassis components. Because the modifications in this book require precise layouts, it is very important to have clean surfaces to work on. Additionally, high temperatures under the hood and around the exhaust systems (especially the catalytic converters) can ignite grease and oil. Coin-operated high-pressure car washes, along with a few gallons of grease cutter, are the best way to go.

Squareness

One of the most important points to address prior to venturing into any modification is to make sure your car is square. If your car has been involved in a crash or has a lot of miles on it, it is extremely important that you have it checked. Even if it has never been bent, have it checked! When I built the original *Slot Car Mustang* prototype, the frame was found to be misaligned slightly from the factory. This was a new car with only 125 miles on it. If the frame is misaligned when you weld the various braces in place, you will have a very stiff car that will require your complete and undivided attention when you dive into that first corner or drop the hammer on your 500 hp street machine. Take your

Non-D.O.T.-approved slicks have no place on the street and will only serve to attract the attention of the police.

car to a reputable frame shop with a quality laser frame machine and someone who knows how to operate it. When buying salvage parts, always ask to see the car they came from. Use common sense and don't buy parts that may have been affected by a crash (like control arms from a front end crash). This book was written for the racers without the means to have a competent major shop do the work. Don't be afraid of good, low-mileage salvage parts. They will work just as well on the track as new parts. In other words, don't let new part prices keep you in the back of the pack.

Rule Books

If you are going to run in a specific racing class, get a rule book first. Read the rules for allowed and disallowed modifications. Go to the races and check out race cars in your class. Look for subtle changes, take good notes and always be a good listener, especially to the conversation of the mechanics. The race classes available to the Mustang are hotly contested, with new tricks and technology evolving at every event. Although the modifications that follow will provide the necessary basics to establish a solid race car, it is very important to visit as many racing events as possible. Take along a simple 35mm camera (preferably with a built-in flash) loaded with 200-speed film, and cruise the pits where your competitors are parked. Take as many pictures as possible of the suspension setups on every car in the class. Then, take the same set of pictures of a completely stock Mustang. Try to take the pictures from the same angle on each car for comparison purposes. Some racers and enthusiasts are glad to allow you to take pictures and will explain what they are doing; others don't respond quite so kindly, so be prepared.

When you have developed the pictures, lay them all out on a table with the pictures of each separate car lined up in a row and aligned so the pictures taken from the same locations and angles can be compared. The rows of pictures should be arranged with the stock Mustang at the top followed by the fastest to slowest cars. Carefully examine the pictures and look for subtle changes to suspension pickup points and angles of their inclination. Pay particular attention to the suspension pickup points. Compare swaybar thicknesses, spring sizes, coils and wire diameter, as well as Panhard bar mounting locations. Study the photographs and shift the stock Mustang pictures above a particularly interesting set of pictures to get a good perspective on the changes. It is amazing what you can learn this way.

Keep in mind your findings as you make the modifications provided in this book. Before you start, get a three–ring binder. Include ruled paper, graph paper, and blank sheets in this binder. As you modify your car, you will be adding copies of the data sheets in the Appendix of this book for specific record-keeping. Keep this with you whenever you work on the car or go to a racing event. Note any changes made to the car before, during and after a race. At a race, take notes about competitors' cars and anything interesting they may be trying.

With all of these considerations in mind, give some thought now on how you want to proceed, then turn the page and start reading! ■

Before modifying your chassis, it is imperative that you have the frame alignment checked by a reputable shop with a quality laser frame machine. Laser frame machines and a properly trained operator, such as the one found at Hahn's Body Shop in Nacogdoches, Texas, are necessary to ensure a square platform to build your race car.

BASIC SUSPENSION GEOMETRY

2

uilding a Mustang with the ability to stick in a turn like a train on rails or launch like Glidden's Pro Stock Mustang can be accomplished with the suspension modifications presented in this book. Making these modifications work, however, requires a minimum understanding of suspension geometry. In this chapter we will explore the key items that define the suspension dynamics of Ford's most popular hot rod,

understand how to take some important measurements and recognize the limitations that dictate compromise.

If you are a road racer you have probably read or heard engineers discuss all kinds of neat chassis engineering terms like roll center, instantaneous center, steering axis inclination, bump steer, polar moment of inertia, mass centroid axis and other weird phrases they learned in school. Now this stuff can really cause brain failure. Most of us

who like to drive fast could care less about all these swell terms. This is especially true if your thing is to rocket in a straight line, so I'll limit the discussion to only those areas necessary for a basic understanding of the specific effects of the modifications that follow.

Take the time to read this, even if you are a straight-line addict. You will find it very helpful when you are trying to dial in your machine for maximum traction for off-the-line launches.

Wide, sticky tires provide a clear picture of the effects of a high center of gravity on this hard-charging Mustang.

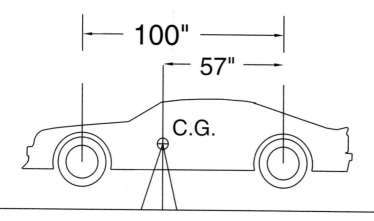

Center of Gravity

100"

57"

C.G.

$$\text{Percent Weight on Front Wheels} = \frac{\text{Rear Distance}}{\text{Wheelbase}}$$

$$\text{Percent Weight on Rear Wheels} = \frac{\text{Front Distance}}{\text{Wheelbase}}$$

Fig. 2-1

CENTER OF GRAVITY

One of the most important characteristics of a car that affects its ability to corner or launch hard is the location of its center of gravity. Center of gravity is generally, thought of in three-dimensional terms: distance between the front and rear axle center lines, lateral or left-to-right location from the centerline of the car, and the height above the ground. Essentially, this represents the location in your car where the laws of physics define the balancing point of the vehicle.

On the typical LX 5.0 Mustang, loaded with approximately 1/2 tank of gas, the front-to-rear center of gravity is approximately 42" behind the front wheels, before you put the driver in. Since cars are not much fun unless we are actually driving them, the real-world center of gravity location in the typical LX 5.0 with a 165-lb. driver is somewhere around 43" rearward of the front axle centerline with the same 1/2 tank of gas. What this translates to is a

driving weight distribution, as defined in percentages, of about 57/43 front to rear. Not bad for an everyday street car. However, when you compare this to the 52/48 ratio found in the average Vette, you can begin to understand why your stock Mustang has difficulty competing with it.

Lateral CG Location

The situation is further complicated (as in poor traction) by the lateral skewing of the weight distribution when you sit in the car. Since the driver's seat centerline sits approximately 16" to the left in your Mustang, the weight of your body will move the center of gravity to the left. For the same LX Mustang discussed previously, with a lateral center of gravity location of approximately 1/2" to the left of center (without a driver), adding your typical 165-lb. pilot moves the same lateral center of gravity to the left an additional 3/4". Big deal, you say. What this translates into is a weight bias shift from 50.8% left to 52.2% left. Again you say, big deal. However, in real world racing, this means that the chassis components, which typically come in matched pairs (springs, shocks, struts and swaybars), will not provide the same traction in equal left and right turns. This phenomenon deteriorates more when you consider the average racer's attempts at lightening his car (or too many trips to the donut shop), thereby increasing the percentage of total racing weight made up by his own body. To the person who likes to corner fast, it is very important to achieve as close to a 50/50 balance as possible for optimum handling.

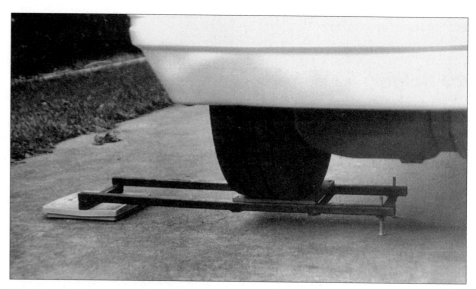

Weight and balance calculations are made by determining the exact corner weights of your car. A simple pair of levered platforms and bathroom scales can be used for these calculations.

Diagonal Balance—One of the small but important things that can pay big dividends to the corner racer is balancing the weight of the car diagonally. The weight distribution between the left front and the right rear should be as close as possible to the right front/left rear. Achieving a 50/50 balance will give your car the same handling characteristics left and right. Typically this requires moving things around in the car and then doing fine adjustments by raising and lowering the ride height at different corners. Once you get the balance close, the distribution can be fine-tuned by modifying the ride height at different corners. It is generally best to start with a heavy corner and lower it to transfer weight. Raising a light corner will increase its weight. Obviously, adjustable spring perches would be great; however, you can shim the springs between the spring and seat to achieve this balance.

By now the quarter-mile group is looking for a new section to read. For those of you still with me, you may be surprised to learn that lateral center of gravity has a significant effect on how your car hooks up. Skewed too much to the left and you can experience traction problems with the right rear tire. This problem becomes more pronounced as horsepower and speeds increase. Balance is important!

CG Height

Center of gravity height in the average Mustang is somewhere around 16.5" above the ground. For the straight-line crowd this is not as important as the front-to-rear and side-to-side location. Generally the Mustang launches harder with a high center of gravity, as fore-to-aft weight transfer is more pronounced in this condition.

To the corner addict, a lower center of gravity translates into higher corner exit speeds. Shifting heavy things lower and rearward, when class rules permit, will

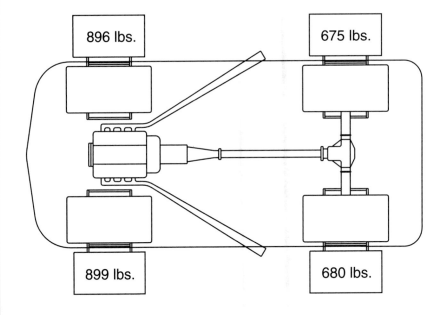

Diagonal Weight Distribution

896 lbs. 675 lbs.

899 lbs. 680 lbs.

Left Front/Right Rear = 899 lbs. + 675 lbs.
= 1574 lbs.
Right Front/Left Rear = 896 lbs. + 680 lbs.
= 1576 lbs.
Diagonal Ratio = LF/RR:RF/LR
= 1574:1576
= 99.8%

Fig.2-2

Achieving ideal weight distribution will generally require the relocation of the battery from the front of the car. Doug Wille moved the battery to the passenger side rear floorpan to improve weight distribution and minimized the polar moment of inertia associated with an object this large.

Roush Double-Wishbone

The only real cure for the limitations of the MacPherson strut suspension is to scrap it and fabricate a double-wishbone system. This slick setup built by Roush Racing for Lyn St. James' Capri provided outstanding handling.

have a marked effect on handling and the location of the center of gravity.

Changing CG Height—Modifying the location of your car's center of gravity can be achieved with something as simple as moving the battery to the rear of the car. Or you may decide to do the more sophisticated change of relocating the engine lower and rearward (upward and rearward to the drag racers). Use of lightweight components obviously helps. In reality, the only significant changes to your car's center of gravity can be made by moving the battery to the rear, removing your air conditioning/heating system, substituting Lexan for the sides and rear glass, raising or lowering the ride height or relocating the engine. Nothing else will have a significant effect.

If you are going to go fast, it is important that you determine where the center of gravity is in your car and how the weight is distributed. This is important for managing the changes you will be making when you race your car.

MacPherson Strut Limitations

The Fox Mustang is built on a unibody platform, utilizing MacPherson strut suspension in the front and four–link,

non–parallel, unequal length suspension in the rear. The MacPherson setup in the front suspension is lightweight and simple in construction. To the bean counters it has that all important feature, low manufacturing cost. This is no doubt the main reason for its use.

To the straight-line crowd the MacPherson strut is also great because it is simple to maintain and gives the added advantage of providing a generous engine bay. Unfortunately, if your thing is cornering speed the fun stops here.

The combination of the lower control arm, spindle, strut and combined pickup points in an LX 5.0 or GT provide the typical Mustang with a low front roll center, instantaneous centers approximately the height of the lower control arm pivots and a very ugly steering axis inclination angle.

Steering Axis Inclination

Ugly is the only way to describe this characteristic of the Fox Mustang's suspension. First, the steering axis inclination is the angle formed when a line passing through the upper strut

This fast and dependable Cobra-R Mustang was prepared by Steeda Autosports to run in the 6 Hours of Sebring, and run it did. While running in second place, there was a credentials dispute that ousted most of the pit crew just before a brake pad change, which dropped the car from a close 2nd overall to 6th.

Steering Axis Inclination

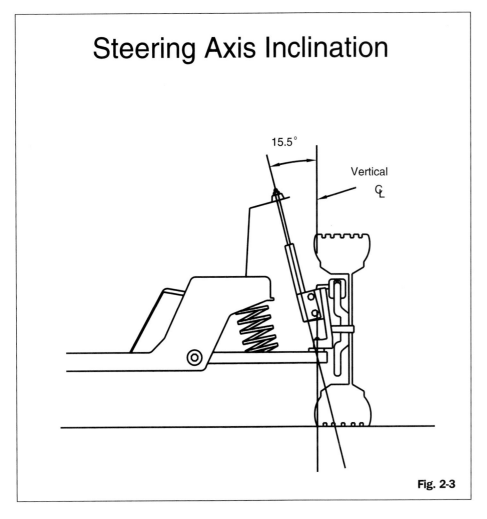

15.5°

Vertical
₵

Fig. 2-3

Using a wide outboard offset wheel, as seen on this 16 x 10, will move the centerline of the tire outward, dramatically increasing the scrub or steering offset radius. Excessive scrub radius can make the car dart about at speeds and make it considerably unstable under hard braking conditions.

mount and the ball joint pivot intersects a vertical line, when viewed from the front (see Fig. 2-3). Basically, if you look at the spindle from the front of your car, you can see that the strut slants toward the engine. For simplicity's sake, that angle represents the steering axis inclination, or *Kingpin inclination,* as it is sometimes known. On the V8 Mustang, this angle is approximately 15.5° at 0° camber. Obviously as we increase negative camber to enhance corner speed, we also increase the angle in direct proportion to the camber change.

Jacking—When you turn the steering wheel to facilitate a change in direction, the spindle on your Mustang passes through a hyperbolic arc, causing the wheel to move away from the lateral centerline of the car toward the road surface, or basically what is known as a *jacking effect.* This effect is very pronounced in some cars. Cars with high

angles of steering axis inclination will show slight lifting of the body as the steering is turned to lock. The greater the degree of steering axis inclination, the more pronounced the jacking effect. Add to this any scrub radius and the effect amplifies.

To the stock passenger car this is not all that bad. When the car is turned going around a curve, this jacking effect helps to counter the body roll that is associated with soft springs. It has the added benefit of helping to center the front wheels much like positive caster does. However, this condition is the pits for the road racer or high-performance nut.

That ugly jacking effect serves to constantly change the roll centers and associated steering geometry. Even large doses of positive caster can not overcome this design limitation of the Mustang's MacPherson strut suspension. Just to

give you a baseline, the best handling results are found with an angle between 2° and 9°. As the angle approaches 0°, the more sophisticated the suspension becomes. Obviously the closer to 2° you get, the closer you get to an Indy car. The late-model Corvette falls well into this category.

Lack of Camber Gain

Probably the most recognized limitation of the MacPherson strut system is lack of camber gain during suspension bump or compression. Unlike the double wishbone, where the shorter upper control arm pulls the top of the spindle inward under suspension compression, the rigid upper strut mount, combined with the long strut length, contributes very little to camber gain. This is further complicated by the attitude of the control arm. If the suspension is not aligned to take this into consideration, the Mustang could operate with a positive camber angle when negotiating a difficult turn.

What to do? Nada. Short of swapping the entire front suspension for a Stock Car Products double-wishbone setup or adapting one of the new T–bird suspensions to your car, you just have to live with it. There are, however, some small tricks you can do that will be covered in the following chapters. However, for the most part this undesirable characteristic has to be accepted and tuned around.

SCRUB RADIUS

In the previous discussion I mentioned the increased detrimental effect of large steering axis inclination angle when scrub radius was added to the equation. Refer to Fig. 2-4, which shows the steering axis inclination line that I referred to in the MacPherson strut confusion. If we extend that same line downward to the road surface, then draw a vertical line through the center of the wheel, we can find the *scrub radius* or *steering offset*. The distance between the intersection of the two lines with the ground surface is the scrub radius.

A simple way to visualize this is to mark a solid 4 x 4 inch patch on your driveway with chalk. Roll one of the front wheels to rest in the center of this square. Reach through the driver's window and turn the steering wheel lock to lock. Next, roll the car backwards far enough to be able to see the image made by the chalk patch (about 20"). Turn the steering to point the tire out and you will be able to see the turning circle created by the chalk. The distance that the center of the tire width is from the center of this circle is the steering offset or scrub radius.

The amount and direction of the offset can be a major factor in how your Mustang will handle at speeds and under braking. Offsetting the wheel centerline to the inside (negative offset) of the steering axis intersection increases the stability of the car in a straight line (common on front-wheel-drive cars) and decreases the steering effort. Offsetting the wheel centerline outside (positive) increases the steering effort and self–centering effect. Unfortunately, as positive offset increases so does the car's tendency to be twitchy at speeds and unstable under braking. Additionally, the car will tend to dart when you first enter a turn. Basically, this phenomenon is the result of the left and right wheelbase lengths changing as the front wheels move through the arc created by the offset length. Obviously not good for achieving high corner entrance speeds.

Most production cars are designed to achieve zero scrub radius. This means things can all be fitted nicely under the fender with minimum wasted space. The Mustang, with its basic 0° camber and caster, follows this line of thinking. Obviously, the large steering axis inclination angle and the hyperbolic arc the wheel passes through, when negotiating a turn, reduce the efficiency of this.

Ideally, we would like to have the steering axis inclination and wheel centerline meet. Fat chance. If you are a corner nut or road racer this is where things really start to get complicated. Throw in some badly needed positive caster, a few degrees of negative camber and, of course, the slick wide wheel with the low and sticky tires on your Mustang, and scrub radius starts to become a problem.

Adding negative camber will move the steering axis intersection with the road surface outward. On a stock width wheel, your Mustang will feel more stable under braking but with a reduced road feel. Add a wider wheel and tire and the centerline of the wheel moves outboard to counter this effect. Unfortunately, the low-profile sticky tires will move the steering axis intersection inboard, increasing the scrub radius. The closer to the ground the car gets, the closer the steering axis intersection with the road surface gets to the ball joint. This results in the intersection point moving away from the centerline of the wheel. Stick on a set of trick Wilwood

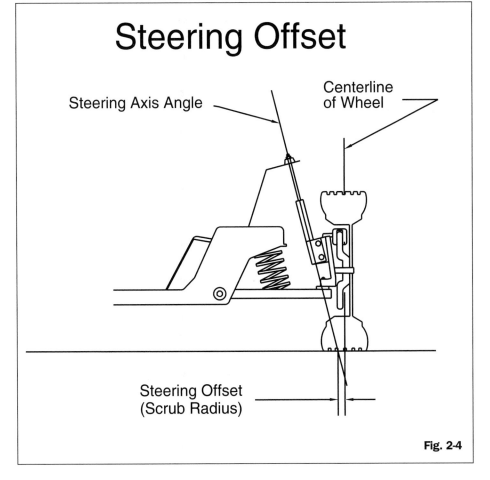

Steering Offset

Steering Axis Angle

Centerline of Wheel

Steering Offset
(Scrub Radius)

Fig. 2-4

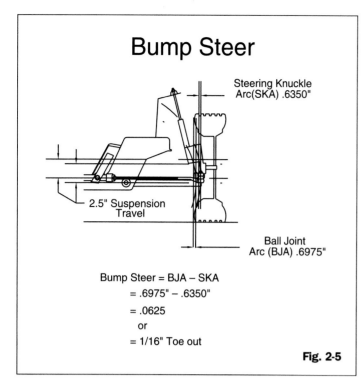

Bump Steer

Steering Knuckle Arc(SKA) .6350"

2.5" Suspension Travel

Ball Joint Arc (BJA) .6975"

Bump Steer = BJA – SKA
= .6975" – .6350"
= .0625
or
= 1/16" Toe out

Fig. 2-5

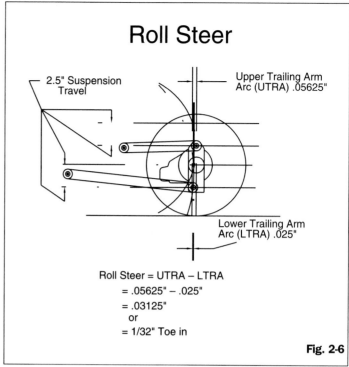

Roll Steer

2.5" Suspension Travel

Upper Trailing Arm Arc (UTRA) .05625"

Lower Trailing Arm Arc (LTRA) .025"

Roll Steer = UTRA – LTRA
= .05625" – .025"
= .03125"
or
= 1/32" Toe in

Fig. 2-6

racing brakes and you move the scrub radius outboard an additional 3/4."

The key to harnessing this situation, like all modifications to a production vehicle, is compromise. Given the limitations of the MacPherson strut suspension, you will have to increase the negative camber to enhance your corner speeds (depending on the roll stiffness). If you are planning to run wide wheels, you'll have to manage the inboard offset to agree with the profile of the tires. Obviously, wider wheels with more outboard offset will increase the roll stiffness needed to match previous roll rates. As the wheel moves outboard, the mechanical advantage of the lever acting on the springs and struts (distance from lower control arm mount and centerline of wheel) increases. Remember, every change you make affects something else.

BUMP & ROLL STEER

This section is about one of the most significant areas of suspension dynamics in Mr. Ford's Mustang, toe steer. Basically this refers to the changes in toe–in or toe–out as the car's suspension travels through its range of motions. For the front suspension, this is commonly referred to as *bump steer*. This term is derived from the pronounced jolt felt at the steering wheel when a single front wheel encounters a bump, causing the steering to jerk to that side. At the rear, a change in toe is called *roll steer*. As the name implies, when the car rolls left or right in a turn a change in toe settings occurs.

Bump Steer

To understand bump steer we will need to view the suspension from the front of the car, as shown in Fig. 2-5. You can see that the spindle, which maintains the direction of the wheel, travels through an arc, defined by the lower control arm, as the suspension compresses and rebounds. The direction of the wheel attached to the spindle, or toe, is controlled by the steering tie rod, which also swings an arc. If these two arcs are not equal length and the rack centerline to tie rod/steering knuckle points are not in the same horizontal plane, bump steer occurs.

Measuring & Adjusting—Bump steer can be measured using a simple gauge that has been around for a long time. It can easily be fabricated from plywood and a couple of hinges and

bolts. Use your imagination and you can rig one of these from almost anything. In Chapter 10, p. 160, I have included drawings to fabricate a more sophisticated gauge.

Ideally there should be no change in toe through 100% of the wheel's travel. Realistically, eliminating toe changes through 90% of the travel is satisfactory. Chances are if your suspension is compressed or extended beyond 90% of its travel on a road course, bump steer is the least of your worries.

To the corner nut or road racer, bump steer translates into tire scrub and a loss of adhesion in the turns and, if severe enough, unstable directional control over rough road surfaces. The Mustang is notorious for this problem when the ride height has been changed. The cure for bump steer in the Mustang typically is to relocate the rack and pinion upward and/or replace the stock tie rods on the pre-'90 car with the newer pieces. Even running some additional caster can eliminate a significant portion of the bump steer problem. Heating the steering knuckle on the spindles and bending them to achieve a perfect match with the rack and pinion is another option. However, after heating them you must have them Magnaflux inspected and re–heat treated. Bring plenty of money. To measure and adjust bump steer follow Step 12 in Chapter 10, p. 155.

Roll Steer

Toe changes at the rear of the car, or roll steer, can be measured using the same gauge and method as used for the front. Unfortunately, correcting roll steer in the Mustang is difficult at best, since this is a characteristic of the design. To minimize roll steer, the lower trailing arms must be relocated and the ride height must be changed. Even these changes will not eliminate roll steer in the Mustang. A stock Mustang typically has as much as 3/8" of wheelbase change at 2.5" of bump in the rear. Obviously this has a pretty dramatic effect on toe.

Other undesirable handling characteristics sometimes require accepting a little roll steer to achieve maximum cornering exit speed. Too much roll steer and your car will develop an abrupt trailing throttle oversteer (consequently a tendency to spin) or be unstable in high-speed turns or straights that may be a little rough. Management of roll stiffness becomes very important to control this characteristic of the Mustang.

ACKERMANN STEERING

When you are negotiating a turn in your Mustang, the outside wheel must travel through a wider arc than the inside wheel. The tighter turning radius on the inside wheel requires a greater steering angle to achieve proper tire contact. The difference between the inside and outside turning angles is called *Ackermann steering*. Ackermann steering is the relationship between the lower control arm ball joint, the tie rod attaching point on the steering knuckle and the center of the rear axle assembly. Basically, you draw lines that bisect the ball joints and the tie rod pivots, extending them until they intersect. To achieve 100% Ackermann, that intersection should occur exactly at the center of the rear axle. The percentage of Ackermann steering increases rapidly as the intersection moves forward to the centerline of the front spindles. If the intersection of those lines is behind the rear axle, as is the case with the Mustang, Ackermann steering is reduced.

Lack of Ackermann steering will cause tire scrubbing and reduce grip. What this translates to is a loss of cornering speed, increased tire wear and unreliable tire temperature readings. Unfortunately, the stock steering system on the Mustang is not designed to provide for Ackermann steering. You could get the torch out and heat and bend the steering knuckle on the spindle. However, it is difficult and expensive. Fear not, a few tricks do exist to change this and will be addressed in following chapters.

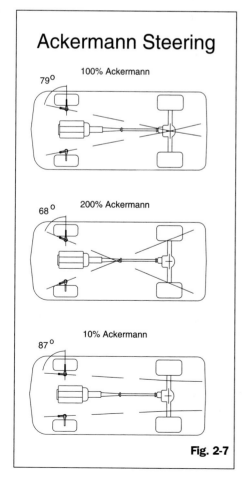

Fig. 2-7

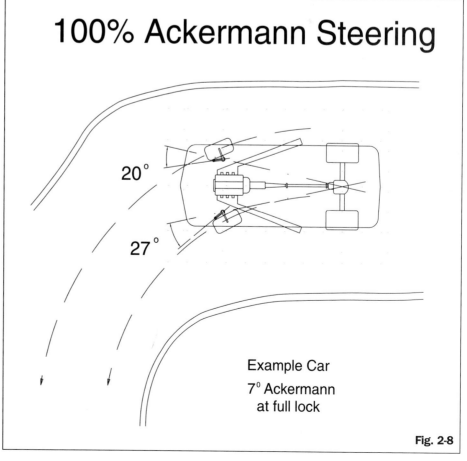

Fig. 2-8

SQUAT & DIVE

There are two characteristics that have been a part of the Mustang's heritage since 1965; nose-dive when braking and squatting at the rear under acceleration. Given all the wonderful things you have learned to this point about suspension geometry, it doesn't take a genius to figure out that these are most uncool characteristics for stability and cornering speeds.

Anti-Dive

The nose-dive characteristic of the Mustang is defined by the relationship of the lower control arm mounting angle and the strut mount as viewed from the top and side. Looking from the side, draw a line through the lower control arm mounts extending rearward and another line through the upper strut mount that is exactly 90° to its length. The distance to the intersection of these lines defines a significant piece of the anti–dive percentage of the car. Additionally, the angle from the centerline of the car that a line passing through the lower control arm pivots creates, also contributes to the anti–dive characteristic of this car. Basically as the intersection of the two lines (either from the side or top view) moves closer to the control arm, the angle widens and the percentage of anti–dive increases.

Too little anti–dive and the front suspension compresses significantly, changing the suspension geometry and causing poor corner entrance speed. Too much anti–dive and the front suspension locks up, preventing suspension compliance and causing tire chatter under braking or hard cornering. As the suspension is modified and anti–dive approaches the maximum to achieve greater cornering speeds, the forgiving early warnings found in the stock suspension become more pronounced and sudden. When the driver abruptly brakes hard while approaching a corner in a car with excessive anti–dive, the

The steep nose angle under hard braking on John Cairn's beautiful 1985 1/2 SVO provides a graphic reminder of the low anti-dive percentage built into the Mustang. Lack of sufficient anti-dive percentage causes excessive weight transfer and makes the car very unstable when braking.

suspension locks against the countering forces and the car will tend to understeer. More brakes and the understeer becomes more pronounced. Realizing the futility of this, the driver experiences brain failure, releases braking pressure suddenly, and oops! The car returns to a normal oversteer condition as the steering is turned to lock. Generally, the driver and car spin off into the tules. Here again, balance is the key.

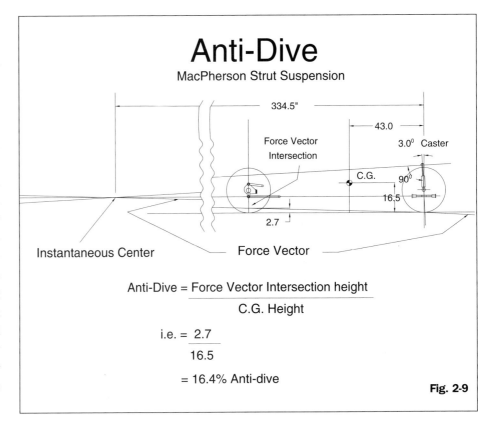

Anti-Dive
MacPherson Strut Suspension

$$\text{Anti-Dive} = \frac{\text{Force Vector Intersection height}}{\text{C.G. Height}}$$

$$\text{i.e.} = \frac{2.7}{16.5}$$

$$= 16.4\% \text{ Anti-dive}$$

Fig. 2-9

Squat

If you have ever observed a stock GT Mustang as it launches from a light or is slammed into 3rd gear, you have seen the body of the car squat on the rear axle. Like the forward pitching associated with dive, squat distorts the front and rear suspension geometry, skews weight transfer away from the front and generates a loss of traction. The resistance to the forces driving the body down is defined as a percentage of anti–squat. Anti–squat is defined as the percentage of the height of the vertical center of gravity. This percentage is found at the intersection of a straight line drawn from the center of the rear tire contact patch through the instantaneous center of the trailing arms (or front pivot on torque arm suspensions as viewed from the side), with a vertical line passing through the car's center of gravity at the front wheel. If that line intersects the vertical CG line at 7.5" above the ground and the CG is 16.5" above the ground, then the anti–squat is calculated as 7.5/16.5 or approximately 45%. This translates into a force that pushes up against the body of the car equal to 45% of the acceleration force pushing down on the car. The instantaneous center is defined as the intersection of lines drawn through the trailing arm pickup points on the axle housing and the frame when viewed from the side. Basically this operates as a lever against the weight of the car. Small changes in the distance and height of that intersection have dramatic effects on how hard the tires plant and how much lift is experienced by the front end.

The four-link suspension of the Mustang complicates anti–squat. The location, angles and distances from the axle centerline of the suspension mounting points, the diameter of the tires, and the ride height all affect this force that counteracts acceleration. Changing the mounting points of the trailing arms can increase anti–squat to

A well-balanced rear suspension provides no noticeable squat as the car accelerates. Jackie Mutschler's fast 1986 CP Mustang demonstrates no squat as she accelerates hard from a tight turn.

the point where it creates a perfect balance between the acceleration forces and the traction necessary to stick in the turns. This is clearly evident from the use of relocated mounting points, as seen in the very fast 1992 World Challenge Mustang of Hal Baer. Extend the lower trailing arm axle mounting points further, and the forces of anti–squat will exceed the acceleration forces and generate longitudinal body lift. Obviously this will unload the front suspension when power is applied, in turn causing the car to transition to an understeer condition.

Drag Racing—To the drag racer, excessive anti–squat will cause the car to expend too much energy rising, which will slow the launch and transfer 100%

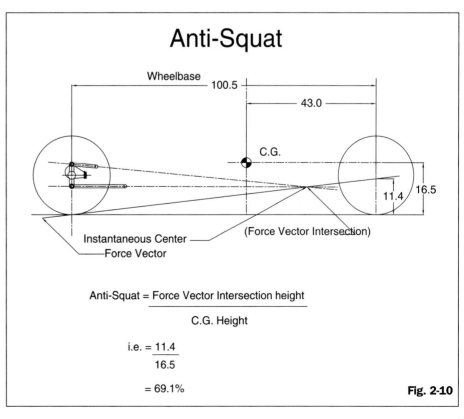

Anti-Squat

Anti-Squat = $\dfrac{\text{Force Vector Intersection height}}{\text{C.G. Height}}$

i.e. = $\dfrac{11.4}{16.5}$

= 69.1%

Fig. 2-10

of the weight to the slicks, possibly generating too much bite. The successful drag racer learns about this effect early on or gets trailered in the first round.

To the drag racer, the operation of the four-link system is defined in terms of chassis lift and rise (axle separation) rather than anti–squat. The twisting force generated by the rear axle as power is applied combines with the acceleration forces against the body. Essentially this translates to pull against the upper trailing arm's chassis mounts, generating front end lift, and push against the lower trailing arm's chassis mounts, causing axle/body separation.

The angle of the trailing arms and the distance from the axle centerline to their mounts dictate how lift and push are distributed to the chassis. As the instantaneous center moves rearward (the angle between the trailing arms widens), the lift lever is shortened and the tendency to wheelstand is reduced. Because the force with which the rear

Anti-squat or rise on this trick four-link drag race suspension can be quickly altered to meet changing track and tire conditions. Moving the link pickup points (arrows) and adjusting their lengths can modify the weight transfer and how hard the tires will plant at the launch.

tires are planted is dictated by the percentage of anti–squat, the higher the location of the instantaneous center, the greater the downward force or axle separation. Basically this is what causes the car to rise, seemingly from all four wheels, when power is applied.

The popular South Side Machine Co. traction bars operate with an instantaneous center about 40.5" in front of the rear axle and about 13.75" high on a 28" diameter rear slick. This causes an intersection between the tire, instantaneous center and center of gravity on the average LX 5.0 Mustang about 19.625" high. Using the formula to calculate anti–squat percentage (intersection height/center of gravity height) we find this setup generates 109% anti–squat or rise. This is a very high percentage but necessary to generate enough weight transfer to the rear wheels to launch hard.

Stock Mustangs generally have about 3/4" difference in vertical separation between the axle mounting holes and the chassis mounting holes, or 7" at the axle and 6.25" at the frame. A triangle is formed (when viewed from the side of the car) by the intersection of lines drawn between upper and lower trailing arm mounts on the axle and those extending from the mounting points of the trailing

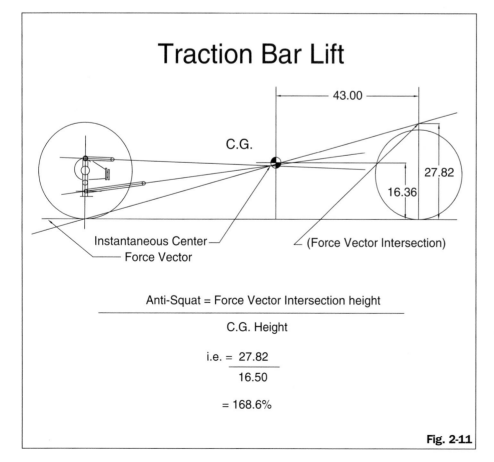

Traction Bar Lift

— 43.00 —

C.G.

27.82

16.36

Instantaneous Center
Force Vector

(Force Vector Intersection)

$$\text{Anti-Squat} = \frac{\text{Force Vector Intersection height}}{\text{C.G. Height}}$$

$$\text{i.e.} = \frac{27.82}{16.50}$$

$$= 168.6\%$$

Fig. 2-11

arms. Given this relationship and some basic rules of geometry and trigonometry, we can calculate the lengths of the long sides. The results of our calculations show the two lines running through the trailing arms, on a stock post-'84 Mustang, intersecting about 90.5" forward of the axle about 10.5" high, creating an anti–squat of approximately 39%. By moving the lower mounting hole down on the axle housing, the angle formed by the intersection of the same two lines increases. Additionally, the intersection of the two lines moves up and rearward. Given the previous discussion, we know the effect of this change is to increase the anti–squat and drive the axle downward under acceleration. Because of this relationship, you will see traction bars replacing the stock lower trailing arms that have their axle mounting holes several inches lower (South Side Machine Co., Texas Turbo, etc.).

Ford lowered both the upper and lower chassis mounting holes on the post-'84 Mustangs. If you are building a race car from scratch it would be prudent to remember this when you are looking for a suitable body. The instantaneous center

on pre-'85 Mustangs will be more forward than the newer cars at the same ride height, requiring more radical control arm locations to achieve the same results. If a lower ride and shorter suspension travel are acceptable, then the pre-'85 body is an option.

Road Racing—On a well-balanced road racing or high performance street chassis, anti–squat should never exceed 50%. Percentages approaching 50% and beyond can cause some very undesirable characteristics, like tire chatter under braking. Worst of all, if the driver has to lift his foot abruptly when accelerating off a turn, the resultant sudden shift in the force vector will unload the rear tires and the car will probably spin. Too little anti–squat and the torque generated by the rear axle under maximum acceleration can cause the rear tires to lift, wasting energy that would have propelled the car forward, resulting in excessive wheel spin. This is real world for the stock Mustang. Unfortunately, the basic design of the Mustang's suspension mandates high anti–squat rates to override some of its other limitations. Basically, these have to be tuned around.

Since the Mustang was designed to serve as both a high-performance vehicle and a fuel-efficient sporty car, Ford designed squat into the suspension. This satisfies the "blue hairs" by providing a stable and forgiving platform and more importantly, keeps warranty costs down. If the Mustang hooked up from the factory instead of spinning the tires, Ford would have to raise the cost of the car significantly to cover for the broken clutches, trannies and driveshafts that would result from the hard launches.

RIDE HEIGHT

One of the most abused modifications to Mr. Ford's Mustang is to the ride height. To the casual enthusiast, a low ride height means righteous cornering. Improved ground effects and low center of gravity are generally associated with a low ride. The ground-hugging plastic cars from GM go sorta fast, so the lower the better, right? Unfortunately this is not so.

The design limitations of the Mustang, principally in the front suspension, do not allow for significant changes to ride height. Even modifications to the suspension pickup points that lower the

This GT Mustang suffers from too low a ride height for the location of the control arms. Since the control arm angle is past horizontal at rest, there is an ever-increasing loss of negative camber as the suspension compresses. (Photo by John Hafemeister)

Due to a high roll center and insufficient roll stiffness, Howard Duffy's 1985 Mustang demonstrates a high positive camber angle on the outside wheel. Although the camber angle is adequate relative to the car's frame, the excessive roll angle negates its functionality. Increased rear roll stiffness (larger swaybar) should help.

car still require that the control arms maintain at least a level attitude. Because the upper strut mount does not move like a true double-wishbone system, the attitude of the control arm affects the camber curve. As the suspension compresses in a turn and the control arm passes through a line from the opposite side's control arm mount through its own mount, extending out beyond the ball joint, the camber curve

goes positive. If your car is lowered with shorter springs, you'll lose negative camber with any compression of the suspension. Setting your alignment with excessive negative camber is not good, especially on a street car, where too much negative camber causes premature tire wear. You already know from the previous discussions that using a small diameter wheel to lower ride height can cause other problems. Such are the limitations of a MacPherson strut suspension.

Obviously a Stock Car Products

double-wishbone setup could cure this. A more subtle approach would be to have a pair of custom spindles made to compensate for the suspension limitations. Either way you go, bring money.

CAMBER, CASTER & TOE

This last section concerns the three components of alignment—*camber, caster* and *toe*. To the racer, especially to the road racer/Conehead, the correct management of these settings can mean the difference between first place and everybody else. Coneheads and road racers live or die by their alignment settings and spend a lot of time searching for the best setup. To the drag racer, mismanagement of alignment can result in increased drag or wander, which results in slower E.T.s.

Camber

Camber, or the angle that the wheel differs from vertical when viewed from the front of the car, is an extremely important adjustment to the corner freak. Camber is defined in degrees from vertical, with an inward till being negative and outward till being positive. For the road racer, negative camber

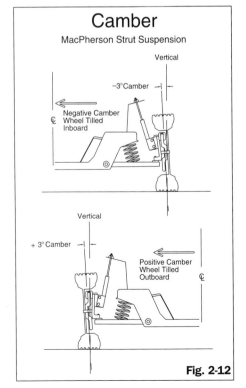

Fig. 2-12

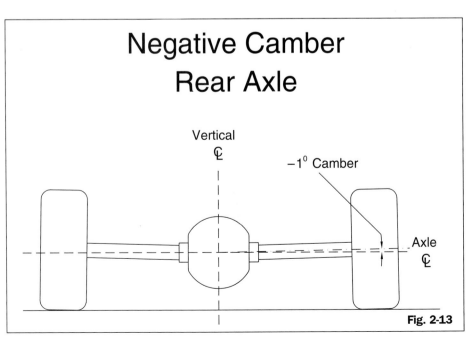

Fig. 2-13

translates into improved traction in the turns. It is generally accepted that a road-race car equipped with radial tires should demonstrate a negative camber angle of –1° on the outside wheel when negotiating a high-speed turn. A negative angle permits the tire to maintain a flat footprint, as the sidewall flexes and rolls under with the centrifugal force acting on the car as it negotiates the turn. Obviously, positive camber acts in the reverse.

In order to achieve the proper camber angle in a turn, the initial camber setting must be sufficient to compensate for camber lost to body roll and suspension design. No doubt you have seen race cars with huge amounts of negative camber to compensate for these limitations. However, camber angles greater than 3° negative affect transient handling (takes too long for the tire's sidewall to roll over and flatten out) and generally indicate a need to make suspension changes elsewhere.

Proper camber selection is especially critical on the Mustang with MacPherson strut suspension. As noted in the section on MacPherson strut suspension, the Mustang suffers from a lack of camber gain as the suspension cycles through bump travel. Large angles of negative camber are generally required of cars equipped with this type of suspension. The championship-winning Sharp Racing Datsun 510's from the early 1970s were some of the first race cars to effectively manage this phenomenon.

Rear Camber—Although not generally considered applicable to the solid rear axle suspension of the Mustang, rear negative camber has been used by many successful racing teams to achieve improved transit corner oversteer. Virtually every successful NASCAR team builds negative camber into the rear axle housings of their Winston Cup cars. Adding negative camber to the solid rear axle of your Mustang is difficult and must be done

precisely to avoid the expense of purchasing a new housing. The benefit of rear axle negative camber is generally restricted to heavy race cars running on high-speed bankings or cars running wheels that are too narrow or on the minimum side of the necessary width for the tires they are using. Like the front suspension, this is done to compensate for excessive sidewall flex. Most Mustangs develop some negative camber from normal driving. Unless you are a drag racer, a little negative camber will help the rear stick better.

As with anything else, excessive negative camber is not a good thing. Too much negative camber and rolling resistance increases. In addition, the lack of a flat footprint on the road surface during straight-line operation reduces the braking efficiency. On a rough track or bumpy street the inward force created by negative camber, or camber thrust, causes an imbalance in side loads when one tire encounters a bump, causing the car to wander. Again we see that the interaction between driving conditions and suspension limitations dictates compromise.

Caster

To the drag racer and the conehead alike, caster is an important consideration in suspension setup. Positive caster is the rearward inclination from vertical that a line passing through the upper strut mount and the lower ball joint creates, when viewed from the side of the car. It provides the driver with road feel and increased straight-line stability from the self-centering torque effect, with negative camber generating the opposite effect. Increased positive caster equals better road feel. Given the fact that positive caster provides the driver with better road feel and stability, why not run 10°? Unfortunately there are four very significant reasons not to.

First, the increased stress placed on the steering and suspension systems can

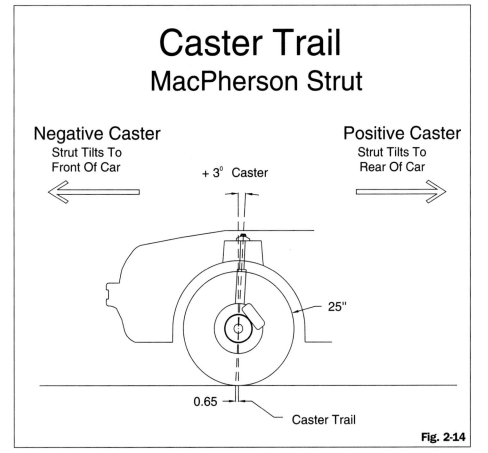

Caster Trail
MacPherson Strut

Negative Caster
Strut Tilts To
Front Of Car

+ 3° Caster

Positive Caster
Strut Tilts To
Rear Of Car

25"

0.65

Caster Trail

Fig. 2-14

cause premature wear and system failure. As the angle of inclination increases, so does caster trail. Caster trail, much like scrub radius, is the distance between the intersection of the caster angle with the road surface and a vertical line that passes through the center of the wheel, except it is viewed from the side of the car. As the steering is turned, the hyperbolic circle (U–shaped) created by the spindle means the steering must overcome the jacking effect that takes place when the car is turned. This is tough on rack and pinions, tie rods and ball joints.

In conjunction with the previous discussion of caster trail, like excessive steering axis angles, positive caster causes the body to rise and fall as the steering is turned to lock. Unlike excessive steering axis angles, positive caster causes the outside wheel to rise, dropping the body in relation to the track, with the inside wheel causing the reverse effect. This translates into an increased lateral inertia, or the centrifugal transfer of the car's weight, not to mention the changes in roll center locations and camber angles.

The additional stress on your suspension or the change in body attitude may not be as convincing as the increased tire scrub that occurs as caster is increased positively. Just like the description implies, the tire scrubbing that occurs as the steering is turned causes a reduction in the coefficient of adhesion, or traction. This, of course, is not good. At the point when traction means cornering speed, any loss of it translates into understeer and additional tire wear as well as unreliable tire temperature readings.

One of the least known disadvantages of caster, for our purposes positive caster, is the detrimental effect it has on bump steer. Typically a 1° change in caster will cause a 1/16" to 3/32" change in bump steer. For this reason, it is very important that you test and correct bump steer after

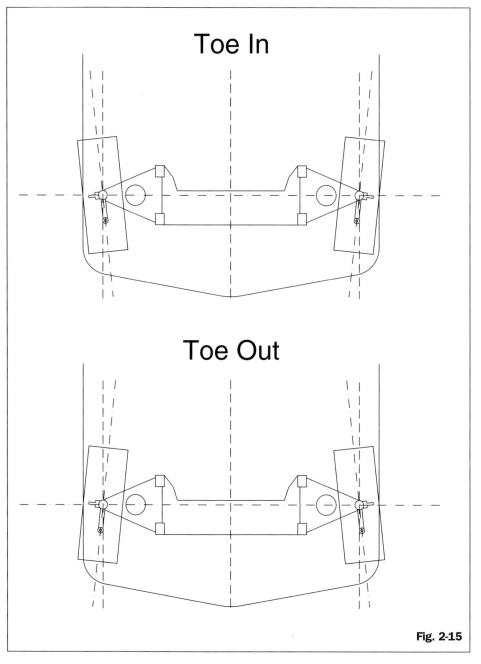

Toe In

Toe Out

Fig. 2-15

you have set the caster you are going to race with.

Caster Settings—Like living with a little scrub radius, caster and the associated caster trail must be compromised to achieve maximum performance. Driver preference typically sets the limits here. It is generally accepted that caster should not be increased more than 2° positive from factory specifications on a production car. However, light cars and small diameter wheels generally mandate more positive caster. The Mustang seems to respond to large amounts of positive

caster when autocrossing, as the lateral weight transfer seems to reduce transient corner understeer. For a well-prepared road racer a few degrees seems to be the key.

To the quarter-mile drag racer, high-speed instability, as in wandering about the lane, is very disconcerting and second only to traction in achieving a satisfying run where a change of underwear is not required. One of the culprits to high-speed wander is the loss of positive caster that occurs when the typical drag racing Mustang's front end lifts at speed. This is especially significant when you consider the Mustang starts with 0° caster. A cursory examination of the trick Alston front chassis reveals that large positive caster angles are needed. Furthermore, several degrees of positive caster will help the stability of your Mustang on the top end.

Toe

The difference between the horizontal distances of the centerlines of the tires, when measured at center height in the front and back of the tire, defines the toe setting of that pair of wheels. When the front measurement is less than the back, the tires are said to have toe–in (like standing with your toes pointed inward), with the reverse being toe–out (like standing with your toes pointed out). The amount and direction of this setting affects how the car will handle at speeds in a straight line, and to the road racer/conehead, corner entry understeer. Front toe settings vary in and out on a high-performance car, depending on how and where the car is being driven.

Rear toe is always 0" on solid axle-equipped cars such as the Mustang. Toe–in is required on cars with independent type rear systems. Bushing and linkage flex allow the wheels to toe–out at speeds, mandating a toe–in setting. The unpredictable reactions of a car with rear toe–out demands that this be avoided.

On a rear-wheel-drive vehicle such as the Mustang, front suspension toe–in is necessary to counteract the normal flex of the steering linkage and soft suspension bushings that induce toe–out at speeds. Toe–in generally promotes straight-line stability and corner entry understeer.

For the drag racer, straight-line stability is very important. However, like excess caster or camber to the road racer, too much toe–in increases tire scrub or rolling drag and absorbs horsepower that would otherwise contribute to lower E.T.s or lap times. Unfortunately, the typical bracket racer spends a lot of time looking back at his opponent trying to avoid breaking out. Obviously, if you're looking back, you're not watching where you're going. It is for this reason toe–in of 1/8" is commonly used to keep the car straight during those lapses of concentration.

Autocrossers and road racers know toe settings can be used to fine-tune their car's suspension and improve corner entry understeer. Racing around the orange cones can generally be improved by adjusting your toe setting to provide toe–out. On a stock suspension Mustang this has a pretty dramatic effect. Essentially toe–out compensates for a lack of Ackermann steering by inducing transient corner oversteer. Although this can improve your pylon times, on a road course the car can become difficult to manage down the straights. Too much toe–out and the car will dart about with every ripple on the track. Additionally, transient oversteer can become quite abrupt and induce a spin when the rear suspension is not set up to counter-balance this effect. Again compromise and balance are important.

SUMMARY

If you have waded through the preceding confusion you know any change you make will affect something else and not necessarily as you had planned. If you run short springs you contribute to a faster positive camber curve; run wide offset rims and you create a scrub radius; too much caster and you give up traction in the turns; excessive anti–dive or anti–squat and your car can become unstable under braking; too low a center of gravity or inadequate anti–squat and your quarter-horse will not launch properly at the lights; and so on. The dynamics of your Mustang's suspension are obviously complex, with every change creating a reaction somewhere else.

A well-balanced approach to suspension modifications, coupled with a basic understanding of what those changes also affect, is essential to maintaining a competitive edge. It is very difficult to dial in your car to the track conditions if you don't understand how the car works. Take the time to digest this chapter. If you are a road racer or conehead and want a more in–depth presentation, read Fred Puhn's book, *How To Make Your Car Handle*, also by HPBooks. ∎

Doug Wille, driving Capt. Marvel's CP Mustang, provides a clear picture of most of the major faults associated with the Mustang chassis. Excessive weight transfer and lack of roll stiffness have unloaded the rear suspension to the point where the inside rear tire is nearly off the ground. (Photo by John Hafemeister)

CHASSIS MODIFICATIONS

3

The purpose of this chapter is to help you build a stiff platform from which to develop your racer. Chassis flex is the weakest point of the Mustang. No doubt you have seen the wrinkles that form on the edges of the roof above the door entrances of high horsepower Mustangs. These wrinkles are the direct result of the body twisting in the middle when the chassis is loaded. Sticky, wide tires transfer such great torsional loads to the chassis that a lack of proper bracing can result in serious damage to the body. Twisted roof lines, doors that won't close and cracked windshields are all too common. Continued launches without minimum chassis bracing will flex the chassis (the car will not be square) and the tires will not contact the pavement correctly, much less track straight. Since your slicks will not be planted squarely, your launch will be squirrelly the instant you drop the hammer. You probably don't need to be reminded of how NHRA and IHRA frown on the use of your competitor's lane during any point of your run.

Anyone who cruises about orange cones on a Sunday afternoon or finds pleasure in pursuing a tight apex at a race track or curvy back road knows the detriments of a weak chassis. Regardless of how much effort you put into the design and setup of your suspension, if the chassis is not rigid, the geometry will

Meticulous, total car preparation is what wins races. On a typical Sunday afternoon, you can find the well-prepared and fast Mustang of Brian Cunningham doing cone wars with other Coneheads in the Houston Region of the SCCA.

change when you negotiate a turn. Your best efforts are rendered useless. If you are serious about razor-sharp handling then you must complete this chapter before moving to the next step.

Much of the information in this chapter is for the hard-core racer. However, even if you don't fit into this category there are still modifications that will apply to you, even if you just want better street performance or are a drag racer. For instance, subframe connectors are an absolute must for any type of performance application. Certain autocross classes do not permit this modification or the addition of rocker panel reinforcements, so check your rule book.

To complete this chapter you will need a MIG-welder, and you'll have to purchase or fabricate the parts listed in the chart below. Before you start you must decide whether or not you are going to purchase the necessary parts or build them. Don't start without the completed parts in your hands. It will save a lot of frustration.

If you want to fabricate the subframe connectors, rocker panel reinforcements, or a roll bar/roll cage see the figures beginning on p. 41. The most important thing to remember is to take your time.

Get a rule book before you start. It will save you untold dollars and time by telling you what you can and can not do to the car to qualify for the particular class you'll be racing in. For example, some classes do not allow the use of subframe connectors. This is definitely something you'd need to know before firing up the MIG and welding them in. Also, following the rule book will save you considerable hassle during that first tech inspection.

Replacing pieces that you screw up because you got in a hurry eats into your high–performance budget. If you want to save time, there are several suppliers that will be glad to sell them to you. However, check around your area. The cost of buying some pieces such as a roll cage or roll bar is magnified by the freight it takes to get it to you. A local vendor is definitely the way to go.

TURNING OR GOING STRAIGHT

As with most chapters of this book, the modifications that follow are grouped and named according to the type of performance you want: street/autocross, road racing or drag racing. Obviously many of the modifications or steps are identical for each group and will not be repeated but referred back to when applicable.

Street/Autocross—For cruising the cones you will be limited to those modifications that your class or conscience allows. Since you are permitted to upgrade to newer-year model parts in the stock classes, specific combinations of various pieces from different years will generally provide the best results and will be covered in the appropriate chapters. For the street, you must consider handling and ride comfort. The stiffer the chassis, the more bone-jarring the ride.

Road Racing—To set up the Mustang for sanctioned road racing, Solo II autocrossing or something like the Silver State Classic, the object will be to stiffen the chassis as much as possible

Parts Required For Chassis Stiffening:

	Autocross/ Street	Road Racing	Drag Racing
Subframe connectors	X	X	X
Rocker panel reinforcements	X	X	
Rear shock tower brace	X		
Two–Point interior body brace	X		X
Strut tower brace	X	X	X
Approved roll bar/roll cage		X	X
Roll bar padding	X	X	X
PPG DP–48 or equivalent paint	X	X	X
Small plastic bags		X	X
Marks–A–Lot		X	X
3M Weld–Thru Coating (051131–05913)	X	X	X
Congenial and helpful friends	X	X	X
Approved libations	X	X	X

The complete disassembly of your car is the best approach for serious race car modifications. Everything that can be removed without a torch is removed, cleaned and inspected before it is modified or reinstalled.

without adding excess weight within the parameters of the rules for your class. This type of setup is the most difficult of the three categories and generally requires considerable skilled manual labor. The construction of a proper roll cage is of the utmost importance, and you must have considerable fabricating and welding skills to do the job properly. With the right parts, the Mustang is capable of speeds near the 200 mph

mark. You screw up for just a few nano–seconds at half that speed on a race track or back road and you'll get a first-hand look at how well your cage is constructed.

Drag Racing—If your thing is the quarter mile, you can strengthen the existing chassis platform or go the whole hog route and install an Alston kit. Because the focus of this book is to provide the average Mustang enthusiast

or racer of limited means with the information to modify his car, installation of the Alston kits will not be addressed.

Modifying the existing Mustang platform for drag racing requires the addition of specific braces. At a minimum you'll need to plan on a roll bar, welding certain suspension pickup points and making modifications to the rear wheelwells for tire clearance. The roll bar or cage will be dictated by the speed of the class you intend to run. Most sanctioning bodies require at least a 6–point roll bar for cars running 11.99 or faster. When the E.T. drops to a 9.99 you are generally required to have at least an 8–point cage. In reality, anyone driving at these speeds without a full roll cage is a full bubble off anyway.

CHASSIS MODS FOR STREET/AUTOCROSS

The cure for the Mustang's chassis flex requires that subframe connectors and rocker panel reinforcements be installed and if possible, that all main unibody seams be welded. Unfortunately, if you are running in a Production class, the addition of these braces to stiffen the

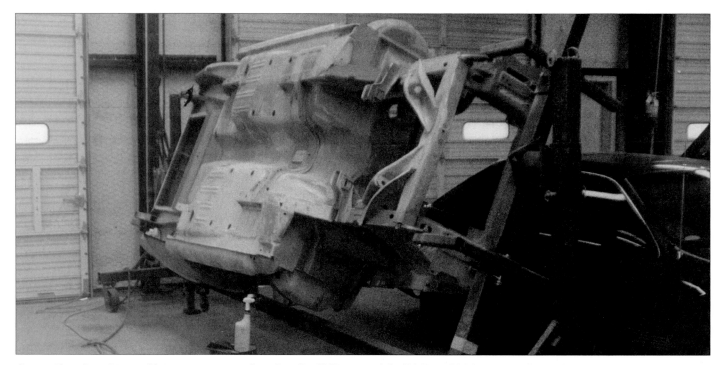

A car rotisserie makes working on your car much easier. David Flectenstein's '70 Boss 302 is shown here getting the treatment at Hahn's Body Shop in Nacogdoches, Texas.

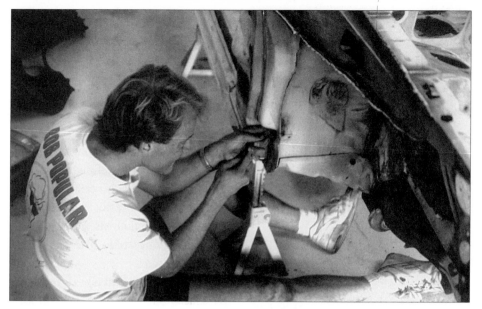

NASA Space Engineer Richard Pedersen demonstrates the art and technique of the most coveted job in race car preparation—the scrape and brush affair. If you are serious about razor-sharp handling, every major body seam must be scraped, cleaned and MIG-welded.

Weld-Thru Coating from 3M is an excellent product to spray on bare metal before welding. This stuff forms a tough zinc coating when welded through, providing a strong barrier to rust. It also works great on the back side of areas that are hard to reach for painting afterwards.

chassis will generally move your car in to a Prepared class. However, these modifications are included as necessary, so you be the judge. If you must remain stock, use the '86 convertible Mustang rocker braces.

If you are running in the fast Prepared or Modified classes you should go to the section on chassis mods for road racing, p. 29 in this chapter. To be competitive in these classes you will need to do the same basic modifications as the road racing cars, with the exception of full roll cages.

Step 1

To begin, mount the car on jackstands that provide at least 18" of floor clearance. The jackstands should be placed under the rear axle and front control arms until the subframe connectors, rocker panel reinforcements and strut tower braces are welded in or fitted. When this is completed, you can relocate the jackstands to the rocker seams at the jack point notches.

Step 2

Remove the seats, carpet and sound deadener underneath it. Using good lighting, carefully examine the floorpan

at and around the driver's seat mounts, the driveshaft tunnel where it intersects the transverse crossmember (at the rear seat platform), just above the axle pinion and around the upper trailing arm mounts. These are common areas where cracks form. At every crack, scrape the area to bare metal and spray with 3M Weld–Thru Coating in preparation for welding. MIG-weld each crack completely, extending the weld 1/4" beyond the crack's visible end.

Step 3: Subframe Connectors

After you have fabricated subframe connectors (see Fig. 3-1, p. 41), carefully align them on the front and rear subframes where the nose of the connector is 1/8" behind the transmission crossmember mount on each side. Scribe a line around the rear section and sand to bare metal along the edges in front of the scribed lines in the rear, as well as the edges to be welded on the connectors. It is very important that clean bare metal be exposed before welding. Any paint–or worse, undercoating–will cause poor weld penetration and the possibility of de–lamination. Take care and don't over-sand the subframe on the car. Use a

high-s   d sander with coarse grit discs. The meta   is very thin. Spray the exposed bare metal with 3M Weld–Thru Coating. If you find the connectors are too long, trim them at the rear before you weld. Quality control on some of the earlier cars dictates you custom-fit each piece.

Step 4

Use a jack to lightly press the connectors against the subframes, then MIG-weld them completely along the edges at the front subframe and along the entire contact surface at the rear using ER70S–6 (.030") wire. *Warning: Do not acetylene weld!* Mustangs use high-carbon steel in the frame that can be ruined with excessive heat. The wire specified, ER70S–6, is designed for this type of metal. Be sure to weld both ends also. It is important to note that the nose of the connector should fit with the slanted tip forward and sloping rearward away from the car.

When you have welded both ends, clamp the reinforcement plates on each side of the front subframe and the connector, and scribe its location. Scrape

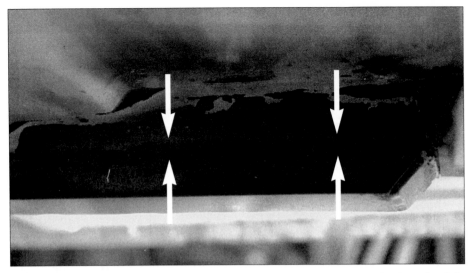

When installing subframe connectors, it is important not only to weld them in place, but it is also important to weld them completely along their entire contact with the subframe as seen in this photo. This subframe connector, based on Fig. 3-1, is properly fitted by butting its forward end up to the transmission crossmember mounting bracket.

Step 5: Rocker Panel Reinforcements

This step involves the installation of the inside rocker panel reinforcements. These braces are very important to the structural rigidity of the Mustang. They tie the front and rear sections of the car together and, when combined with the subframe connectors, eliminate most of the body flex and the related camber changes commonly associated with these cars. For production-based Solo II cars, install the convertible Mustang inside rocker panels.

Aftermarket Units—If you have purchased one of the aftermarket kits, then install them according to the instructions, except again, I suggest you MIG-weld them in place instead of using the screws. The screws will work but will not provide sufficient rigidity.

If you have fabricated reinforcements from the drawing in Fig. 3-3, p. 45, it will be necessary to fit the right angle braces to the front and rear sections of the inside rocker panel. The better you fit them the stronger the structure will be and the more rigid the chassis. Take your time and carefully fit the brace around the rear of the rocker panel and the transverse

or sand the paint away and spray with the Weld–Thru Coating. Re–clamp the pieces and MIG-weld to the frame and the connector. Do the same for the rear. Be sure to weld the complete circumference of the hole in the braces to ensure a strong brace and to distribute the stress over a wider area. This will insure a long life and less chance for cracking with severe use. Be sure to spray the bare metal with 3M Weld–Thru Coating prior to welding to prevent corrosion.

This is a heat-activated zinc-plating process that is used by good body shops when welding together areas that are impossible to paint.

Aftermarket Connectors—If you have purchased aftermarket subframe connectors, I strongly suggest you weld them in place. The units that bolt–on will not stay tight long and will weaken the frame. The bolt–on versions are easier to install but are not up to severe performance use.

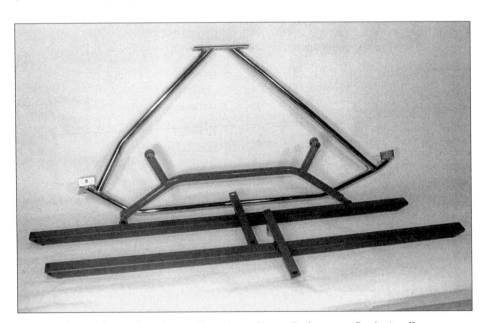

If fabricating subframes is not your thing, Kenny Brown Performance Products offers an excellent subframe kit that also provides bracing for the rear seat mounts. Anyone that has road raced or autocrossed a Mustang knows of the cracks that eventually form in the floorpan around the seat mount. Also shown are strut tower and G-load braces.

It is very important to completely scrape the corner insulation before fitting and welding the inside rocker panel braces. Not only will this stuff spoil a good weld, the fumes from the fire it starts are not good for human consumption.

interior crossmember. Also, be sure to drill the holes for the seat-belt bolts. Before you drill the holes for the bolts, measure the location of the holes by marking the inside of the car just below the attachment, lay the fabricated brace in position and scribe the correct location. Although the two most common locations have been indicated in the drawings, there can be significant differences from car to car. If you fail to do this and weld the brace in place, you will use all the expletives you learned as a teenager the first time you try to put the seat belts in. Take your time.

MIG-weld 1" beads along the edges of the reinforcements with a 2" gap between the beads. It is not necessary to weld the long edges completely. However, it is important to completely weld the 4 or 5 inches of each end. Remember to use the correct welding wire as stipulated in Step 4 above.

Please note that this design will not fit the convertible Mustang without considerable modification to the seat mount. The convertible rocker panel was changed to provide more stiffness. It angles outward and consequently requires a brace with a bend greater than 90°.

Step 6: Strut Tower Brace

To improve front-end handling it is necessary to add a strut tower brace.

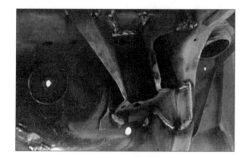

Stress from high "g" corners or drag slick equipped launches can cause the factory spot welds on the upper trailing arm bracket to tear out. MIG-welding all the seams will greatly reduce this potential problem.

The Ford convertible outside rocker panel braces can be used in stock classes that do not permit subframe connectors. These braces (FORD PN# E6ZZ-66102B66-A & E6ZZ-66102B67-A) are fitted using structural adhesive and about a million 1/4" pop rivets. The new Solo II rules allow them to be welded like the Cobra R so weld them if you can.

Check the rules for your class if you are an autocrosser. Some classes permit a single crossbrace between the strut towers while other classes allow a three-point attachment. For the street, install a three-point brace to keep your front-end righteous after a full diet of potholes.

Aftermarket Units—There are about a zillion manufacturers of these braces today. Most are pretty good and will add significant front chassis stiffness. The ones sold by Project Industries, Central Coast Mustangs, BBK or Saleen seem to be the best. However,

A strut tower brace, such as this piece from Kenny Brown Performance Products, will add much needed rigidity to the Mustang's front end. These braces are generally simple to install. All you need to do is drill a few holes for fitting.

the key point is simply to have a crossbrace.

This brace is not difficult to fabricate, however. To do so, you will need access to a 1" conduit bender and MIG-welder. Fig. 3-2 on p. 42 illustrates how to construct a simple two- or three-point brace.

If you are fabricating a brace, first locate the tabs on the front inside corners of the strut towers. Drill the holes in the strut towers and tightly bolt up the tabs. Examine Fig. 3-2 closely to determine the attaching points for the crossbrace.

Use a stick of 1/8" gas welding rod and make a pattern for the crossbrace. Be sure to provide adequate clearance for the Mass Air hose, distributor and oil filler cap (leave sufficient room to remove the cap and put oil in the engine). Use the pattern to mark the length to cut a section of 1" x .065" wall tubing, adding 2" for fitting. Examine the drawing carefully, then bend the section of tubing to fit the pattern and carefully trim the ends to fit flush against the tabs on the strut towers. MIG-weld the crossbrace to the tabs taking care to move all wiring and coil cover to prevent damage from the heat. If your class rules do not permit the strut-to-cowl bracing skip the next two paragraphs.

Fabricate the cowl plate and reinforcement doubler per the drawing in Fig. 3-2. Carefully locate the center of the cowl just above the windshield washer hose. Drill the three holes for the attaching bolts, and bolt in the plate and doubler.

Again, using sticks of 1/8" gas welding rod, form patterns for the strut tower-to-cowl braces. Take care to provide adequate clearance for the Mass Air hose and intake plenum. Cut and bend the two braces to conform to the patterns. Trim the ends to fit flush against the cowl plate between the center bolt and outside bolts (leave sufficient room to get a socket on the bolts) and the crossbrace just outside the strut tower.

Tack-weld the two pieces in position and remove the brace for complete welding. When the bar has cooled down, sand the tubing and tabs, clean with a grease and wax remover (PPG DX–330) and paint with an epoxy primer and your choice of enamel paint.

This completes the construction of the brace. Install it if you are not going to do any engine work next.

Step 7: Interior Brace

This step involves the installation of a two–point interior body brace. If you wish to install a roll bar or roll cage see the *Road Racing* section of this chapter for details. However, if a full roll bar is not part of your requirements, because of class rules or you still wish to use the rear seat, this simple chassis stiffener can be fabricated (Fig. 3-4), and still provide some small measure of rollover protection. The two–point interior body brace has been around for some time and can be purchased from most high–performance Mustang dealers. Fig. 3-4 on p. 43 shows how to fabricate the hoop if you have access to a tubing bender (not the kind found at the muffler shop but one designed to bend steel tubing without kinking it). Alternately, a local chassis shop can bend this for you or build the complete brace from Fig. 3-4.

Before you start, remove the shoulder harness guides on the door pillars. Make certain you know how the strap is indexed before you remove the retaining bolt. It makes reassembly a lot less unpleasant.

Be sure to paint the brace with an epoxy primer (PPG DP–48) before fitting. It is extremely difficult to spray the top of the brace once it has been welded in the car. Over time, the exposed metal will rust and look most uncool.

If you are going to build this yourself, begin by fabricating a hoop from 2" x .120" wall D.O.M. (Drawn Over Mandrel) tubing per Fig. 3-4 as well as the two footing plates and shoulder harness tabs. Although I have provided the proper angles for attaching the footings to the hoop, which enables you to fabricate this before installation, a

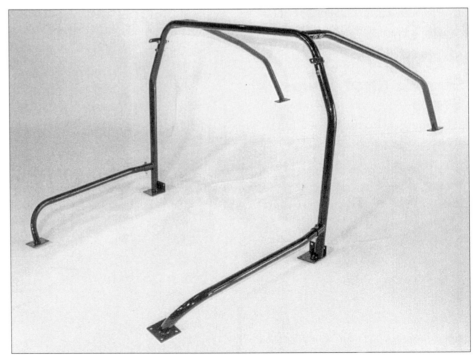

For the street, autocross and drag race enthusiast, bolt-in roll bars such as this Super Street Cage™ from Kenny Brown Performance Products can provide the driver with some measure of protection as well as increase the rigidity of the chassis. (Photo courtesy Kenny Brown Performance Products)

better fit can be achieved if you fabricate the footings and fit them to the transverse interior crossmember before attempting to weld the hoop on.

Install the footings with bolts rather than by welding so the bar can be removed later if the interior ever has to be serviced. Before welding the main hoop to the footings, check the ends to make sure they are square to the angle of the footing plates. This is very important to ensure a strong weld. With the help of a friend to hold the hoop, center the bar in the car over the footing plates and check to make sure it is vertical. If the car is sitting level (use a carpenter's level on the rocker panel brace to check) then a vertical level against the main hoop will properly set the 90° angle of the bar. If the ends of the bar do not sit flat against the footing plates when the bar is vertical it will be necessary to trim the ends of the bar so that they do.

Once the bar is set vertically, tack-weld each leg to the footing plates and re–check for alignment and vertical angle. If everything is satisfactory, weld completely around each leg at the footing plates. Fit the side tabs that attach the brace to the shoulder harness bolts by slipping the hole in the tab over the shoulder of the harness attachment hole. Clamp the tab to the brace in this position and MIG-weld it in position, tapping the tab with a hammer to wrap it around the bar as you weld. The tabs should be fabricated from .125" mild steel, approximately 1.5" x 5" in size, and wrapped partially around the bar for maximum strength. This is by no means a roll bar. However, it will add significantly to the stiffness of the chassis.

Step 8

At this point you have completed all of the basic chassis-stiffening procedures on your cone or street racer and must paint the exposed metal to prevent corrosion. Clean all welded surfaces, seams, and attachments with a wire brush or sandblast them. Carefully mask off all areas to prevent any overspray from getting on exterior painted surfaces. Using PPG DX–330 Acryla–Kleen or an equivalent, wipe all areas to be painted and apply two coats of PPG DP–48 (or any of the other four colors, black, yellow, green or red). This is an epoxy primer that is extremely durable. You should also paint the primered surfaces with color to match your car. Be aware that epoxy primers cure in about five days. Unless the color coat is sprayed within a few hours of the last primer coat, it will need to be sanded before applying paint, usually with a red Scotchbrite® pad. If you fail to do this, any color coat you spray will not stick.

This completes the chassis stiffening for the autocross/street section of this chapter. If you are building a car for this use, then go to Chapter 4 for street/autocross suspension modifications. If you are building for road racing, see below. If you are building for drag racing, see p. 37.

CHASSIS MODS FOR ROAD RACING

To build a competitive Showroom Stock, A Sedan, or World Challenge racer requires major commitments in time and labor. In addition, to compete in the World Challenge series you must hold a professional license and bring large quantities of money! This is when sponsorship becomes a big deal.

Like all groups of modifications in this chapter, be sure the car is square and clean before you start. If you still haven't done so, take your car to a frame shop and have it checked and/or straightened.

Step 1

Follow Step 1 as in the street/autocross section, p. 25.

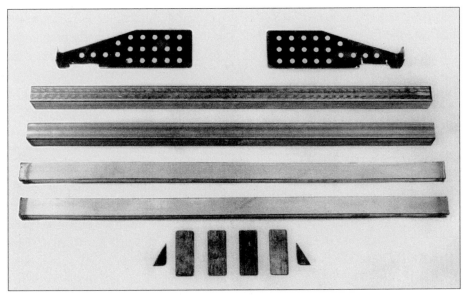

Griggs Racing offers this chassis-stiffening kit (MFK 1000) to tie the front and rear subframes together. Similar to the full-length subframes described in the text, this kit requires that the floorpan be notched in several places to insert the square tubing.

After cutting the tubing for the full-length subframes per the drawing, the rear tip must be drilled for the 3/4" trailing arm bolt sleeve and welded at the correct angle.

This modification requires that a 2" slot be cut in the floorpan from the base of the firewall and front subframe to the transverse crossmember with a Saws-all or a torch to fit the new full-length subframe connectors.

Two 3/4" x 2 1/2" long (.120" wall 4130N) trailing arm bolt sleeves must be machined. These sleeves provide a very strong support for the lower trailing arm, virtually eliminating the flex commonly associated with the stock chassis.

Step 2

Next, fabricate the subframe connectors and follow the procedures outlined in Steps 3 & 4 on p. 25 of this chapter unless you are building a World Challenge race car. Currently full-length subframes are approved for this class.

If you are purchasing subframe connectors keep in mind that the large square units and the round units will provide less ground clearance than the rectangular units shown in Fig. 3-1. Several companies make the rectangular design and offer them at a reasonable price. You make the call.

Full-Length Connectors—To fabricate the full-length subframes for

World Challenge racing cars, you will need 12' of 2" x 3" x .120" wall steel tubing. Before you start this modification, check the current rules, because this procedure is extremely difficult to reverse. Fig. 3-5 provides the specifications to fabricate these. In order to fit these connectors, you must remove the front subframe just as it turns upward, cut a notch in the floorpan extending to the rear subframe and finally cut a slot in the rear subframe that extends 2" beyond the center line of the lower trailing arm access hole. Large quantities of work.

Use an adjustable-depth carpenter square and draw a vertical line on each side of the factory front subframes approximately 3/8" rearward of the point it turns upward. With a body chisel or heavy-duty sabre saw, cut the subframes to the floorpan. Drill out the zillion spot welds that hold this section of the subframes to the floorpan and remove.

On the inside edge of each rear subframe, draw a vertical line 1-3/4" rearward from the vertical centerline of the trailing arm bolt holes. Extend this line across the bottom of the subframe to the beginning of the outside radius on the trailing arm side. With the help of a friend, snap a chalk line from the intersection of the bottom line you scribed with the outside radius to the outside edge of the front subframe and the floorpan. Move to the inside edge and snap a second chalk line. Essentially you are marking the lines that must be cut to insert the new subframes.

Measure 2-1/2" up the vertical lines on the inside of the rear subframe previously marked and draw a horizontal line along the side to define the upper edge of the new subframe. Check your measurements several times and give it the smell test before proceeding. When you are satisfied with your layout, use a body chisel, heavy-duty sabre saw or better yet, a plasma cutter, and cut the slots for the new subframes.

Fit the new subframes into the slots

In this photo, the nose of the full-length subframe is being trial-fitted in the front subframe. Once the nose has been properly aligned, the edges of the stock subframe that were not removed in this installation will be trimmed and prepped for welding.

with the forward tip fitting flush against the inside upper surface of the factory front subframe. There should be a 1/4" lip from the factory rear subframe that overlaps the new subframe. Insert a spacer with a 1/2" I.D. the length of the factory trailing arm bushing between the trailing arm attachment holes, and then insert a 6 1/2" x 1/2" bolt through it and the new subframe pin from the inside out. Torque the bolt in place and spray all areas to be welded with 3M Weld–Thru Coating.

Hammer the 1/4" lip on the rear subframe to fit flush against the new subframe. This is necessary to create a strong fit between the two. MIG-weld the new subframe along all sides. Before removing the trailing arm bolt, weld the pin in the new subframe connector in position.

Drill two 3/4" diameter holes in the factory subframe at the forward tip of the new subframe. MIG-weld the edges of these holes to the tip of the new subframe. Complete the installation by welding the transmission crossmember mounts to the new subframes.

Step 3

Follow Step 6 in the street/autocross section, p. 27 and install a three-point strut tower brace.

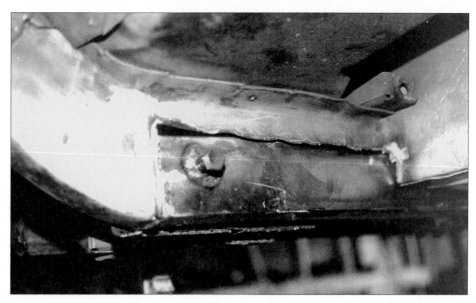

At the rear, the new full-length subframe has been fitted with the trailing arm bolt being used to secure it in proper position. Before cinching down the 6-1/2" bolt for fitting the bolt sleeve and subframe, be sure to insert a trailing arm (or sleeve of equivalent length) to prevent distortion of the stock frame.

Step 4

Lower the car from the jackstands and remove the hood, nose piece, fenders, and doors. Remove the engine and transmission as a unit. Re–clean the engine bay. Remove wiring, radiator, A/C condenser and any components that are next to a body or frame seam.

Step 5

Set the car up on jackstands mounted under the rocker panel seams, with the jackstands located in the jack notches, providing at least 18" of floor clearance.

Step 6

Disconnect the flexible rear brake line at the frame, taking care not to get brake fluid on anything important. Remove the rear end assembly, including the trailing arms. Remove the shocks and the horizontal dampeners. Disconnect the

At the base of the stock front subframe, just in front of the nose of the new full-length subframe, drill two or three 3/4" holes for welding the tip to the stock frame.

After the installation of both full-length subframes, the floorpan must be skip-welded to the tubing and the seams filled with a body seam filler.

swaybar and trailing arms from the axle housing.

Step 7

Move to the front of the car and remove the struts, springs, spindles, control arms and rack and pinion. Examine each part for any unusual wear if you are going to use it again. Scribe lines on the frame at the rear edge of the lower rear crossmember to frame mounts as a reference point. Finally, remove the four large bolts and the four small bolts that hold the crossmember to the frame and remove the crossmember.

Step 8

Next, purchase a case of your friends' favorite beverage and invite them over for a little scrape and brush party. At every body seam in the front section, along the rocker panel seams, door opening seams, front and rear frame seams, trailing arm attachments, and inside wheel tub seams, scrape and brush the paint to expose clean metal and spray with 3M Weld–Thru Coating.

With the help of a propane torch, heat and scrape all the tar-like sound deadener in the footwells, the rear seat area, on the driveshaft tunnel and in the trunk area. This stuff is heavy and a fire hazard so remove it all.

Step 9

Using good lighting, carefully examine the floorpan at and around the driver's seat mounts, the driveshaft tunnel where it intersects the transverse crossmember (at the rear seat platform), just above the axle pinion and around the upper trailing arm mounts for cracks. These are the most common areas where cracks form. Scrape the areas along every crack to bare metal and spray with 3M Weld–Thru Coating.

Step 10

MIG-weld every body seam and trailing arm bracket that was cleaned in

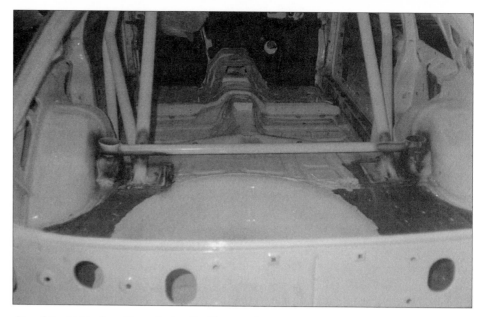

One of the biggest problems facing the Mustang is the flexing of the rear shock towers. This effect becomes particularly acute when the car is equipped with a Carrera coil-over conversion kit. A simple section of tubing welded between the two towers can eliminate this problem. In this photo, the brace is also welded to the roll bar to provide additional rigidity.

Step 9 using ER70S–6 (.030") wire. Lay down 1" beads approximately 1" apart to prevent warping, then weld in the spaces between the first beads. (Again, do not acetylene weld! Mustangs use high-carbon steel in the frame that can be ruined with excessive heat. The wire specified, ER70S–6, is designed for this type of metal.) Be sure to weld completely around the trailing arm attachment brackets. These things have been known to pull out under severe usage. This can be very disconcerting when negotiating a turn at 100 mph. If you will be installing a torque arm or three–link rear suspension do not weld the upper trailing arm brackets.

Make one last check for cracks, then MIG-weld each crack found in Step 9 completely, extending the weld 1/4" beyond the visible crack's end. This will ensure that the hairline fractures that typically extend beyond the visible ends will be fused, preventing new cracks at the same location.

Step 11: Rear Shock Tower Brace

Before you can proceed with the installation of a roll cage, it is necessary to fabricate the rear shock tower brace first. This piece adds considerable rigidity to the rear section of the car, essentially halting the inward flex of the shock towers, allowing more precise shock function. I have included a drawing of it (Fig. 3-6, p.45) if you wish to fabricate this yourself. There are several high–performance shops that sell rear shock tower braces, although most are bolt–in types. When you have completed the fitting of the roll bar with the shock tower brace, weld it in place even if it is a bolt–in unit, unless the rules for your class stipulate otherwise.

Fabricating Your Own–Begin fabricating the rear shock tower brace by fitting the short 2.5" pieces of tubing atop the shock towers centered around the shock mounting washers and cushions. MIG-weld these in place. Next you must custom-fit the length of the crossbar, especially on the earlier cars, as quality control was not up to current standards. Once you have fitted the cross–brace, do not weld it in place if you are going to mount the roll bar braces on the frame next to the shock towers. You will be able to tie the rear shock tower brace to the roll bar braces for maximum strength and rigidity if you carefully fit the roll bar braces. This can be accomplished by first laying the shock tower cross-brace in place. Then locate the roll bar braces at a point on the frame next to the shock towers, where the upper roll bar braces contact the shock tower cross-brace. This will permit welding the two systems together to provide maximum strength and rigidity.

Step 12: Roll Cage

This step involves the installation of a roll cage. If you are going to road race or run the high-speed autocross series in SCCA, you must have an SCCA-approved roll cage that is constructed according to SCCA specifications. These are different and considerably more complex than required of NHRA/IHRA. For the Ford Mustang, SCCA currently requires a roll cage from 1-7/8" D.O.M. steel tubing with a minimum wall thickness of .120". The size of the bar is dictated by SCCA and is dependent on the normal weight and anticipated speed capability of the car. Check the latest rules before you buy the tubing. I have included drawings and specifications of the current minimum

This bolt-in roll cage was designed with ease of installation as the primary goal. Unfortunately, this cage locates the rear mounting plates outside the usual stress points, greatly reducing its ability to provide much-needed rear chassis rigidity.

SCCA construction requirements.

Bolt-In Cages—Although maximum strength is achieved by welding the cage in place, the Showroom Stock class requires roll cages to be bolted in and removable. Total insanity! The bolt–in units work well but lack the rigidity found with a welded–in bar. Clearly why you are not allowed to weld the bar in. The moral of the story: check the rules before you buy a kit or build the roll

cage. Because of the difficulty and expense of fabricating a bolt–in cage that meets SCCA requirements, a purchase is definitely in order. Autopower Industries (3424 Pickett Street, San Diego, CA 92110, 619/297-3300) has these for your Mustang. Just follow the instructions that come with the cage and skip the rest of this step.

Most roll cage kits come with a main hoop bent to fit and several straight pieces of tubing that require custom fitting. Not all kits are made with D.O.M. tubing (some actually still use E.R.W.), so ask before you write the check.

For the do–it–yourselfers, I have included specifications to bend the main hoop if you wish to construct the entire cage yourself. The savings from bending and fitting the tubing yourself will pay for a mechanical tubing bender, provided you don't screw up too much tubing. Generally it will take about 100' of tubing for the main cage and an additional 20' to 30' of smaller tubing for cross braces. Using 4130N chrome-moly steel was the trick setup. SCCA no longer allows this though.

Building a roll bar requires the correct placement of the main bar and the rear braces. Although the bar is designed primarily as a safety device, fitting the rear braces so they tie into the frame at high-stress locations, such as those shown in this photo, can also serve to reduce the flex associated with a stock chassis.

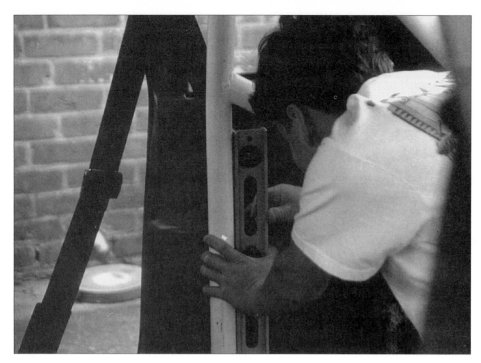

Before welding the main hoop to the footing plates, it is important to level the car at the rocker panels and then level the bar. Jeff McClure is shown here checking the vertical alignment on the author's SVO Mustang's roll bar.

Building a Cage—Building a roll cage is not difficult but it is time consuming. If you are not a good welder just tack the plates and bars in place and have someone else do the welding. This is the one area in a race car where the best is cheap.

Footing Plates—Begin by fabricating all of the footing plates. Place them in the correct locations and scribe around the edges. Strip away the paint approximately 1/2" on each side of the perimeter lines for welding. The footings for the main hoop should be in the corners of the rear footwells extending up the side of the rocker panel ("L" shaped). The front hoop footings should approximate the front edge of the door openings, with the rear footings placed on the frame next to the shock towers on the front edge of the shock towers. If your class rules do not permit the use of the shock tower brace, then be sure to attach the rear braces to the shock towers.

MIG-weld the plates in position by first tack-welding each of the four sides. Next, lay down 1" beads with 2" separation, and then weld the entire perimeter between the 1" beads once again to prevent warpage. Don't forget to spray the bare metal with 3M Weld–Thru Coating prior to welding.

Main Hoop—The main hoop of the roll bar should be located on the floorpan just in front of the transverse interior crossmember. Check the distance between the rocker panels before you bend the bar and be sure you understand that measurements on the inside of the car will be equivalent to the exterior-most sides of the bar. Subtract the diameter of the roll bar from the inside measurement (1/2 the diameter from the vertical measurement) in order to achieve a tight fit. The bar should fit against and be welded to the rocker panel and as close as possible to the roof for the greatest strength. Remember, the lengths specified in the drawings should be correct, but always cut a little long and trim to make a good fit.

Before welding the main hoop, check the ends to make sure they are square to the angle of the footing plates. This is very important to ensure a strong weld. With the help of a friend to hold the

hoop, center the bar in the car over the footing plates and check to make sure it is vertical. If the car is sitting level (use a carpenter level on the rocker panel brace to check) then a vertical level against the main hoop will properly set the 90° angle of the bar. If the ends of the bar do not sit flat against the footing plates when the bar is vertical it will be necessary to trim the ends of the bar to attain this fit. This is very important! Essentially the bar should be able to stand on its own once the ends are flush against the footing plates.

Once the bar is set vertically, tack-weld each leg to the footing plates and re–check for alignment and vertical angle. If everything is satisfactory, weld completely around each leg at the footing plates.

Braces & Tabs—When the main hoop has been completely welded to the footing plates, you must fit the braces and shoulder harness tabs. If you do not have access to a tubing notcher it will be necessary to cut the notches with a plasma cutter, torch or grinder. If you have decided to use 4130N steel (chrome-moly), do not cut it with a torch! It can be difficult to get the correct normalization in the metal when you do this and consequently the bar could crack. Grind or notch only. There must be one brace within 6" of the top of the main hoop legs and in a parallel direction (to the length of the car) at an angle of at least 30° from vertical on each side of the main hoop. The best location is in the center of the bend (see Fig. 3-8, p.47).

Fitting Braces—Fitting the braces is normally a very difficult process for most people. However, you can use a 1" x 2" length of wood as a guide to determine the exact angles to cut the braces. Simply trim the end of the wood where the brace mounts to the rear footing plate (while holding it against the main hoop at the estimated angle to the rear footing) until you have achieved a flat mate with the footing plate. Next, carefully trim the

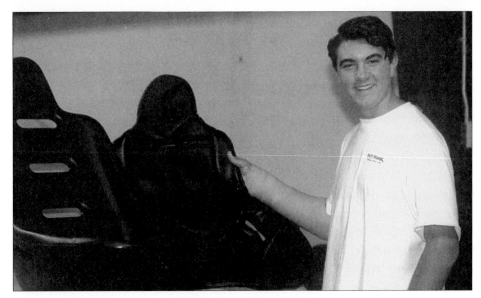

If you are going to go fast, a comfortable and rugged seat is imperative. The Racer Components Inc. seat and cover shown by Major Mathis is the most popular setup on the market today.

length of wood to exactly fit the back edge of the main hoop. Lay the length of wood alongside the tubing for the brace and cut the end that mates with the rear footing plate to match the side angle.

Lay the wood guide against the tubing again and carefully mark the attachment angle to the main hoop. This angle designates the extremes for the notch that fits the brace to the main hoop when viewed from the top and bottom. It is at this point that most people screw up, so slow down and take your time. Be sure to take into consideration the side angle of the main hoop if you attach your braces at the bend. (Study Fig. 3-8 before you cut the notches.)

Cut the tubing off approximately 1/2 the diameter of the main hoop tubing beyond the mark for the notch extremes (7/8" on a 1.75" bar). This should be at the approximate angle of the notch when viewed from the side of the triangle formed by the brace and the main hoop. Next, cut a half circle on the top and bottom of the brace to match the edge of the main hoop tubing. These half circles should approximate the extremes of the attachment angle as noted by the side mark from the wood guide. Be careful not to cut too much. You can always trim additional amounts to provide a tight

fit; however, if you cut too much off, you will have to scrap the piece and start over. Use this same method for each type brace on one side (rear and side door braces), the transverse and horizontal braces.

To facilitate the construction of the bars for the other side, a mirror image can be made by wrapping tag paper (manila file folder) tightly around the notched end (tape sides together), and, using a sharp knife, cut the notch out of the paper. Slide the template you have made off and onto the tubing for the

second brace and mark the end for notching. Make certain you have the two notches of the second bar properly indexed before making your cuts. Remember, although it will be a mirror image, the inward slope of the side angles cause the notches to rotate in the opposite directions on each side. Check it closely before you cut. This is a simple and fast way to fabricate the second set of bars.

Horizontal Bracing—Horizontal and diagonal braces must be installed in the main hoop for all approved roll cages. This bar should be approximately 24" from the floor to facilitate the installation of shoulder straps. The shoulder straps attach brackets must be welded to the bar and should be designed to prevent penetration into the back of the seat in the event of a severe rear impact. This attachment should be constructed to sandwich the harness tips between two plates, putting the attaching bolt in double shear. The mounts should be wide enough to fit the driver's shoulders, approximately 4" to 6" apart. Do not use the "Y" type shoulder straps, as they have been outlawed by SCCA.

Side Hoops—The next step is to fabricate the side hoops. Typically the side/door bars originate on the main hoop

No race car is complete without an approved safety harness. This popular Simpson harness provides excellent 5-point support with shoulder, lap and submarine belts to contain and protect the driver.

at the intersection of the horizontal brace. This should be observed as this provides the maximum strength. There must be at least one bar on each side running horizontally from the main hoop at the intersection of the horizontal bar to the front hoop; and at least one bar running diagonally from the intersection of the horizontal braces' intersection with the main hoop, and the intersection of the front hoop with the floor footing. The best bet is to cut the interior panel from the driver's door and extend three horizontal bars, equally spaced, into the door. A fourth horizontal bar should run straight across between the main and forward hoops along the inside base of the door. Add two sets of vertical braces between the four bars, dividing the distance between the two hoops equally. Obviously this is more difficult but also provides considerable peace of mind to the driver.

Use 1/8" gas welding rods or 3/16" brake line to form a pattern for these bars. Start at the main hoop intersection with the rear braces and follow the upper door opening forward and down the windshield pillar to the cowl and straight down to the floor along the forward door opening. Check the fit carefully then cut a section of tubing approximately 1" long on each end and bend the bar accordingly. Once you have the bar close, cut fish-mouth notches in the main hoop end and trim small amounts at a time until the front tip fits flush against the center of the floor plate. Like the main hoop, this bar should fit against the rocker panel also. If you will be using the minimum door braces (one horizontal and one diagonal) be sure to fit this bar just forward of center of the footing plate to accommodate the diagonal bar.

Bend a mirror image of the first bar for the other side using the completed bar as a pattern. Tack-weld these two side hoops in place.

Fit a horizontal bar between the upper bends of the side hoops using a template

as described for constructing the rear braces. Additionally a second bar is necessary that will run between the side hoops just above the steering column. This bar should be mounted at the intersection of the upper horizontal door bars. Generally the steering column is attached to this bar.

Finally, the forward foot protection braces should be attached at the intersection of the top door safety bar and horizontal front bar and extend forward and downward to the frame. The footings must be welded to the frame just where the frame turns down below the strut tower in the wheelwell. This brace will pass through the body structure, from the side hoop, to the frame in the wheelwell. Typically these braces are fitted after the #2 crossmember has been installed so they can extend down and tie into it as well.

Additionally, you must drill a 3/16" hole in the main hoop at least 3" from any bend so that the tech inspector can check the tubing thickness. Normally this hole is just below the bend on the driver's side (see Fig. 3-8) Be sure to add side tabs to tie the main hoop to the door pillar at the factory shoulder harness

attaching point and about halfway between the shoulder harness tab and the rocker panel braces. Also, it is very important to extend additional braces from the main hoop to the interior side of the upper trailing arm mounts. Be sure to use an appropriate footing plate for strength. Higher speeds, fatter tires, and more horsepower can cause the floorpan to flex (or even tear out) at this location, which will cause undesirable suspension geometry changes.

This completes the basic roll cage construction. For the safety conscious, additional bracing such as a "Petty Bar" may be added to provide additional rollover protection. Generally the main hoop's rear braces have diagonal braces forming an X between the top of the hoop and the base of the braces to strengthen the cage. The additional weight of a few extra braces may seem questionable now, but in the unlikely event you get to test your roll cage, you'll be glad you added them.

Step 13: Rear Wheelwells

Whether or not you modify the rear wheelwells is dependent on the class

When the rear seat is a must and drag racing is your thing, the rear brace can be angled over the seat and bent downward to a footing plate located on the rear frame (see Fig. 3-12 for bending details).

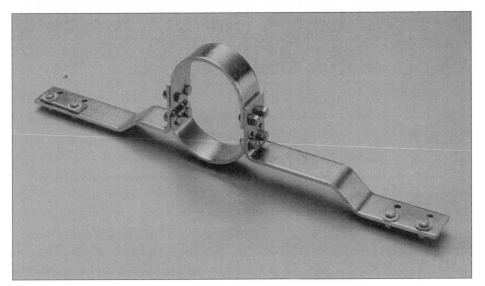

Whether you hurdle around corners or blister strips of quarter-mile pavement, if high horsepower is part of the package a front driveshaft hoop is mandatory. This photo shows the new NHRA/IHRA approved Lakewood Industries hoop that is specifically designed to be a direct fit for the Mustang (PN18015).

rules. Generally, this modification is not allowed in Showroom Stock classes. Additionally, when running the World Challenge Series, any fender modifications must be made to conform to the original wheelwell opening design.

The following procedure is meant to provide some measure of tire clearance for the stock and sedan classes. Using the huge 275/40ZR-17 Goodyear GS–CS tires will generally require reworking of the wheelwell opening by a skilled body repairman. Know which tires you will be using before attempting this.

To complete this modification with minimum damage to your paint, you will need a sandbag to absorb the harmonics when you hammer the inside lip. The easiest approach is to use one of the bags designed as a rifle or pistol shooting rest. They are typically leather and quite durable. If not available, one can be fabricated from one of the cotton canvas bags that shotgun shot pellets are sold in, or virtually any heavy cotton canvas bag. Fill the bag with coarse foundation pad sand (available at most lumber yards or soil centers), being sure to pack it tightly, fold the open end over and sew it shut. Cut the excess cloth off so it's easy to handle.

Next, cut approximately 1/2" from the inside lip of the fender. The best method is to have someone experienced with a body air chisel do the cutting. Most body shops will be glad to accommodate you for a nominal fee. If it is not possible to do, then don't worry about it. Instead use a hacksaw and cut slots in the fender lip to within 3/8" of the outside edge. These should be spaced approximately 1" apart.

Hold the sandbag you fabricated against the outside edge of the wheelwell opening and slowly work the inside lip down and out with a 2-lb. ballpeen hammer. Take your time, using light blows at first. Don't over-hammer as the paint will de–laminate at the fender's edge.

Once you have completed this modification, clean the hammered surface and spray a thin coat of 3M Undercoating to prevent rust. Obviously painting the fender lip would be better.

CHASSIS MODS FOR DRAG RACING

The modifications provided in this section have been used by several quick racers to put their cars in the 9's, most notably the Joe Rivera-prepared twin–turbo 5.0 Mustang of Mario Meza.

This is the ultimate shoestring chassis setup. Joe is the owner of EFI Hyperformance in Houston, Texas, and he was kind enough to share his setup.

If you have ever read any of the articles on the very fast Pro 5.0 Class cars (Stormin' Norman, Brian Wolfe, Gene Deputy, etc.) you know these cars are very light, weighing in between 2,500 and 2,800 lbs. It is extremely important to keep this in mind. Unless something adds to the speed or safety of your car or is required by class rules, it is only slowing you down. That incredible 200-watt sound system with the four 22-lb. woofers may be the "in" thing but you pay the price on your time slip. For every 100 lbs. of weight you save you can expect 1/10 of a second reduction in your E.T. in the 11- to 12-second cars.

It is important to note that some of the changes to your car to achieve better launch and traction control for drag racing will have a detrimental effect on its ability to negotiate a turn, even small ones. Sudden directional changes at speeds, like swerving to avoid your neighbor's cat, could plant you against the curb or on your roof. Keep this in mind until you have adjusted to the difference in steering response.

Step 1

Like the previous chassis sections, begin by mounting the car on jackstands that provide at least 18" of floor clearance. The jackstands should be placed under the rear axle housing and front control arms until the subframe connectors are welded in. When this is completed, set the car with the jackstands under the rocker panel seams at the jack point notches.

Step 2

Follow Step 6 in the *Road Racing* section, p. 31, and remove the rear axle assembly, except store the unused parts in a box or toss them (these items will not be used).

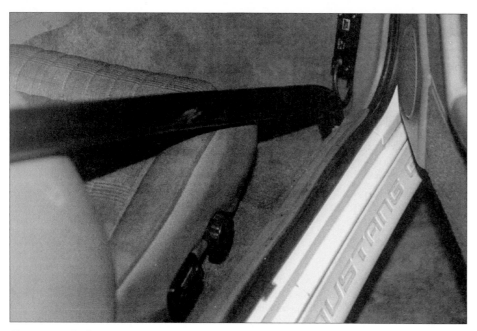

If your sanctioning body or club allows a 6-point roll cage (NHRA/IHRA) and ease of entry and exit are important, the front side brace should angle down from the main hoop to just in front of the rocker boxes. A slight bend at the tip as demonstrated in this photo and the accompanying drawings in Fig. 3-12, p.51, will provide for easier installation.

Step 3

Remove the seats, carpet and sound deadener. Using a strong putty knife and a propane torch, de–laminate and peel back the tar–like sound insulation directly above the upper trailing arm mounts inside the car. This is to prevent a fire when you do the welding. If you have difficulty locating the proper spots, just look for the spot welds and compare to those under the car on the brackets.

How much of the sound deadener you remove is a matter of personal choice. This stuff is quite heavy and should be removed for the more serious racer. Once again, if it doesn't make it safer or go faster you probably don't need it.

Brush and scrape away the paint around the seams of the upper trailing arm brackets on the chassis, making sure you have clean bare metal. Spray the exposed bare metal with 3M Weld–Thru Coating.

As in the *Road Racing* section, use good lighting and carefully examine the floorpan at and around the driver's seat mounts, the driveshaft tunnel where it intersects the transverse crossmember (at the rear seat platform), just above the axle pinion and around the upper trailing arm mounts for cracks. Scrape the cracks to bare metal and spray with 3M Weld–Thru Coating.

If you are not satisfied with the inconsistent 60-foot times that a stock chassis generally provides, then drag your trunk of $100 bills over to one of the top chassis shops and have a real chassis built. Photographed here is a new Comp Car chassis being built at one of the top shops in America, Zander Action Products in Houston, Texas.

Twisting frames can unload the left slick, causing some pretty scary rides. When high horsepower and fat slicks are involved, proper bracing of the subframes is critical.

Step 4

Follow the instructions in Step 10 of the *Road Racing* section, p. 32 for MIG-welding.

Step 5

Follow Steps 3 & 4 in the *Street/Autocross* section, p. 25 and install the subframe connectors that are specified in Fig. 3-1, or weld-in aftermarket units.

Step 6: Roll Bar

This step involves the installation of a 6-point roll bar. See Fig. 3-12, p. 51, to fabricate the main hoop if you have access to a tubing bender. Be sure to paint all the bars, especially the main hoop, with an epoxy primer (PPG DP–48) before welding.

Pre–fabricated drag race roll bars come in all shapes and sizes. Current NHRA/IHRA requirements specify a .120" wall D.O.M. steel tubing diameter of 1.75" for roll bars and cages. Since these steps are for modifying a street car, a 6–point roll bar is recommended. If your car will never see the 11's then a two–point interior body brace will provide significant strength to the chassis and some rollover protection.

There are many variations of roll bars and kits sold today, including beautifully chrome plated ones. Oftentimes these have rear braces that are bent to clear the rear seat. Very convenient but not very strong. Additionally, most racing organizations do not permit chrome-plated roll bars. The chrome plating can embrittle the metal if it is not baked at 300° for several hours just after it is plated to de–hydrogenate. The chrome plating also makes it very difficult to see cracks. The best bet is to avoid those shiny bars and spend your savings on go-fast stuff.

Installation—Most roll bar kits come with a main hoop bent to fit and three straight pieces of tubing (5 on the 6–point bars) that require custom fitting. There must be one brace at least in the upper 1/3 of the main hoop legs and in a parallel direction (to the length of the car) at an angle of at least 30° from vertical on each side of the main hoop. The upper braces should extend to the rear frame near the taillight panel with an 8" radius bend at the end if you are to retain your rear seat. Although this is an acceptable location, it is not the optimum position to achieve maximum stiffness in the chassis. The best location is to attach the braces to the rear shock tower or frame next to the shock towers.

If you attach the rear braces to the shock towers, the inside rear interior panels will have to be modified to fit around the main hoop and roll bar braces if the interior is to be retained. This is a real pain and requires a great deal of patience. No instructions—just approximate the location of the necessary holes and fit an oversize plate made of .032" 2024–T3 aluminum that fits tight around the bars. Use screws with rivet–nuts or pop rivets to attach the plates to the interior panels to cover the unsightly holes you will probably make.

Begin fitting the roll bar by finding the approximate location of the main hoop just behind the driver. The location of the bar is dependent on the normal seating location of the driver. Competition rules generally require that the bar must pass overhead within 6" of the driver's head, so be sure you know that location. If the driver's seating position permits, the bar should be located atop the lower trailing arm torque box just behind the transverse interior crossmember. This is a very strong point in the car and will go a long way toward stiffening the chassis.

Unfortunately, locating the main hoop in this position can require significant modifications to some interior panels to fit. If this is a problem (like for a street car) then mount the bar atop the transverse crossmember, being sure to bend the footing plates to contour the 90° edge with approximately half the footing plate bent downward.

Basically, to install the main hoop, turn to Step 12 of the *Road Racing* section, beginning on p. 34 with the section titled "Main Hoop," and follow the instructions from there through fitting the rear braces and shoulder harness tabs.

Horizontal Brace—Although technically not required for a street machine, a horizontal brace should be installed in the main hoop and is a requirement for NHRA/IHRA-approved roll bars. The same warnings and specs apply as outlined on p. 35.

Locate the side bar footings in the front floorpan next to the rocker panel, centered at the base of the forward door opening. After the footings have been located and installed, the side bar must be fabricated. Typically the side/door bars originate on the main hoop at the intersection of the horizontal brace. This should be observed as this provides the maximum strength.

To construct the side/door bars make a template from 1/8" gas welding rods or 3/16" brake lines. It may be necessary to put a bend at the forward end of these bars to provide adequate clearance and fit around the seats. If so, bend the bar at the forward end with a 2" downward extension.

Trim the forward tip so it fits flush against the footing plate at the correct angle to the main hoop. Next, notch the main hoop end of the bar so it fits tightly to the hoop. Take your time and make a good fit. This is very important for strength. Once you have completed one bar make an exact duplicate of it for the other side.

Complete the construction of your 6-point roll bar by MIG-welding the door bars to the main hoop and the footing plates.

If a full roll bar is not part of your requirements, a simple chassis stiffener can be fabricated that will not delete the rear seat while offering some small measure of rollover protection. Follow Step 7 in the *Street/Autocross* section, p. 28, and install a 2-point interior body brace.

Step 7

This involves the modification of the rear wheelwell openings to accommodate larger rear tires, such as the M&H Streetmaster slicks. Generally these 275–50/15 tires require an 8" or 9" wheel to react properly. I have seen these slicks used on a stock 7" Mustang wheel with marginal success, although it is not recommended. This modification is an optional step for the street machine and is only required to prevent tire chaffing when utilizing the larger tires or slicks.

Follow Step 13 in the *Road Racing* section, p. 36. Additionally, using the same or heavier hammer, pound the inside corners and along the lower inside edge of the inboard wheelwell. The inside lower edge will require approximately 1/2" inboard relocation. The area in front of the spring perch will require the greatest modification, typically as much as 1.5" inboard in the corners. This is where the larger tires (28" diameter on 10" wide wheels) rub the most, so pay close attention to this modification.

At this point you have completed all the basic chassis stiffening on your street machine and must paint the exposed metal to prevent corrosion. Follow Step 8 in the *Street/Autocross* section.

SUMMARY

Obviously it does not take a Rhodes scholar to see this chapter is for the serious racer. Even if you are just looking to improve the handling of your street car, at least install the rocker panel reinforcements and subframe connectors. Like virtually all unibody cars, the Mustang has a tremendous amount of flex in stock form that translates into a very dramatic and negative effect on handling, be it drag racing or corner burning. These modifications are the minimums. The next three chapters entail designing and building the suspension for specific applications. Chapter 4 is for *Street/Autocross;* Chapter 5 is for *Road Racing;* and Chapter 6 is for *Drag Racing.* However, some of the steps in these chapters are repeated in the others, so it is best if you read them all through first before performing any more work. If you don't have the fabricating skills and/or time, I've outlined the most popular bolt-on suspension kits in Chapter 7, if that is the way you want to go. ■

Modifying the fender flares is generally necessary when running the 275 series tires or the 28 x 10 drag slicks. Trimming the inside lip and then cutting slots to within 3/8" of the outside edge will permit easier modification.

Subframe Connector

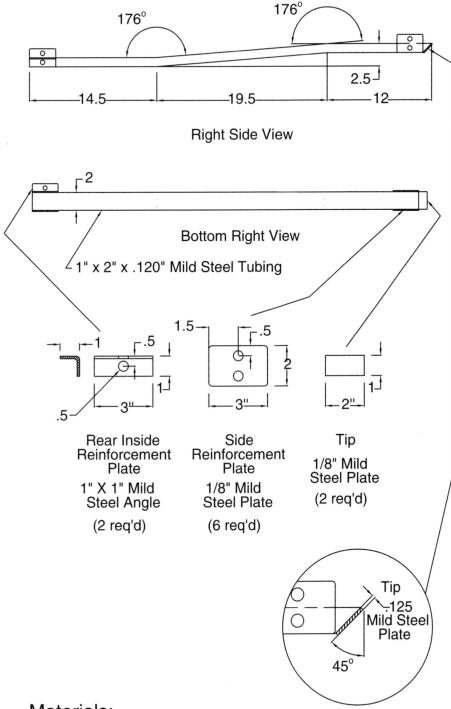

176° 176°

Right Side View

2.5

14.5 19.5 12

2

Bottom Right View

1" x 2" x .120" Mild Steel Tubing

1 .5

1.5 .5

.5

2

1

.5

3" 3" 2"

1

Rear Inside
Reinforcement
Plate

1" X 1" Mild
Steel Angle

(2 req'd)

Side
Reinforcement
Plate

1/8" Mild
Steel Plate

(6 req'd)

Tip

1/8" Mild
Steel Plate

(2 req'd)

Tip
.125
Mild Steel
Plate

45°

Materials:

(2) 1" x 2" x .120" Mild Steel Tubing
(2) 1" x 1 7/16" x .125" Mild Steel Plate
(6) 2" x 3" x .125" Mild Steel Plate
(2) 1" x 1" x .125" Mild Steel Angle

Fig. 3-1

Strut Tower Brace

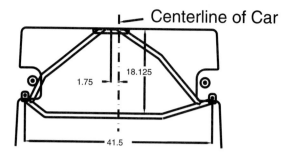

Centerline of Car

18.125

1.75

41.5

All Sizes are Approximate...Fit to Your Car

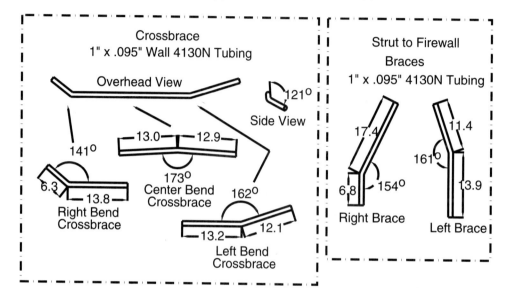

Crossbrace
1" x .095" Wall 4130N Tubing

Overhead View

141°

Side View
121°

13.0 — 12.9

6.3
13.8

173°
Center Bend
Crossbrace

Right Bend
Crossbrace

162°

13.2 — 12.1

Left Bend
Crossbrace

Strut to Firewall
Braces
1" x .095" 4130N Tubing

17.4

11.4

161°

6.8   154°

13.9

Right Brace

Left Brace

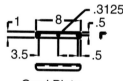

1

8

.3125

.5

3.5

.5

Cowl Plate
1" x 1" x .1875"
Mild Steel Angle

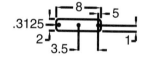

8

5

.3125

2

1

3.5

Cowl Reinforcement Plate
2" x 8" x .125"
Mild Steel or Aluminum
Plate

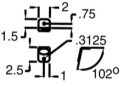

2

.75

1.5

.3125

2.5   1

102°

Strut Tower
Tabs
2" x 4" x .1875"
Mild Steel Plate
(2 req'd)

Materials:
(1) 1" x 10' x .095" Wall 4130N Tubing
(1) 1" x 1" x .1875" Steel Angle
(1) 2" x 8" x .125" Mild Steel or Aluminum Plate
(2) 2" x 4" x .1875" Mild Steel Plate
(3) AN5-14A Bolts (5/16")
(4) AN5-12A Bolts
(7) AN315-5 Nuts
(7) AN935-S Lock Washers
(4) AN960-5 Flat Washers

Fig. 3-2

2-Point Body Brace

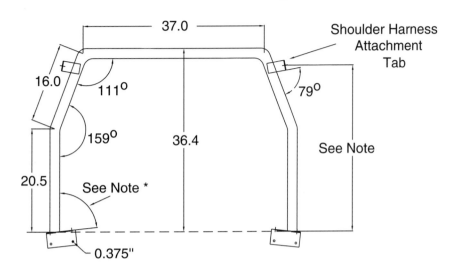

37.0

Shoulder Harness
Attachment
Tab

16.0

111°

79°

159°

36.4

See Note

20.5

See Note *

0.375"

Footing
(Passenger Side)

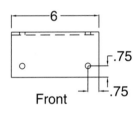

6

.75

.75

Front

90°

Side

.375

1.25

3

1.75

Top

6" x 6" x .1875" Mild Steel Plate
(2 req'd)

Shoulder Harness
Tab

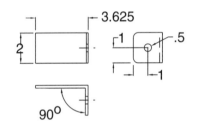

3.625

2

1

.5

1

90°

2" x 5 5/8" x .1875"
Mild Steel Plate
(2 req'd)

* Note:
Different year models
and body types have
unique dimensions. Fit
to your car.

Footing Doubler

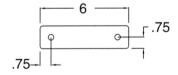

6

.75

.75

1 1/2" x 6" .1875"
Mild Steel Plate

Materials:

(1) 1 7/8" x 10' x .120" Wall D.O.M.
    Steel Tubing
(2) 6" x 6" x 3/16" Mild Steel Plate
(2) 2" x 5 5/8" x 3/16" Mild Steel Plate
(4) 1 1/2" x 6" x 3/16" Mild Steel Plate
(8) AN6-14A Bolts (3/8")
(8) AN315-6 Nuts
(8) AN935-5 Lock Washers

Fig. 3-4

Full-Length Subframe Connectors

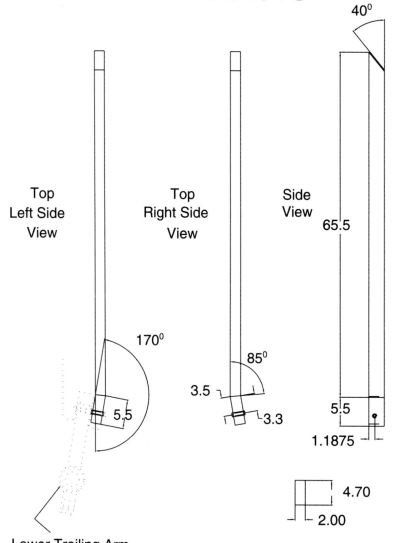

Top
Left Side
View

Top
Right Side
View

Side
View

40⁰

65.5

170⁰

85⁰

5.5

3.5

3.3

5.5

1.1875

Lower Trailing Arm

4.70

2.00

End Plate
2" x 4.7" x .1875"
Mild Steel Plate
(2 req'd)

Materials:
(2) 2" x 3" x .120" Square
Mild Steel Tubing
(2) .75" x 2.5" x .120" Wall Rd. Tubing
(2) 2" x 4.7" x .1875" Mild Steel
Plate

.75

2.5

Pin
Trailing Arm Bolt
.75" x 2.5" x .120" Wall

Fig. 3-5

44

Rocker Panel Reinforcement

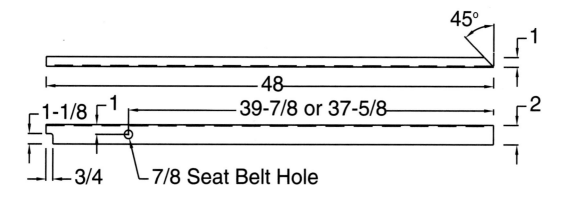

45°

48

1

1-1/8   1   39-7/8 or 37-5/8   2

3/4   7/8 Seat Belt Hole

Materials:

(2) 1" x 2" x 48" 10 Gauge Mild Steel

or

(2) 1" x 2" x 48" 10 Gauge Junior Angle

Fig. 3-3

Rear Shock Tower Brace

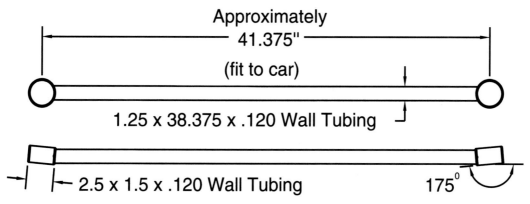

Approximately
41.375"

(fit to car)

1.25 x 38.375 x .120 Wall Tubing

2.5 x 1.5 x .120 Wall Tubing   175°

Materials:
(1) 1.25" x .120" Wall Mild Steel Tubing, approx. 38.375" long
(2) 2.5" x .120" Wall Mild Steel Tubing, 1.5" long

Fig. 3-6

1   Roll Cage

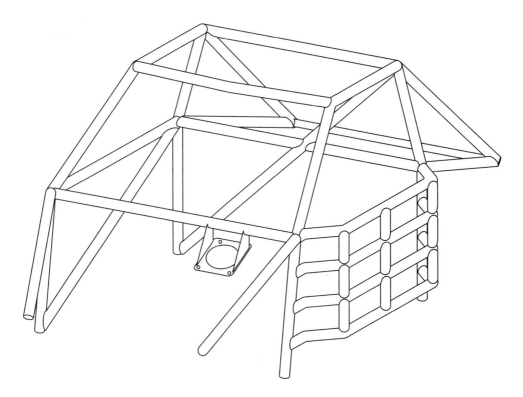

Construction Steps:

(1) Locate and attach footings.
(2) Fabricate main hoop.
(3) Fabricate and attach rear braces.
(4) Fabricate and attach side roll bars.
(5) Fabricate and attach front upper roll bar.
(6) Fabricate and attach dash brace.
(7) Fabricate and attach door braces.
(8) Fabricate and attach front braces.
(9) Fabricate and fit steering column attachment and fit to driver's position.

Fig. 3-7

2 Roll Cage
Main Hoop & Braces

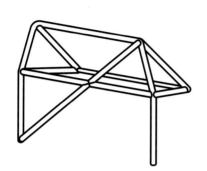

Materials:
32' x 1 7/8" x .120" Wall
    D.O.M. Mild Steel Tubing
(1) 1 1/4" x 42" x .120" Wall
    D.O.M. Mild Steel Tubing
(4) 6" x 6" x .125" Mild
    Steel Plate
(8) AN6-12A Bolts
(8) AN315-6 Nuts
(8) AN935-6 Lock Washers

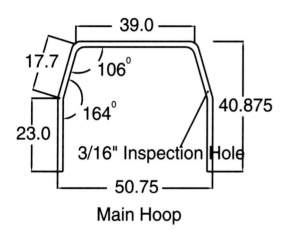

Main Hoop

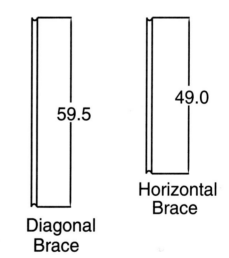

Diagonal
Brace

Horizontal
Brace

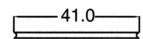

Upper Rear Brace
(2 req'd)

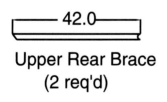

Horizontal Brace
Shock Tower to Shock Tower
1-1/4" x .120" Wall D.O.M
Mild Steel Tubing

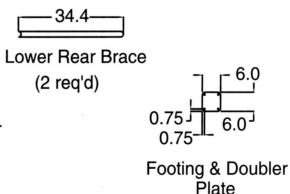

Lower Rear Brace
(2 req'd)

Footing & Doubler
Plate
(4 req'd)

Fig. 3-8

47

3 Roll Cage
Shoulder Harness Attachment

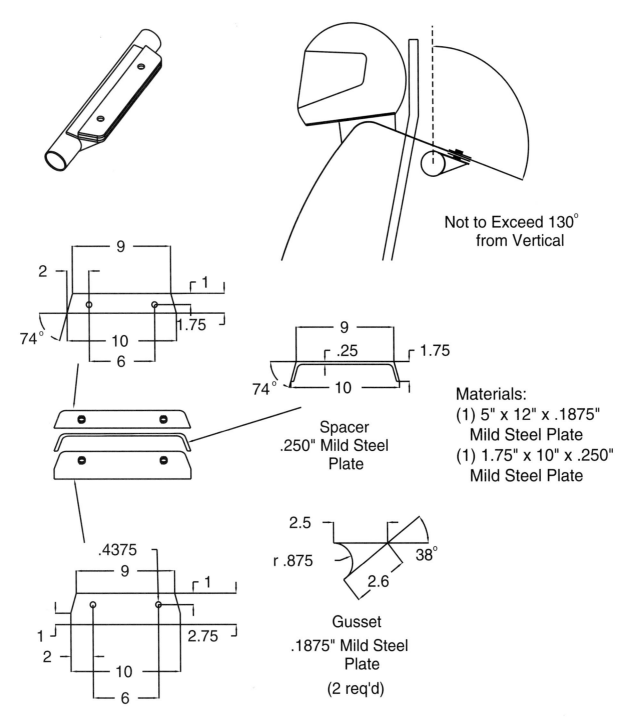

Not to Exceed 130° from Vertical

Spacer
.250" Mild Steel Plate

Materials:
(1) 5" x 12" x .1875" Mild Steel Plate
(1) 1.75" x 10" x .250" Mild Steel Plate

Gusset
.1875" Mild Steel Plate
(2 req'd)

Fig. 3-9

4 Roll Cage
Side & Front Bars

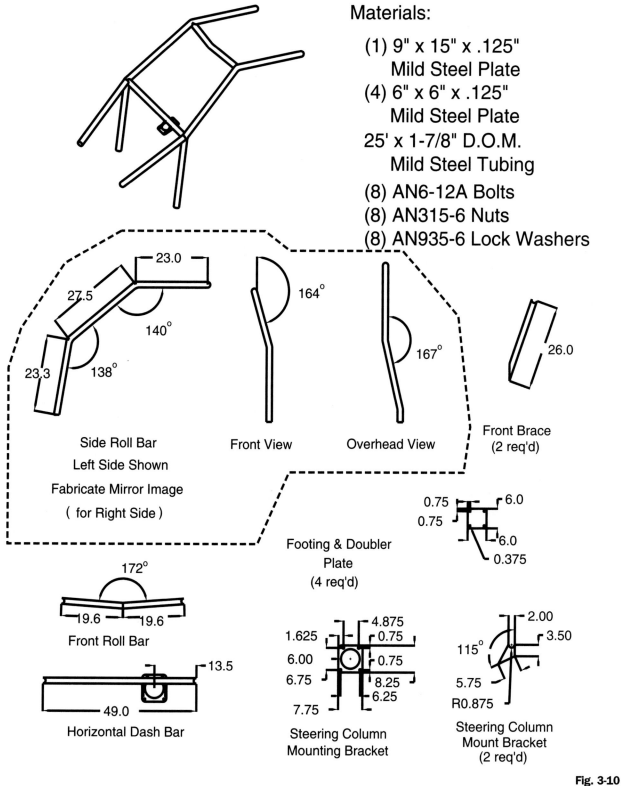

Materials:

- (1) 9" x 15" x .125"
  Mild Steel Plate
- (4) 6" x 6" x .125"
  Mild Steel Plate
- 25' x 1-7/8" D.O.M.
  Mild Steel Tubing
- (8) AN6-12A Bolts
- (8) AN315-6 Nuts
- (8) AN935-6 Lock Washers

23.0
27.5
140°
138°
23.3

Side Roll Bar
Left Side Shown
Fabricate Mirror Image
(for Right Side)

164°

Front View

167°

Overhead View

26.0

Front Brace
(2 req'd)

0.75
0.75
6.0
6.0
0.375

Footing & Doubler
Plate
(4 req'd)

172°
19.6
19.6

Front Roll Bar

13.5
49.0

Horizontal Dash Bar

4.875
1.625
0.75
6.00
0.75
6.75
8.25
6.25
7.75

Steering Column
Mounting Bracket

2.00
3.50
115°
5.75
R0.875

Steering Column
Mount Bracket
(2 req'd)

Fig. 3-10

5 Roll Cage Door Braces

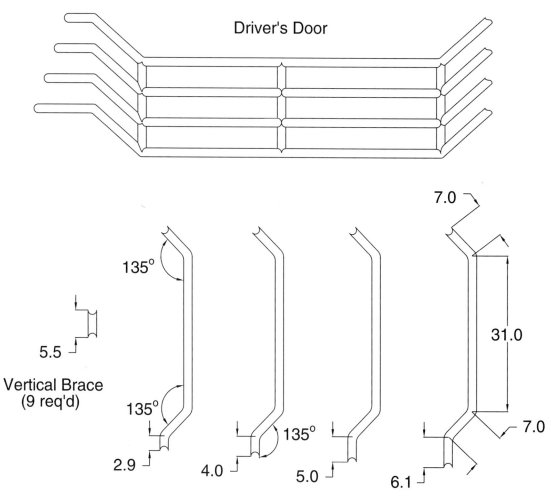

Driver's Door

135°

135°

135°

135°

Vertical Brace
(9 req'd)

5.5

2.9

4.0

5.0

6.1

7.0

31.0

7.0

Driver's Door

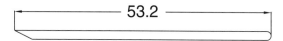

53.2

Diagonal Passenger Door

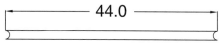

44.0

Horizontal Passenger Door

Materials:

30' x 1-7/8" x .120" Wall
    D.O.M. Mild Steel Tubing

Fig. 3-11

6 Pt. Roll Cage

All sizes are approximate.

Materials:
40' x 1-7/8" x .120" Wall
   D.O.M. Mild Steel Tubing
(12) 6" x 6" x .125" Mild Steel
   Plate (Footings & Doublers)
(24) AN6-12A Bolts
(24) AN315-6 Nuts
(24) AN935-6 Lock Washers

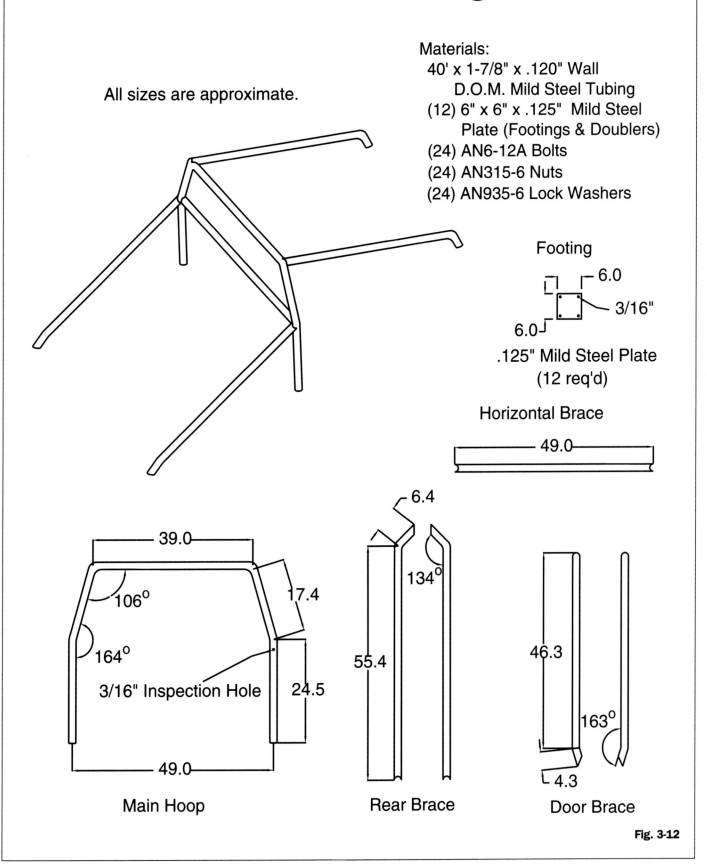

Footing

6.0

3/16"

6.0

.125" Mild Steel Plate
(12 req'd)

Horizontal Brace

49.0

6.4

134°

55.4

Rear Brace

46.3

163°

4.3

Door Brace

39.0

106°

17.4

164°

3/16" Inspection Hole

24.5

49.0

Main Hoop

Fig. 3-12

51

STREET/AUTOCROSS SUSPENSIONS

4

I n this chapter of the book we will address setting up the Mustang suspension for autocrossing or high–performance street handling. The modifications specified in this chapter are geared for the individual who wants to improve the handling of his car without major fabrication work. If you are an autocrosser (Conehead), then you already know that modifying your car can put you in some pretty fast classes. Obviously, these changes are

meant for the Conehead running outside the Production class. SCCA rules allow specific modifications in each class, so before you start, get a rule book.

Read this entire chapter and Chapter 5, *Road Racing Suspensions*, before you begin modifying your car. You may find that a more radical approach is what you want. You will find that many of the modifications in Chapter 5 are also applicable to autocrossing and high–performance street. When mixing

modifications, be aware that it is important that the springs, shocks, and struts are compatible.

Every shock has specific parameters in which it will function properly. A spring rate that is above the operating range of the shock will overpower it and handling will deteriorate. In addition, the shock's life is shortened significantly. If you are using red Konis then limit the front springs to 650 lbs-in. The yellow Sport struts should function properly up to an

Autocrossing the Mustang provides an inexpensive outlet for the auto enthusiast to test his or her driving skills. The modifications in this chapter are designed for competitive autocrossing. However, these modifications also work well for high-performance street driving. (Photo courtesy BBK Performance)

Parts Required:

	Autocross	Street
Chassis:	G–Load brace	G–Load brace
Springs:	Eibach Competition Pro	Eibach Competition Pro or M5300–C Motorsport
Struts:	Koni Sport Yellow	Koni Sport Yellow
Shocks:	Koni Red	Koni Red
Dampeners:	Koni 25–1215	Koni 25–1215
Swaybars:		
Rear	Stock or Lincoln LSC	Suspension Techniques 3–034 Kit
Front	GT, V6 & 4-Cyl. Mustang	
Suspension:	SVO trailing arms	SVO trailing arms
	(upper) M5500–A	(upper) M5500–A
	(lower) E2BZ–5A649–A	(lower) E2BZ–5A649–A
	Ford axle housing bushings	Ford axle housing bushings
	Offset Rack Bushings	Offset Rack Bushings
	Urethane Control Arm Bushings	Urethane Control Arm Bushings
	Urethane Swaybar Bushings	Urethane Swaybar Bushings
	Camber Plates	Camber Plates
	Borgson Steering Shaft	Heavy-Duty Steering Coupling Insulator
Spindles	'94 GT Mustang	'94 GT Mustang
Pre-'90 Cars:	'90–93 Tie Rods	'90–93 Tie Rods
Brakes:	Lincoln LSC Mk VII Calipers	Lincoln LSC Mk VII Calipers
	On pre-'87 Cars, use '87–'93 Rotors	

Coil Springs

Modifying the front and rear suspensions requires the removal and reinstallation of the springs. Proper safety procedures must be adhered to when making these modifications. A compressed coil spring can be very dangerous and cause severe physical injury or even death, as well as property damage, if not handled properly. Use the right tools and safety precautions for removing a coil spring.

800 lbs-in. rate. When utilizing a spring beyond 800 lbs-in. you should stay with the SPSS. The same balance should be observed with the rear shocks, except limit the SPSS shock to smooth high-speed race tracks only.

Before proceeding, you must decide on what combination of parts you will use for your car. Make sure you have the parts in your hands before you start. You may already have an idea of what you want; however, the combinations listed in the chart at left should provide significantly improved handling over the factory setup.

FRONT SUSPENSION

This group of modifications is designed to improve caster, reduce bump steer and add a few degrees of Ackermann steering. A tighter, more aggressive ride will be the result.

It will be necessary to either fabricate the offset rack and pinion bushings and the spindle bushings or buy them from one of the many suppliers. I have provided drawings of these if you wish to machine them (see Figures 4-3 and 4-6). The spindle bushings that are required when utilizing the SVO/Continental spindle are more difficult to make and can be expensive to have fabricated. Fortunately these can be purchased from several suppliers for a very reasonable price.

Step 1

If your car is not already up on jack-stands, do so now. Place the jackstands under the rocker seams at the jacking notches. Be sure to provide at least 18" of ground clearance.

Step 2

Move to the front of the car and remove the struts, springs, spindles and control arms. Examine all parts as you remove them for any unusual wear unless you intend to replace them. Re–clean the control arms, spindles, and rack and

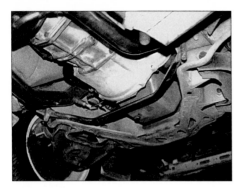

High-speed cornering stress can cause the #2 crossmember to flex inward, destroying suspension geometry and handling. The brace pictured here, commonly referred to as a "G-load brace," is typical of the many braces available that are designed to help control the flexing that disrupts handling.

pinion before beginning. You'll work a lot happier without having to peer through grease and grime.

Step 3: G-Load Brace

One of the ugly things about the chassis design on the Mustang is how the crossmember flexes inboard at the rear control arm mount under severe cornering loads. Because the outside front wheel must control the majority of the centrifugal forces acting on the car, this mount receives the brunt of the cornering loads. Because this section of the crossmember is at the long lever end of a large "V," the high loads experienced when cornering are dissipated by bending. If your chassis is not rigid, your suspension geometry goes down the toilet.

This most uncool characteristic can be cured by the use of a strategically located brace, commonly referred to as the G–load brace. With all the suspension off the crossmember it would be a good time to fit one of these to your car.

Aftermarket Units—If you have purchased one of these, check the fit to your crossmember before reinstalling the control arms. The quality control is not real good on some of these, so take the time now and tweak it as necessary to fit. There are several braces on the market today. The ones sporting four mounting points are the strongest. If you want to

Production Class Autocrossing

Production autocross racing stipulates that the car must be stock in all respects other than shocks, struts, dampeners and tires. However, the rules do allow you to swap pieces on your car for those of other year models as long as it is a Fox Mustang. To that end I have compiled a list of those production items that should be included on your stock Mustang. Additionally Production-Class rules allow the use of a torque arm provided the trailing arms are retained. Using a torque arm in this class means replacing the upper trailing arm brushings with soft foam.

Crossmember:	'90-'93 GT
Control Arms:	'85-'93
Upper Trailing Arms:	SVO (Motorsport M5500–A)
Lower Trailing Arms:	SVO (Ford E2BZ–5A649–A)
Axle Housing Bushings	TRW 12584
Tie Rods:	TRW ES 3091 (Ford F0ZZ–3A130–A)
Convertible Rocker Reinforcements:	E6ZZ-66102B66-A & E6ZZ-66102B67-A
Convertible Underbody Brace:	SVO M5024-A
Front Swaybar:	V6 Mustang with stock 4-link rear suspension V8 GT Mustang with torque arm
Rear Swaybar:	Stock GT
Spring perch pads:	Earlier GT for street (delete for racing)
Springs:	800 lbs-in. front/260 lbs-in. rear w/4-link 750 lbs-in. front/450 lbs-in. rear w/torque arm
Strut mounts:	SVO "Onion Head" mount for street Camber plates for racing
Struts:	Koni 8741–1121
Shocks:	Koni 8040–1026
Dampeners:	Koni 25–1215 (delete Torque arm)
Brake Pads:	Quality Semi–Metallic
Front Calipers:	'85/86 SVO
Spindles:	'85/86 SVO Mustang
Rotors (pre-'87 Cars Only):	Upgrade to '87 rotors or newer

build a brace, Fig. 4-1 shows how to fabricate a very strong piece without a great deal of hassle. The measurements provided in the drawing are standard. However, the measurements should be checked against your crossmember before you cut and drill the tubing. The most important thing is to find the center of each lower lip to ensure a strong and easy installation.

Fabricating Your Own—To begin, use a felt-tip pen and your middle finger as a guide, and draw a line in the center of the lower lip from the rearmost bend extending forward along the edge 3". Use a mirror and check the relationship of this line with the topside to be certain you have marked the center of the flattest area. This lip is pretty narrow so alignment is important.

Next, lay the 1-1/2" wide side of the tubing flat on the two edges of the crossmember where the rearmost edge (of the tubing) intersects the inside corner (where the rear control arm pickup attaches) of the crossmember. Mark the ends of the tubing for cutting length and cut to size. The tubing should extend to the outside edges of the lips. Trim the ends to achieve the correct taper as noted in Fig. 4-1, p.65. This is to provide easy access to the attaching fasteners.

Clamp the finished section of square tubing to the crossmember, and use the previously drawn lines as references. Drill 3/16" pilot holes through the tubing and the lips on the crossmember. The holes should be separated by 3/4". Drill one hole at a time and insert a 3/16" bolt or #10 machine screw in each successive hole, checking the alignment as you go. When you are satisfied that you have a good fit, remove the tubing and drill out all the holes to 5/16". De–burr both sides of all holes by spinning a 7/16" drill bit against the edges of the holes with your fingers.

Install the brace using any 5/16" bolts to test final fit. After you have completed the fitting, remove the brace for painting. Use 5/16" x 1" NC or NF grade 8 fasteners and crimped locking nuts for actual installation.

On some cars, the G–load brace may interfere with headers or the oil pan, particularly those cars with the engines lowered. If this is the case, you will find it necessary to space the brace away from the crossmember, generally with flat washers on purchased braces. On some

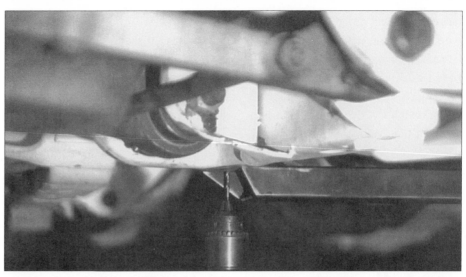

Fitting a simple G-load brace as provided in Fig. 4-1 requires drilling two holes on each side in the lower lip of the crossmember to attach the brace. This design works great in vehicles with stock or shorty tube headers.

four-point braces, such as the Project Industries piece, it is very difficult to achieve this with the forward mounting brace going on top and the rear mount going on bottom; however, it can be done. For the brace design in this book you simply cut 1-3/4" strips of 3/4" wide aluminum or steel, drill holes to match those on your brace (should be 3/4" apart) and sandwich between the brace and the crossmember using longer bolts (aircraft grade only).

Step 4: Strut Modification

This step is designed to move the strut more closely to the centerline of the spindle and provide for better shock action as well as the ability to elect more negative camber. On some struts, in particular the Koni SPSS racing struts, this modification is unnecessary as they are already set up this way. *Warning: This modification will move your strut closer to the wheel and could cause some tire interference with wide wheels with increased inboard offset or fat tires on narrow rims, so check first.*

Per Fig. 4-2 on p. 66, scribe the areas to be removed from the strut–to–spindle mounting holes on each strut. Be sure to use an adjustable depth square when marking the parallel lines to ensure holes

that are square in relation to the spindle mounting holes. Also, take care that both struts are modified identically.

When you have completed the grinding, do a trial fit on each spindle and file as necessary. If you screw up a hole it will be necessary to scrap the strut. It is very dangerous to try to repair a mistake by welding, as these things can explode.

Touch up the bare metal with paint matching the strut. If you will be replacing your stock brakes with Wilwood brakes, you must modify the spindles before reassembling (see p. 134 in Chapter 8). Otherwise, assemble the strut and spindle with the spindle as close to the strut housing as possible, using Loctite on the threads and torque to 150 to 175 ft-lbs. Again, make sure both sides are identical.

Replacing Spindles—If you can find them, replace your stock spindles with '82/83 Lincoln Continental units. These spindles have a steering knuckle that is 5/8" longer than the stock Mustang piece. This added length will generate a few badly needed degrees of Ackermann steering. Although the longer steering knuckle on the Continental spindle slows the steering rate down, the additional Ackermann steering provides for better corner entry transition and will give a feeling of quick steering response, especially if you mill the rack mounting bosses as provided in the *Road Racing Suspensions* chapter.

In order to use these spindles, you will need a ball joint bushing, as the ball joints on the Continental have a shank that is .100" larger than the ones found on the Mustang. Fig. 4-3, p. 66, gives the dimensions for these if you wish to machine them, otherwise purchase them from one of the several suppliers, like Central Coast Mustangs (805/925-8848).

Step 5: Urethane Control Arm Bushings

The soft bushings found in the Mustang's control arms allow camber changes when they deform from high lateral loading in the corner. The loss of negative camber is not cool for optimum cornering speed. This can be cured by replacing the stock bushing with polyurethane pieces such as those made by Energy Suspension, whom I highly recommend.

To replace the sponges in your control arms, press out the factory rubber inserts using a torch to heat the bushing shell to release the rubber (or burn them out with a torch, which is very messy). Next, make four 1.5" x 1.5" plates from .125" steel and weld inside the gaps at the bushing ends for reinforcement. See Fig. 4-4 for details.

Clean the bushing shells until there is no rubber residue remaining. Before installing the Energy Suspension

bushings it is important to cut two equally spaced shallow grooves around the inside of the bushings to store grease. Lubricate the bushings with a light grease and press them into the factory bushing shells. Leave the steel insert out for now. Turn the control arm upside down and drill a 1/8" hole, at a 45° angle from vertical toward the ball joint, through the center of the bushing shells to the center of the polyurethane bushing. Remove the polyurethane bushings. Drill the holes in the bushing shells out with a #21 bit (.159") and thread with a 10–32 tap. Clean everything up and lubricate the polyurethane bushings and steel inserts with the glue-like grease that comes with these bushings. Install straight zerk grease fittings in the bushing shells for future lubrication (see Fig. 4-5, p. 66). This will prevent the very annoying squeaks associated with polyurethane bushings.

Alternatively, you can use the aluminum bushings made by Global West. These are the best thing going and should be used if your budget permits. They are generally not as noisy as the urethane bushings and come with a lifetime guarantee. However, they are generally difficult to install and also expensive. You make the call.

BBK Performance offers a complete set of replacement swaybar, strut mount, end link and steering rack polyurethane bushings for high-performance street use. These are a must to reduce bushing deflection. (Photo courtesy BBK Performance)

Step 6: Rack and Pinion Bushings

In this step you will be installing offset rack and pinion mounting bushings to reduce bump steer on the car that has now been lowered more than 1" in the front. Generally, what you will be doing is raising the rack up to improve the rack-to-control-arm relationship. This will eliminate some of the bump steer associated with a lowered car and also improve Ackermann steering when used with the SVO/Continental spindles. It is important to understand that the amount your car has been lowered defines the distance the rack housing must be relocated. Generally if your car has not

To improve front suspension compliance, the soft stock rubber control arm bushings must be replaced with polyurethane or aluminum bushings. Pictured are the replacement bushings sold by Energy Suspension Systems.

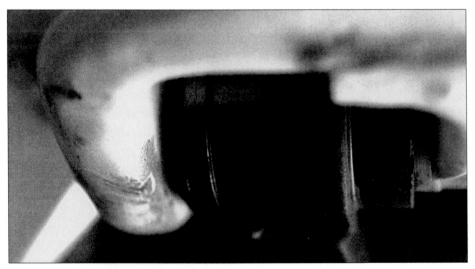

The solid aluminum bushings for the control arms that are sold by Global West are precision pieces that provide outstanding suspension compliance and no squeaking. Unfortunately, they are more expensive than their polyurethane counterparts. If you own an SVO Mustang, these are the only bushings available.

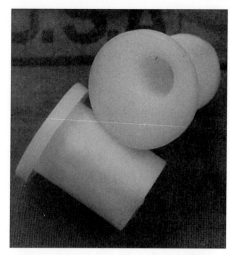

Running short springs can create a bump steer problem. When changing to the '91-'93 long shank tie rods will not cure the problem, installing offset rack and pinion housing bushings can provide relief as well as generate a few degrees of Ackermann steering. The bushings photographed here are made of U.H.M.W. polyethlene (for the street use) and sold by Central Coast Mustang.

been lowered more than 1" and is already equipped with the '90 or newer FOZZ–3A130–A tie rods, offset rack bushings are not required. Adding them will only increase the bump steer problem you already have. Typically 3° of positive caster will eliminate most of the bump steer on a car that has been lowered 1". If your car has not been lowered, stick with the stock tie rods and run 3° of positive caster.

Steering Upgrade—If your car is not a factory GT or a late-model SVO, you must check to see if it has the high–effort 15:1 power steering. If your car was equipped with the standard 20:1 power steering system, you must upgrade to the high–effort 15:1 rack and pinion and related power steering pump (E6SZ–3A674–B). Do not use a standard power steering pump with the high-effort rack and pinion! The standard pump is not compatible with the high–effort rack and pinion and can cause the steering to momentarily lock when attempting to change direction quickly. This phenomenon is exaggerated on those cars with engines sporting the underdrive pulley kits, especially when

the engine is at or near idle while shifting gears in a switch–back turn. I had the misfortune to experience this first-hand in my 351-powered '82 Mustang. Most uncool!

After you have sorted out the rack & pinion confusion, remove the two long bolts that hold the rack housing to the crossmember. Do not disconnect the power steering lines unless you are masochistic. Introducing air into the system will cause you to spend several hours wishing you hadn't.

Secure the rack housing in the factory position with large clamps and check the bump steer at 1" compression (see p. 155 on how to check bump steer). If you are experiencing bump steer, move the rack up 1/16", return the suspension to center ride height, zero the bump gauge and check it again at 1". Keep doing this until you find the ideal location that eliminates the toe change. Check the bump steer at 2, 3, and 4 inches and adjust the rack height until you achieve the minimum overall changes. Carefully measure the distance the rack has been moved from the vertical centerline of the hole in the crossmember. This distance will be the correct distance to offset the hole in the rack bushing you will be fabricating, as per the instructions in Fig. 4-6.

When you have completed the test for locating the offset bushing holes, push the factory bushings out and clean the holes in the housing thoroughly. Press the newly machined offset bushings in from the front, aligning the mounting hole at the base of the housing (6 o'clock). The distance between the two mounting holes in the offset bushings should be identical to the distance between the centers of the bushing holes in the rack & pinion housing and on a perpendicular line with the rack centerline. This is important. If the rack is offset to the right or left you will bias the steering to one side, causing bump steer to be different from one side to the

other and the handling will really be screwed up.

On Mustangs equipped with sleeves and rubber bushings, it is necessary to cut the protruding sleeve off that normally fits inside the factory rack bushings so it fits flush with the crossmember mounting surface. This is necessary since you will be replacing the soft factory bushings with a solid bushing that mounts tightly around the bolt and against the crossmember. On early Mustangs that use the large bolt, you must drill the front holes in the crossmember out to 7/8" and either install modified sleeves from a newer Mustang or fabricate them from steel tubing. Additionally, you must use the small diameter mounting bolts from the '87 or newer Mustang. This is necessary to achieve the maximum height of the rack. With the large bolts, you are limited on how low the centerline of the offset hole can be placed, which reduces the amount of bump steer that can be eliminated.

Reinstall the rack and be sure to check for interference with the rack housing and the tubing/hoses on the left engine mount. Some bending may be necessary for the steel tubing to clear. Also, you may have to trim the outer edge of the housing, at the tubing mount, slightly to clear the underside of the engine mount. Check it carefully. On some cars it may be necessary to trim the lower front edge of the right engine mount for the rack housing to fit flush on the crossmember. Check the outer edge of the crossmember where the rack bellows pass when the steering is turned full lock. If the bellows rub, use a large Crescent wrench (large hammer optional) and bend the lip rearward just enough to provide a 3/8" clearance. Don't overdo this, as you could cause interference with control arm travel.

Step 7: Tie Rods

If your car is not a '90 or newer and it

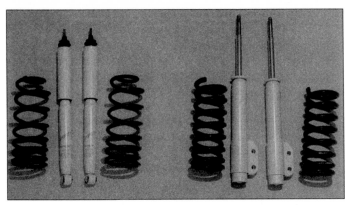

BBK's specific rate and progressive springs lower the car 1-1/2 inch, and are designed to work well with the stock shocks and struts, or replacement Konis or Monroe Formula GP's. They provide much-improved handling without affecting ride quality, characteristics that are nice to have on the street. The specific rate springs are 650 lbs-in. front, 260 lbs-in. rear. (Photo courtesy BBK Performance)

Precision handling requires dampeners that are matched to the springs they must control. Upgrading your stock dampeners and springs with a matched set, such as this kit sold by Steeda Autosports, can provide balance that equates into much-improved handling.

has been lowered, replace your tie rods with ones from the '90–'93 Mustang for better bump steer control. These tie rods have a slightly longer shank than prior years (see Fig. 4-7). This allows the tie rods and inner socket assemblies to hang lower. This reduces the difference between the angle it forms from horizontal and that angle formed by the lower control arm. The closer these two angles are to one another, the less bump steer.

Before removing the stock tie rods, measure the tip-to-tip length. This will allow you to approximate the alignment when installing the new tie rods and reduce the hassles during final adjustment.

Step 8: Steering Shaft Upgrade

Next you will be upgrading the steering shaft. Be sure you have the heavy-duty steering coupling on the steering shaft of the rack (the bracket the soft insulator attaches to). The heavy-duty steering coupler (D9BZ–3A525–A) is made of forged steel, whereas the light-duty unit is stamped steel and very weak. Replace the soft insulator with one from a Boss 302 or equivalent aftermarket unit. These are laminated reinforced rubber and provide much better road feel. They are generally available at most auto parts stores in the

red "help!" bubble packs.

Optionally, you can install a Borgson universal joint steering shaft. This steering shaft is very strong as well as narrow for that additional clearance around those big tube headers. There is, however, an increase in road noise that is transmitted through the steering column and wheel. If yours is a street car where bumpy roads are the norm, then stick to the stock steering shaft and replace the soft rubber insulator.

Step 9: Camber Plates

Reassemble the front suspension using a pair of adjustable camber plates, except wait until Step 10 to install the swaybar. Do not leave the rubber sleeves and spring perch pads off your springs for the street. The squeaks and groans that are normally drowned out by a race car's exhaust will probably drive you crazy on the street.

Aftermarket Plates—If you are purchasing camber plates, be sure they provide for an additional 1" of strut travel

Replacing your stock steering shaft with one fitted with a Universal joint can provide better road feel. Improved road feel allows the driver to make precise steering changes with improved lap times.

Kenny Brown has developed his "Caster Plus Kit" for high-performance street and autocross racing that provides improved caster and strut compliance without the road noise typically transmitted through the more serious camber plates. This is an excellent kit similar to the SVO "onion head" upper strut mount, except with more positive caster.

the Konis and change the settings on the struts during a race and screw up the handling. You can waste a lot of time chasing something as simple as this at a race. This is the voice of experience speaking.

Step 10: Front Sway Bars

On the street, the best front swaybar for the GT/5.0 LX Mustang is the Suspension Techniques kit. It is larger than the factory performance bar and will provide the additional roll stiffness necessary for improved handling when combined with spring rates your kidneys can live with on the street. The matching rear bar provides a good balance to reduce understeer.

If you are a conehead you will need to scour the local salvage yards and procure a V–6 and 4-cylinder Mustang front swaybar to go along with your stock GT bar. Don't forget to get the frame mounting brackets for each. On each bar, replace the factory swaybar bushings

to keep the strut in the middle of its stroke on a lowered car. When you use shorter springs, it is imperative that the upper strut mount be designed to allow the additional travel. Of the factory mounts, only the "onion head" mounts used on the SVO, and some specialty cars, move the mounting point upward, albeit a small amount. Testing has shown that the same car equipped without the additional travel will run slower lap times. So, ask the supplier before you buy.

Fabricating Plates—I have included drawings (Fig. 4-8, p. 68) on how to build camber plates for the fabricator types. These are not difficult to make, however the bearing retainer should be TIG-welded to avoid damage to the bearing. Just follow the drawings and take your time.

As noted previously, you will need to modify the hood's inner brace to clear the adjustable Koni struts when using a camber plate that raises the upper strut mount. After you have re–installed the struts and adjusted their location to approximate the appropriate alignment settings, place a dab of silicone on the end of the strut and carefully close the hood until it touches. Cut the holes to

match the location where the silicone touches. Be sure to take into consideration the additional space needed when you adjust the camber and caster for different street and competition settings. If these holes are too small, they can rub the protruding adjustment tips of

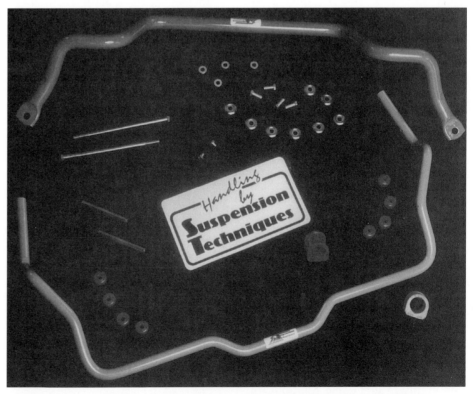

The Suspension Techniques swaybar kit is a well-balanced package that will make a substantial improvement in the understeer common to a high-performance Mustang. These bars are well made and have been seen on some pretty fast machines, including the 175 mph Silver State Classic-winning Mustang of Richard Holdener.

The stock front swaybar bushings are made of soft rubber and allow considerable movement of the bar during cornering. Replacement of the bushings with a pair of Energy Suspension polyurethane pieces is a must for the autocross and high-performance street addict.

with the black polyurethane pieces from Energy Suspension. You will need all three of these bars to tune your suspension for the various tracks and conditions you will encounter on a Sunday afternoon. Most fast Mustangs on the autocross circuit use a smaller-than-stock front swaybar to allow increased weight transfer and improved corner entry transition. For the rabid Conehead, the Fairmont and '83–'86 LTD swaybars will also fit the Mustang. There are eight different-size bars that were installed on these cars, varying from .875" to 1.250". Think of the combinations!

When installing your front swaybar, you should note that the factory swaybar comes stock with the lever ends (ends that attach to swaybar end links) being parallel to the frame mounting holes of the control arms at normal ride height (see Fig. 4-9). It is very important that you maintain that same relationship when installing the end links. If you are running shorter springs, it will be

necessary to trim the sleeve and use a shorter bolt between the bushings to achieve this relationship. On newer Mustangs, it will be necessary to replace the factory solid end links with the older style bolt & sleeve in order to make the necessary adjustments and fit. Once you have assembled your suspension and the car has settled, fine adjustments to the end links can be made to remove any side-to-side bias by using washers under the sleeve. This is important to ensure a balanced left–right handling characteristic.

Warning: Don't forget to cut the slots in the inner hood brace to clear the Koni strut before slamming the hood.

REAR SUSPENSION

In this group of modifications, we will remove some of the slop that is so common with the rear suspension on the Mustang. This involves replacing the stock axle bushings with higher durometer rubber pieces. In conjunction with this, we will also be replacing the stock trailing arms with heavy-duty pieces from the Ford parts bin that also have higher durometer bushings.

Torque Arm Setup

Since the fall of 1992, the torque arm rear suspension has become very popular with the corner racing crowd. This comes as no surprise to those of us who have been doing battle with the GM bunch, especially on the autocross circuit. The torque arm setup has been around for a long time and is standard issue on Camaros and Firebirds.

The long single bar that attaches to the center of the rear axle provides very stable and solid rear tire hookup. So good are the rear tires at hooking up that most Mustangs seen autocrossing with them will pick up the inside tire on a hard turn. And I bet you thought only German cars did that.

Picking up the front tire clearly demonstrates the dramatic change to the

roll center this system makes. The torque arm setup moves the roll center significantly lower than stock, increasing the rear weight transfer and body roll. Additionally the anti–squat percentage is increased over stock. Obviously, increased rear roll stiffness and alternate suspension settings must be used with this setup.

Like everything there is a price, and price is the key here. To install a torque arm you must either build one or purchase it from one of the several suppliers. Currently the Griggs Racing Torque Arm (285 Prado Road #A, San Luis Obispo, CA 93401, 800/655-0336) is the most popular kit available. Because this setup eliminates the upper trailing arms, the installation is complicated by the need to use a Panhard bar that is bull stout and welded in place. By the time you buy everything for this rig and install it, you can spend the better part of $1,000. Additionally, these things are a bit fragile and have a history of breaking when abused with drag race-type launches.

If you like this system then skip this part of this section and go the torque arm installation step, pp. 93-94 in Chapter 5.

Step 11

If the car is not already on jackstands follow Step 1 from the front suspension section.

Step 12: Disassembly

Disconnect the flexible rear brake line at the frame, taking care not to get brake fluid on anything important. Disconnect and remove the shocks and swaybar. Next, disconnect the trailing arms from the axle housing. Remove the rear end assembly and the trailing arms.

Step 13: Replace Upper Trailing Arm Bushings

With a big hammer, long drift pin and short section of 2 x 4 lumber (oak being the best), drive the existing stock upper trailing arm bushings from the axle housing. This particular modification is a real pain. Unless you have access to a heavy-duty slide hammer with the correct attachment, or the factory bushing removal tool (T78P–5638–A), there is no easy way to do this. Attempting to do this while the axle is still attached to the car, via the lower trailing arms, without the special tool is ludicrous. Obviously, if you are replacing your axle assembly with one of the Ford Motorsport units, this step would be an exercise in futility and clearly the action of someone who enjoys hitting his thumb with a large hammer.

Once the stock bushings have been removed, lubricate the new high durometer bushings with light oil and drive them in until the inside edge of the bushing's lip is approximately .300" from the face of the axle ear (see Fig. 4-10). Use a 2" socket or short section of pipe with a 1-3/4" I.D. to avoid deforming the new bushing. At this time a break would definitely be in order.

Step 14: Increasing Anti-Squat

One of the limitations of the Mustang's suspension configuration is the inadequate percentage of anti–squat built

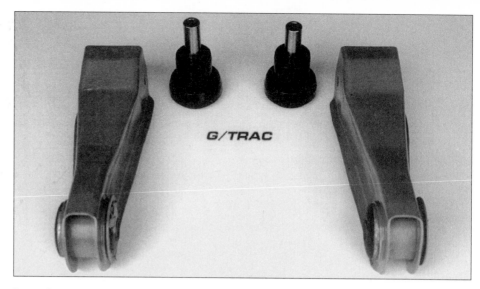

Improving rear axle compliance is critical to high-performance handling. Steeda Autosports offers these heavy-duty upper trailing arms with urethane bushings to eliminate the drift and movement associated with soft stock bushings.

into the design. This problem is further exaggerated when the already inadequate anti–squat percentage deteriorates and becomes more pronounced as the rear ride height is decreased. Shorter springs and smaller diameter tires lower the instant center and reduce this percentage. What this translates to is squatting on the axle under acceleration, which changes the suspension geometry and reduces corner exit speeds. Fear not. The percentage of anti–squat can be raised with a simple procedure while the rear axle is out of the car.

To accomplish this modification, you

must remove the axles and rear brakes. Balance the axle housing upside down on jackstands under the axle tubes by using a jack under the pinion part of the housing. Attach a magnetic inclinometer to the face of the yoke and adjust the jack to achieve an angle of 0°.

Place a level vertically on each side of the trailing arm brackets with an edge that bisects the trailing arm bolt holes (see Fig. 4-11, p. 69). With the level held vertically level and one edge bisecting the center of the hole, draw a line from the edge of the hole to the edge of the bracket. Draw a parallel line on the

When modifying lower trailing arm brackets, an inclinometer or level should be used to set the pinion angle at 0° before marking the bracket (see Step 14).

Once the pinion angle has been set at 0°, the trailing arm bolt holes are then marked with a vertical line. Layout dye, a metal level and a scribe should be used. Use the metal level to bisect the hole vertically, then scribe the line.

If your class rules require stock trailing arm bushings, or if the urethane bushings are just too stiff and noisy for you, the original SVO trailing arms (E2BZ-5A649-A lower & M5500-A upper) with the high durometer rubber are your best choice. The SVO piece is the one with the round bushings.

pinion side of the first line with a gap of .030" between the two lines. Mark a point on the second line 5/8" up from the perpendicular center of the hole. This should be approximately 3/8" from the edge of the hole.

Use a center punch to mark the points for drilling. Drill 1/8" pilot holes at each of the four punch marks. Check the alignment of the holes carefully. If they are off, MIG-weld them closed and try again. When you are satisfied with the location of the pilot holes, drill each one out with a 15/32" bit.

Cut four 1/2" diameter discs from 3/16" steel and MIG-weld them in the original holes. Dress the welds smooth.

Step 15: Trailing Arms

One of the weaknesses of the Mustang's four–link system is the longitudinal twisting of the trailing arms that occurs in a hard turn. Adding a plate to box–in the trailing arms will provide considerable resistance to the twisting action. Don't waste your time boxing in the stock trailing arms unless they are the SVO or Motorsport upper arms (M5500–A). The bushings in the stock units are too soft. You can utilize your stock trailing arms, both upper and lower, provided you replace the soft rubber bushings with the Energy Suspension 88 durometer polyurethane bushings.

Upper Arms—Once you have the correct upper trailing arms (M5500–A Motorsport or SVO) follow the instructions and dimensions in Fig. 4-12

and fabricate reinforcement plates from 10-gauge mild steel. Center the plates on the bottom open side of the trailing arms and tack-weld at all four corners and midway down the sides. MIG-weld each side starting with 1" beads that are 1" apart to prevent warping. Then go back and weld in between the first beads. *Warning:* Most factory trailing arms are galvanized steel. The off-gassing that occurs when welding galvanized steel can make you very sick. Try not to breathe the fumes, and wear a respirator at all times. Do not weld galvanized steel without one.

Lower Arms—Twist in the lower trailing arms is very prevalent in cars using sticky autocross tires and must be eliminated. Either replace your stock lower trailing arms with the SVO Mustang units or replace the bushings with 88 durometer Energy Suspension polyurethane bushings. Follow the dimensions in Fig. 4-13 on p. 70 and fabricate a reinforcement plate from 10-gauge mild steel. Use the same welding procedure as noted above. Trial-fit the swaybar you will be using and trim the

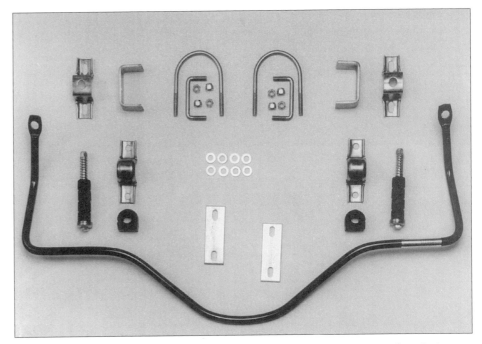

Increasing the rear roll stiffness is generally recognized as an important step in reducing understeer in the Mustang. One of the most popular approaches is to install one of the Steeda Autosports adjustable rear swaybar kits. This kit allows the driver to dial in additional roll stiffness to suit his driving style.

Spring rates are defined based on the number, diameter, and spacing of the coils in conjunction with the wire thickness. Shown here are two front springs manufactured by Eibach. The spring on the left is a 850 to 1000 lbs-in. variable rate while the one on the right is a specific 700 lbs-in. rate. The differences in wire diameter and coil spacing provide a graphic example of why one spring is stiffer than the other.

hole for 3/8" clearance on all sides.

Clean the welds and paint the trailing arms with an epoxy primer (PPG DP–90). Follow the basic instruction for removing the rubber bushings and fitting the new polyurethane bushings as noted in Step 5 on p.56.

Step 16: Rear Swaybar

Before you install the axle assembly you must select a rear swaybar. Generally the stock rear swaybar is adequate for most applications. However, the larger bar offered by Suspension Techniques, Helwig, and Rancho or the adjustable bar from Steeda make an excellent balance for the autocrosser since they will generally help understeer.

Step 17

This step involves the re–installation of the axle assembly. If your car is a newer model you should replace the spongy upper spring pads with ones from an earlier GT Mustang, i.e. 1982. These are much more dense and will provide better suspension compliance.

To begin, reinstall all suspension components, leaving the trailing arms and horizontal dampeners bolts only finger-tight. All brakes, interior, wheels and tires, and the engine and transmission must be installed if you have not done so already. The car should be in driving condition with 1/2 tank of fuel. (Add 6 lbs. to the spare tire well for every gallon of fuel below 1/2 tank.)

On a level floor, jack the car up and insert car ramps of equal height under each wheel or jackstands under the rear

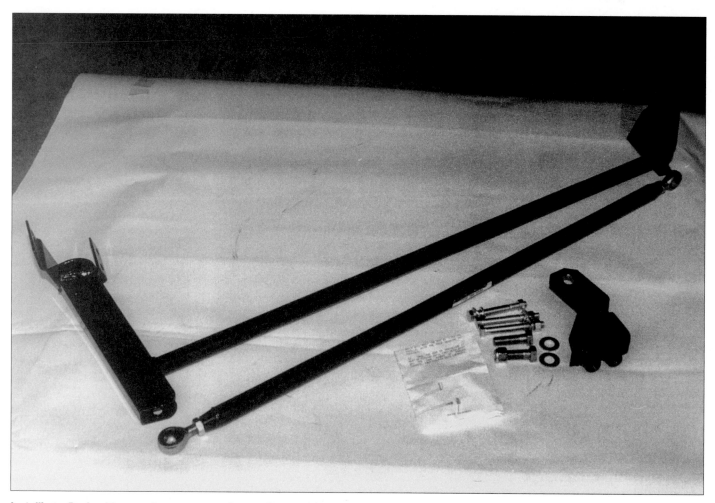

Installing a Panhard bar can improve rear axle compliance and lower the rear roll center. The Panhard bar shown is a light-duty kit sold by BBK. This bar is adequate for autocrossing in Prepared classes or for high-performance street applications. It has a unique double attachment point axle bracket that allows for cars with stock and lowered suspensions.

axle and the control arms. Place weights in the driver's seat equal to the weight of the normal driver or have him sit in the car and joust the suspension several times to settle the springs. Torque the trailing arm bolts, shocks and dampeners to factory specifications.

Step 18: Bleeding Brakes

The final step is bleeding the brakes. If you are inexperienced just follow the procedures outlined in Chapter 8, p. 139.

Step 19: Final Check

Before removing your car from the jackstands, take the time to recheck every fastener, especially wheels. It is very easy to get sidetracked or distracted when making these modifications and forget to torque something down. ■

It is very important when fitting a Panhard bar for a street-driven car to provide adequate clearance around the exhaust pipes. This installation had very little room for movement of the tailpipe and resulted in a very irritating rattle. Leave at least 1/2" clearance or you will suffer the same fate.

The Central Coast Mustang and Saleen Panhard bars are excellent well-built pieces. However, if you subject them to high stress cornering on a real race track or autocrossing in the CP or faster classes, especially on slicks, the bolt-on axle mount will probably break. The best approach is to fabricate a new mount from 1/8" mild steel that is welded to the housing like the example shown here (arrow). This modification is mandatory if your car's ride height does not create the correct geometry with the supplied bracket.

G-Load Brace

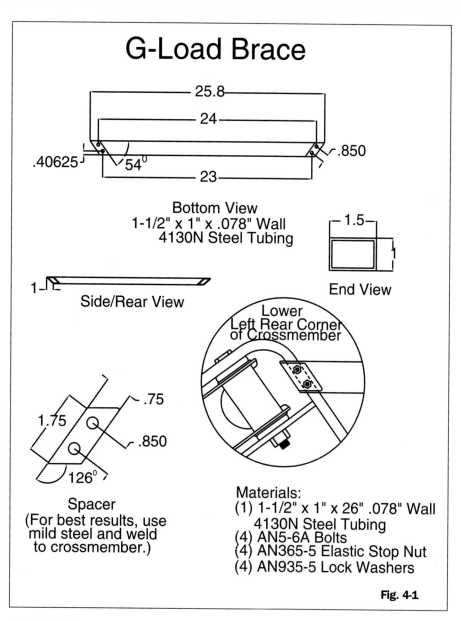

25.8

24

.40625

54°

23

.850

Bottom View
1-1/2" x 1" x .078" Wall
4130N Steel Tubing

1.5

1

End View

1

Side/Rear View

Lower
Left Rear Corner
of Crossmember

1.75

.75

.850

126°

Spacer
(For best results, use
mild steel and weld
to crossmember.)

Materials:
(1) 1-1/2" x 1" x 26" .078" Wall
4130N Steel Tubing
(4) AN5-6A Bolts
(4) AN365-5 Elastic Stop Nut
(4) AN935-5 Lock Washers

Fig. 4-1

G-Load Brace
Installation

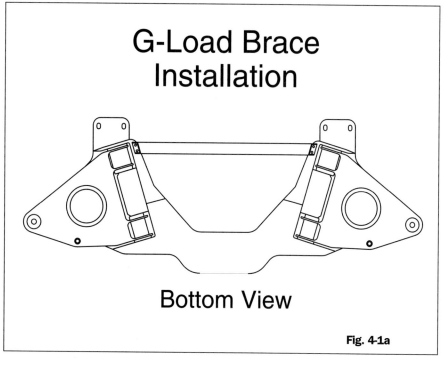

Bottom View

Fig. 4-1a

Strut
Modification

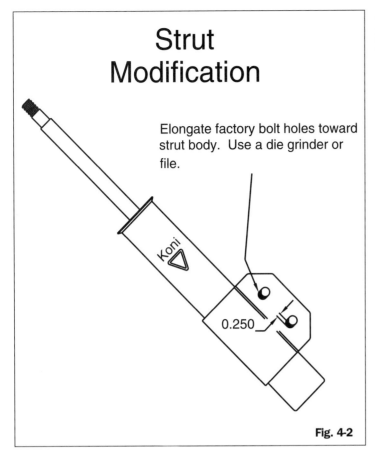

Elongate factory bolt holes toward strut body. Use a die grinder or file.

Koni

0.250

Fig. 4-2

Spindle Bushing

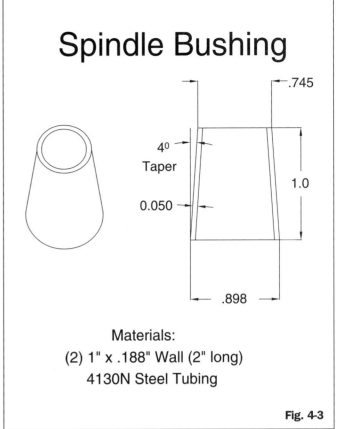

4° Taper

.745

1.0

0.050

.898

Materials:
(2) 1" x .188" Wall (2" long)
4130N Steel Tubing

Fig. 4-3

Control Arm
Reinforcement

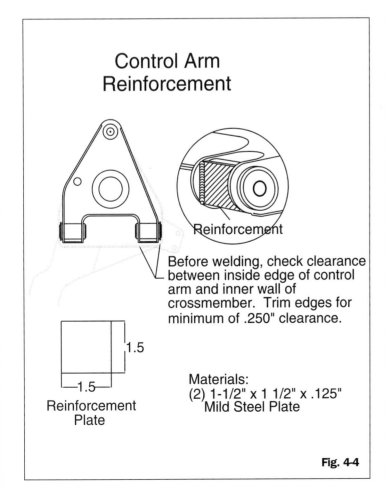

Reinforcement

Before welding, check clearance between inside edge of control arm and inner wall of crossmember. Trim edges for minimum of .250" clearance.

1.5

1.5

Reinforcement
Plate

Materials:
(2) 1-1/2" x 1 1/2" x .125"
Mild Steel Plate

Fig. 4-4

Control Arm
Bushing Zerk

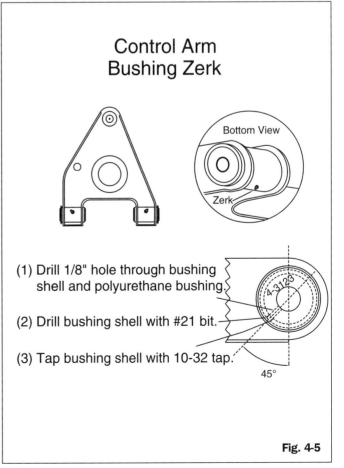

Bottom View

Zerk

(1) Drill 1/8" hole through bushing shell and polyurethane bushing.

(2) Drill bushing shell with #21 bit.

(3) Tap bushing shell with 10-32 tap.

.3125

45°

Fig. 4-5

Offset Rack Bushings

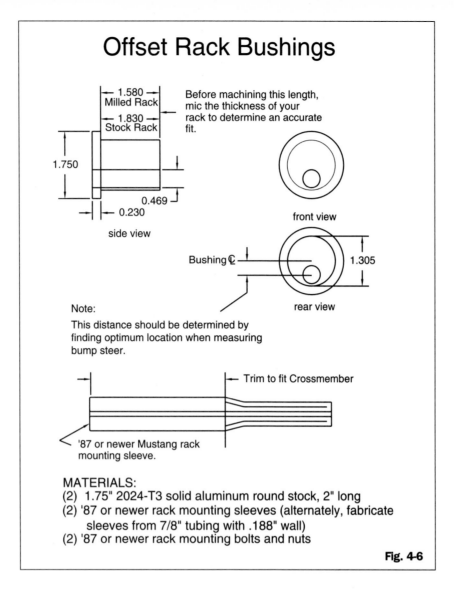

1.580
Milled Rack

1.830
Stock Rack

1.750

0.469

0.230

side view

Before machining this length, mic the thickness of your rack to determine an accurate fit.

front view

Bushing ℄

1.305

rear view

Note:

This distance should be determined by finding optimum location when measuring bump steer.

Trim to fit Crossmember

'87 or newer Mustang rack mounting sleeve.

MATERIALS:
(2) 1.75" 2024-T3 solid aluminum round stock, 2" long
(2) '87 or newer rack mounting sleeves (alternately, fabricate sleeves from 7/8" tubing with .188" wall)
(2) '87 or newer rack mounting bolts and nuts

Fig. 4-6

Tie-Rod Comparisons

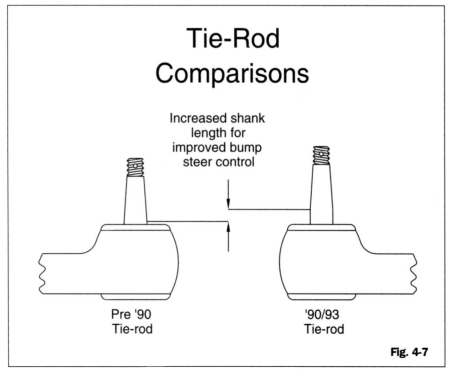

Increased shank length for improved bump steer control

Pre '90
Tie-rod

'90/93
Tie-rod

Fig. 4-7

Camber Plates
'79 - '93 Mustang

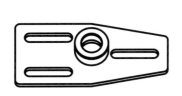

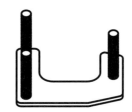

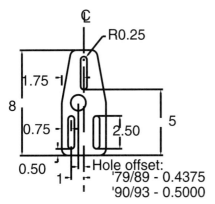

Adjusting Plate
.190" 4130N Steel Plate
(2 req'd)

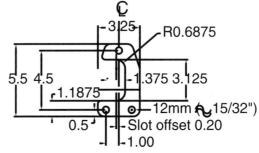

Base Plate
.190" 4130N Steel Plate
(2 req'd)

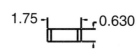

Bearing Sleeve
1.75" x .188" Wall
4130N Steel Tubing
(2 req'd)

Bearing Retainer
.190" - 4130N Steel
Plate
(2 req'd)

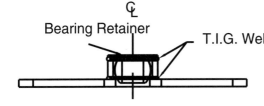

Bearing Retainer   T.I.G. Weld

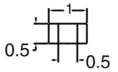

Adjusting Plate Riser
Mild Steel
(12 req'd)

Assembly:

(1) Fabricate 2 of each piece.
(2) Center Bearing Retainer on end of Bearing Sleeve and T.I.G. weld in position.
(3) Insert bearing into bearing sleeve. Fill edges with Loctite.
(4) Examine bearing/sleeve assembly to insure bearing outer shell is flush with edge of bearing sleeve.
(5) Center bearing/sleeve over hole in Adjusting Plate and T.I.G. weld in position. (Tack weld in postion, then skip weld around base. Allow assembly to cool to prevent damage to bearing, before completely welding.
(6) Tack weld head of bolts to base.

Materials:

(1) 8" x 15" x .190" 4130N Steel Plate (or .250" Mild Steel)
(1) 1-3/4" x 1.5" x .188" Wall 4130 Steel Tubing
(2) PWB-12T Aurora Spherical Bearing
(6) 12mm x 60mm Bolts, Grade 10.8
(1) 1" x 13" x .250" Wall Mild Steel Tubing
(2) 70.34.53.000.0 Koni Bump Rubber

Fig. 4-8

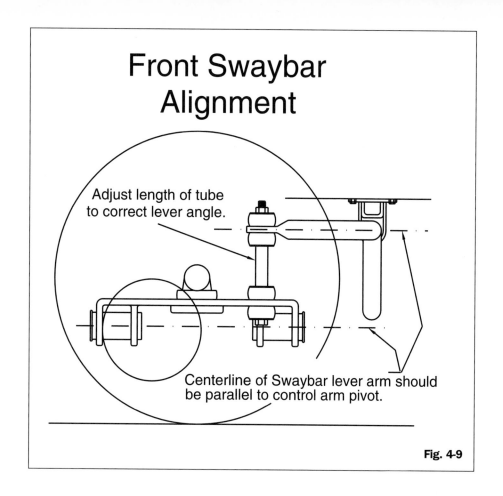

Front Swaybar Alignment

Adjust length of tube to correct lever angle.

Centerline of Swaybar lever arm should be parallel to control arm pivot.

Fig. 4-9

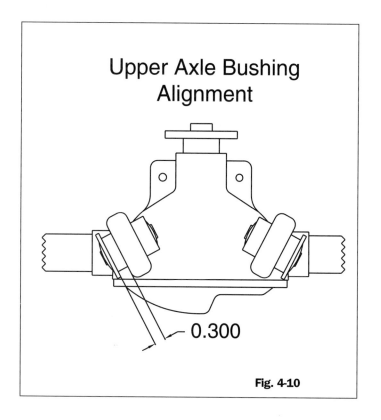

Upper Axle Bushing Alignment

0.300

Fig. 4-10

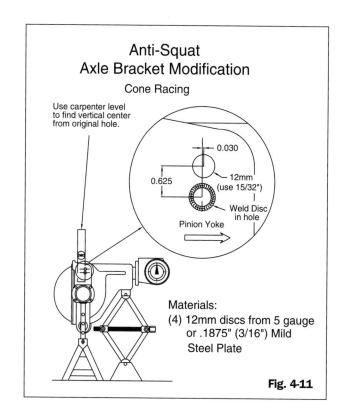

Anti-Squat Axle Bracket Modification
Cone Racing

Use carpenter level to find vertical center from original hole.

0.030

0.625

12mm (use 15/32")

Weld Disc in hole

Pinion Yoke

Materials:
(4) 12mm discs from 5 gauge or .1875" (3/16") Mild Steel Plate

Fig. 4-11

Upper Trailing Arm Reinforcement

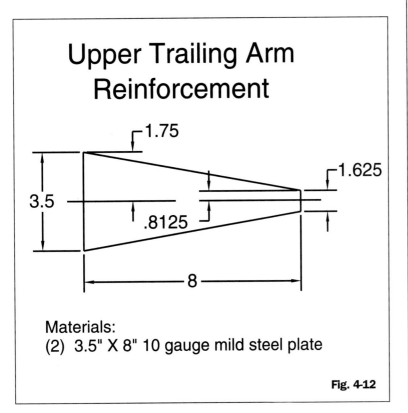

Materials:
(2) 3.5" X 8" 10 gauge mild steel plate

Fig. 4-12

Spring Rate
Calculation

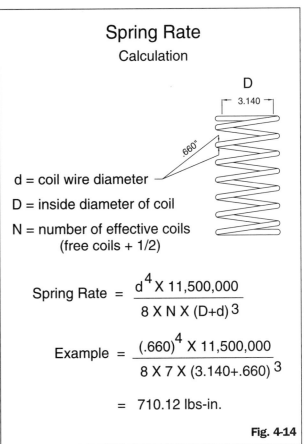

d = coil wire diameter

D = inside diameter of coil

N = number of effective coils
(free coils + 1/2)

$$\text{Spring Rate} = \frac{d^4 \times 11{,}500{,}000}{8 \times N \times (D+d)^3}$$

$$\text{Example} = \frac{(.660)^4 \times 11{,}500{,}000}{8 \times 7 \times (3.140+.660)^3}$$

$$= 710.12 \text{ lbs-in.}$$

Fig. 4-14

Lower Trailing Arm Reinforcement

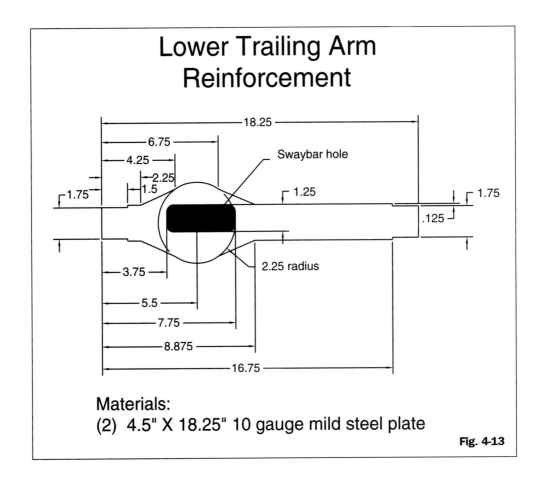

Swaybar hole

2.25 radius

Materials:
(2) 4.5" X 18.25" 10 gauge mild steel plate

Fig. 4-13

ROAD RACING SUSPENSIONS

This chapter of the book is directed at those individuals who are into white-knuckle speeds and high g forces. In this chapter there will be no compromise for ride comfort or bone-rattling stereos, just W.O.T. (wide open throttle, for you neophytes) modifications. If you are modifying your car to compete in a specific class in SCCA or IMSA don't take anyone's word on what is allowed. Get a rule book and read it carefully before you begin. Then go to the races and see what setups the fastest people are running.

CROSSMEMBERS

Contrary to common belief, all front crossmembers are not created equal, and I don't mean the obvious structural bracing (see Fig. 5-1, p. 99). Some of the pre-'88 crossmembers have good control arm locations for modification purposes, such as the '84-1/2 anniversary cars.

However, the '90–'93 crossmembers include lower control arm locations that are 1/2" more outboard than the pre-'88 cars and have a slight increase in anti–dive angle over all previous years—good stuff. Obviously, utilizing the '90 or newer crossmember on a pre-'88 car will widen the front track width 1". The additional track width, when combined with the narrower fender openings on the pre-'90 cars, can cause tire-to-fender interference on those cars utilizing wider

One of the most successful Mustangs in road-racing history is the Baer Racing World Challenge Mustang. This car was purpose-built with modified suspension pickup points and a three-link rear suspension.

wheels. Proper wheel selection is very important and will be addressed in Chapter 9.

The '90–'93 units are manufactured with weight savings in mind and are not as strong as some of the pre '87 units. If you use one of these crossmembers for road racing and the rules permit, add gussets inside between the exterior and interior control arm mounts.

Any V8 crossmember will do for this group of modifications, although the early units ('79–'80) don't permit significant control arm relocation without considerable work. With the control arm pickups moved 1/2" more outboard on the '90–'93 crossmember, there is more room for relocation without having interference problems with the control arms. Although vastly improved over previous years, even these crossmembers are a compromise. The ideal angle of the lower control arm mount is dependent on so many things, that the modifications presented in this section are a good starting point.

SVO Mustang

If you are modifying an SVO you probably already know that the front crossmember is unique to this car. Also, the control arms, brakes, and spindles are from the '82–'83 Continental. No other control arm will work with this crossmember. The SVO/Continental control arms are 1" longer than the regular Mustang units. This is most desirable since the longer the control arm the less change in roll center height as the suspension cycles. However, the SVO/Continental control arms are very heavy (especially the solid steel SVO units) and require expensive aluminum bushings. These bushings are quite large, consequently they will limit how much you can relocate the control arms. Finally, the extra length of these control arms can cause track width problems and tire-to-fender interference when using wide wheels and fat tires.

If you choose to stay with the original SVO crossmember, then you should replace the control arm bushings with aluminum pieces made by Global West Suspension Components. The stock bushings are extremely soft and allow a great deal of camber change in hard cornering. Because of the uniqueness of this vehicle, I would suggest you remove the stock crossmember and control arms and store them. This car will become more valuable as time passes and you may wish you had not modified the original pieces, so save the originals to reinstall if you ever sell it.

Finding Parts

When buying a crossmember from a salvage yard, ask to see the car it came from. It is important to make sure it is a Mustang unit and that it has not been hit in the front or with a side impact that affects the integrity of the front frame area. If the car was hit somewhere in the front half, the crossmember could be bent. If the crossmember is bent it will bias the frame when you bolt it up and make it very difficult to achieve correct frame/suspension alignment. Cross-members are virtually impossible to straighten once bent.

It is an absolute must to have all necessary parts in hand before you begin. Many of the parts here are for racing only and are seldom stocked by local vendors. It can be a real drag to wait several weeks to get the competition parts after you have screwed up your stock parts.

It will be necessary to fabricate or modify several pieces in this chapter. I have provided drawings of most of the parts if you wish to fabricate or machine them yourself. However, some of the items, i.e. spindle bushings and a modified crossmember, are difficult to fabricate. Fortunately these can be purchased from several suppliers at a very reasonable price. See the chart on p. 73 for the list of parts required for the type of suspension you wish to build.

FRONT SUSPENSION

This group of modifications is designed to improve anti–dive, caster, reduce bump steer, add several degrees of Ackermann steering and provide a more stable roll center. Additionally, there is the added benefit of creating better

Relocating the control arm mounts involves moving the holes higher and inboard (arrow). In this photo, a 1980 crossmember has had the rear bolt holes relocated to the point where they touch the rear mount. This was the original crossmember the author built for the prototype *Slot Car Mustang*.

PARTS REQUIRED:

Four–link

G–load Brace

Camber Plates

Offset Rack Bushings

'90–'93 Tie Rods

Polyurethane or aluminum Control Arm Bushings

Polyurethane Swaybar Bushings & end link kits

Racing Springs

Racing Struts & Shocks

'94 GT Spindles

OR

'82–'83 Continental Spindles

'87–'93 Rotors

SVO/Lincoln Mark VII Calipers

Borgson U–joint steering shaft

(2) HMX–6 Unibal Rod End

(2) HF–6 Unibal Rod End

'87–'88 T–bird Control Arms

Urethane #3 crossmember bushings

SVO Trailing Arms

Heavy Duty Upper Axle Trailing Arm Bushings

Suspension Techniques Swaybar

Koni SVO Axle Dampeners

Moser Engineering Axle Kit (9" type kit preferred)

Torque Arm

G–load Brace

Camber Plates

Offset Rack Bushings

'90–'93 Tie Rods

Polyurethane or aluminum Control Arm Bushings

Polyurethane Swaybar Bushings & end link kits

Racing Springs

Racing Struts & Shocks

'94 GT Spindles

OR

'82–'83 Continental Spindles

'87–'93 Rotors

SVO/Lincoln Mark VII Calipers

Borgson U–joint steering shaft

(2) HMX–6 Unibal Rod End

(2) HF–6 Unibal Rod End

'87–'88 T–bird Control Arms

Urethane #3 crossmember bushings

Helwig or Rancho 1" Rear Swaybar

Moser Engineering Axle Kit (9" type kit preferred)

Three–link

G–load Brace

Camber Plates

Offset Rack Bushings

'90–93 Tie Rods

Polyurethane or aluminum Control Arm Bushings

Polyurethane Swaybar Bushings & end link kits

Racing Springs

Racing Struts & Shocks

'94 GT Spindles

OR

'82–'83 Continental Spindles

'87–'93 Rotors

SVO/Lincoln Mark VII Calipers

Borgson U–joint steering shaft

(2) HMX–6 Unibal Rod End

(2) HF–6 Unibal Rod End

'87–'88 T–bird Control Arms

Urethane #3 crossmember bushings

Adjustable Upper Trailing Arm

Suspension Techniques Swaybar

Moser Engineering Axle Kit (9" type kit preferred)

OPTIONAL:

'90–'93 Mustang Front Crossmember

(2) MF–8 Unibal Spherical Rod End (replace tie rods)

Adjustable Upper Trailing Arms

Tubular Lower Trailing Arms

Real Brakes, Wilwood or Baer Racing Brakes Kit (Cobra R Brakes also)

front–to–rear weight distribution when relocating the #2 crossmember— something the Mustang desperately needs.

Many of these modifications require above-average mechanical aptitude and fabrication skills, as well as more sophisticated tools. If you don't know how or don't have the proper equipment, you could waste a lot of money learning. Know your limits and take your time. If you can't do it, then hire a competent professional. Many of the drawings can be given to a fabricator to work from.

Before you begin, it is necessary that you read this entire section first. You must decide about brakes, struts, spindles, control arms and crossmember selection before proceeding. Certain combinations require different modifications, so save yourself the possibility of a lot of grief and read first.

Step 1

If you have not disassembled the front suspension follow Step 7 in Chapter 3, p. 32.

Step 2

The next step is to re–clean the crossmember, control arms, spindles, and rack and pinion before beginning. You'll work a lot happier and can do a better layout of your modifications without having to peer through grease and grime.

Step 3: Welding Crossmember

Before you begin, check that your crossmember is square, then MIG-weld every seam and joint on the crossmember. This is extremely important. Much of the change in suspension geometry in a hard, high-speed corner can be attributed to the flex inherent in the spot- and tack-welded factory crossmember. To eliminate this flex, weld the seams before you proceed any further.

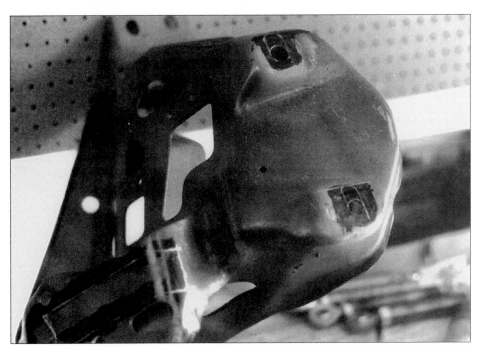

Apply layout dye around the upper mounting holes on both sides and scribe parallel lines the width of the holes toward the rear mounts. This area will be removed with a torch or grinder to allow the crossmember to be moved forward (see Step 4).

Step 4: Crossmember Mounting Holes

In this step you will be modifying the mounting holes on the top front of the crossmember. This will move the crossmember forward 5/8" (1/2" for high–performance street) and provide for several additional degrees of positive caster. It will also move the engine rearward in relation to the centerline of the front and rear wheels. Moving the engine rearward will move the center of gravity toward the rear and reduce the polar moment of inertia for improved steering response. Really good stuff for a Mustang.

The '88 or newer crossmember has a 1" wider track than previous years. Beginning in 1990, a small increase in anti–dive percentage was added. Ford applied some of what it had learned from the Escort Racing Series to provide some badly needed changes. Although the '90-'93 crossmember is an improvement over the older models, significant gains in handling can be achieved by relocating the pickup points and using the longer Thunderbird control arms.

Study Fig. 5-3 on p. 97 and be sure you understand the procedure to lay out the parallel lines on the mounting holes. When you are satisfied, place the crossmember on a flat stable structure or table. Using a long ruler, straight-edge and felt-tip pen (or layout fluid and scribe), carefully draw parallel lines along the sides of the large mounting holes on each side (on top of the spring upper base). Use the centerline of each pair of forward and rearward holes as references. You will note that the holes on each side are not parallel to one another since the frame spreads as it extends forward. This is the reason you must use the centerline as a reference to lay out the parallel lines.

Mark off an area 5/8" (1/2" for high–performance street) toward the rear of the crossmember (to the rear of the car when bolted up) within these parallel lines (see Fig. 5-4, p. 97). Elongate the original holes with a grinder or plasma cutter by removing this area. It may be necessary to use socket head-mounting bolts and a modified AN960–9 flat washer on some crossmembers to achieve a true 5/8" forward relocation due to clearance at the rear edge of the new holes. Additionally, you may want to use a torch to heat the area around the rear edges of the bolt holes inside and next to the spring seat, and hammer a 1/4" radius to ensure clearance for a washer or the head of the bolts. Most crossmembers require this modification to be able to re–install the bolts without pushing the crossmember back to its original location.

Next, go to the lower rear mounting bosses on the crossmember and draw parallel lines for each of the four holes extending rearward. Mark off an area within these parallel lines 1/4" rearward (see Fig. 5-5, p. 98). Once again, using a grinder, elongate these holes toward the rear of the car. There is not sufficient metal to elongate these holes the full 5/8", therefore elongate the holes on the frame toward the front of the car 1/2" to compensate. It will also be necessary to elongate the slots in the frame so the plate nuts for the mounting bolts can be moved forward enough to bolt up the modified crossmember. The additional 1/8" length of the slots on the frame is necessary to allow for some maneuvering during alignment.

Step 5: Control Arm Mounting Holes

To improve the anti–dive characteristic, you will be relocating the control arm mounting points. Examine Fig. 5-6 on p. 98 closely before you start this step. Note the relationship between the new hole locations and the inside centerline of the car. It is extremely important that you take your time doing this modification. You screw this up and you'll get some very weird handling, especially if the right and left sides are not identical.

Use a torch or plasma cutter and cut the inside control arm mounts off at their base and set aside. With the help of a drill and a spot–weld cutter, carefully remove the front and rear reinforcement washers found on the outside mounting holes. Take care not to damage the crossmember. Grind the excess welds smooth and apply layout dye 1" away from the existing holes toward the center of the car.

Secure the crossmember to a flat table or workbench. Using a long straight-edge bisecting the front, then the rear holes, carefully locate the new holes. On

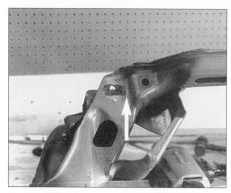

A pilot hole has been drilled in this 1985 crossmember's left front hole to move the hole up 1/4" and inboard 3/4". This is done on both sides in the front in order to use the longer T-Bird control arms, to lower the car and to provide an increase in the anti-dive percentage, as well as maintaining the stock track width.

the '88 or newer crossmember this point should be 3/4" inboard and 1/4" higher than the factory control arm mounting bolt holes on the front outside mount hole (front of car). Check this location several times before you mark it with a center punch. Do the same for the rear mounting hole except locate it 3/4" inboard and 3/4" higher. If you are modifying a pre-'88 crossmember, the holes in the front should be moved inboard 1/4" and raised 1/4", with the rear holes being moved inboard 1/4" and up 3/4". Be sure you are on a parallel line to both sides of the crossmember, left to right, when marking the location of these holes. Again, take your time and reflect on the locations you have marked before proceeding.

When you are satisfied that you have properly located these points, drill a 1/8" pilot hole. Recheck its location carefully. If it is off more than a few thousandths, weld it up and try again. When you have successfully located the holes, drill them out to 1/4".

Before drilling the holes out to size, it will be necessary to fabricate four 2-1/4" diameter reinforcement discs from 3/16" mild steel. Drill a 1/4" hole in the center of each disc. Using 1/4" bolts and nuts, bolt the discs to the new holes, one at a time, and mark the excess inboard edge

The first step in relocating the control arm pickup points is to cut the inside mounts off at their base. They should be cut off as close to the base as possible. After removing the mounts, grind the edge smooth and relatively flat. This is important to ensure a solid fit when the mount is reinstalled.

In this photo you can clearly see where the new rear holes are located, 3/4" up and 3/4" inboard on this 1985 crossmember.

that must be trimmed for the washer to sit flat. Trim the washers to fit against the inside radius on the front, and possibly at the rear, crossmember-to-frame bracket. Take your time and make a good fit. Generally it is necessary to grind a radius on the bottom inboard edge of the discs for the front holes to achieve a good fit without deleting most of the edge.

Bolt the discs tightly in their correct locations using the same 1/4" bolts and nuts. MIG-weld the outside radius of these discs as well as the inside original holes. Remove the 1/4" retaining bolts and dress the welds, paying particular attention to the welds on the original holes. Be sure the surface is smooth and flat on the inside where the control arm bushings rotate. In step increments, drill the new holes out to 5/8" diameter, using a 1/4", a 3/8", a 1/2" and finally a 5/8" drill bit. Deburr the holes.

Next, dress the edges of the remaining inner mount on the crossmember with a grinder before proceeding (see Fig. 5-7, p. 98). Taking small amounts at a time, trim the inside edges of the inner mounts you previously cut off, to align with the new hole locations. This can best be achieved by using a 3' length of 5/8" x .65" wall 4130N tubing as a guide. Work the edges down until the tubing will slide through all four holes without binding. Be sure to use the steel inner bushings from the Energy Suspension control arm bushing set as guides on each side of the mount for proper centering. Make certain you have the front and rear bushing sleeves in the correct location! The front bushing is shorter. If you align the mount with the bushings in the wrong place you will say many ugly things— especially after you have spent the better part of a weekend making this modification.

Once you are satisfied you have the mount correctly aligned, install an unmodified T–bird control arm in the crossmember with the center mount bolted up. Do not weld the mount yet. It may be necessary on some cross-members, especially earlier years, to remove some of the rear edge of the control arm before welding in the center mount. This is necessary to clear the inside of the crossmember. Check the fit and clearance throughout the complete range of motion before you weld. On the older crossmembers ('79–'80), it may be necessary to cut a 3" x 3" hole directly behind the rear control arm mount for clearance. You will then have to fabricate a cover from .125" mild steel to return the structural integrity to the crossmember. Additionally, it may be

Relocating the control arm pickup points per the accompanying text and drawings is designed to use the 3/4" longer '87-'88 T-Bird control arms. By using these longer control arms the arc of the spindle is not as severe as the stock pieces. The slower arc reduces the amount of camber loss as the suspension compresses.

With the new holes completed and dressed, the 2-1/4" x 3/16" steel washer can be fitted and welded in place. Be sure to use the long 5/8" rod as a guide to ensure the discs are properly located.

After the outside holes have been relocated, it is necessary to fit the inside bracket. Follow the accompanying drawings and trim the inside edges, small amounts at a time, until the bracket will fit flush against the crossmember with the long 5/8" rod passing through its holes.

It is necessary to use the control arm bushings' inner sleeves as spacers for the final fitting and welding of the modified inner bracket. Since you need to replace the soft stock control arm bushings with urethane pieces, use the inner sleeve provided with them as guides. Be sure to use the short sleeve in the front.

necessary to cut a small square in the lower rear crossmember-to-frame mount to clear the mounting nut. Once you are sure there is no interference with the control arm, bolt up the control arm with the bolts passing inside out, MIG-weld the nuts in position in the rear, and tack-weld the center mount in position. Remove the control arm and completely MIG-weld the center piece in its new location. Repeat this procedure for the other side.

Step 6: Relocating Engine

The last step in the modification of the crossmember is to alter the engine mount to relocate the engine rearward. How far you move the engine rearward is your choice. Some racers have moved their engines rearward as much as 2" and down 1". However, if you intend to move the engine more than 1" over the stock location, you will have to cut the mounts off of the crossmember with a torch and reweld them in the new location. In doing so, you will suffer the usual problems with headers, firewall clearance, steering shaft linkage, and oil pan. Unless you are a skilled fabricator, limit the relocation to the 1" shown in Fig. 5-8, p. 98. Also, if you are running in SCCA or IMSA check the rules before you do this.

Header Clearance—I have relocated engines rearward 1" and had no problems with any of the popular aftermarket headers built for the 5.0 engines, including the long-tube type. There is always a first, so be aware of the possibility of slight modifications necessary to fit your headers. To avoid interference with the rear axle and fuel tank, the header-to-muffler extension tubes will have to be shortened the amount the engine was moved rearward in relation to the frame. *Warning: If your car is equipped with an automatic transmission, you cannot move the engine rearward more than 1/2" beyond*

In this photo, the guide marks have been laid out for cutting the right-side engine mount to relocate the engine rearward. As with the left side mount, the rectangular box as scribed by the lines will be removed and discarded.

the original engine-to-frame location before the transmission's bellhousing hits the firewall.

Begin by scribing parallel lines down the engine mounts on the crossmember (just behind the tear–drop shaped mounting holes) that are 1-5/8" apart and perpendicular to the centerline of the car. Mark perpendicular lines across and to the front showing the cross cut. Study Fig. 5-8 carefully before you start cutting to ensure you have laid out the proper cuts. It's easy to redraw, but it's tough to re–fabricate. The idea is to remove two perfect 1-5/8" rectangular sections out of the middle of the left mount and one 1- 5/8" rectangular section from the right mount, and then weld the front section to the remaining rear section, thereby moving the mounting location rearward 1" from stock. Remember that you have already modified the crossmember mounting holes that will move the crossmember forward 5/8", making it necessary to remove 1-5/8" to achieve a 1" relocation over the stock position in relation to the frame. (If you moved the crossmember 1/2" forward for high–performance street, you would need to remove 1-1/2" instead of 1-5/8".) Although you will be moving the engine rearward only 1" in relation to the frame,

this, in combination with the fact that the front suspension has been moved forward, will achieve a significant change in the front–to–rear weight distribution.

When you are certain you have the layout correct, mark the cuts with chalk and cut with a torch or plasma cutter. Dress the edges on the remaining mount and the front section that was cut off with a grinder or coarse sander, clamp the front section to the remaining mount, and MIG-weld in place. Be sure to completely fill in the joints as you weld. Dress the welds with a high–speed

sander using an 80-grit sanding disc. This is important for that "stock" look.

It is very important to check the engine mounts very closely for cracks, especially the left mount. If your car has been subjected to frequent drag race launches or the rigorous demands of a high-horsepower engine, the left engine mount is probably cracked. Grind a "v" groove in any crack you find and MIG-weld it back together.

Step 7: G-Load Brace

With all the modifications completed on the crossmember a G–load brace must be installed. Follow Step 3 in Chapter 4, p. 54.

Step 8

Once you have completed these modifications, clean the crossmember and G–load brace with a good grease and wax remover (PPG DX–330), prime with a good epoxy paint (PPG DP–48), and paint with an acrylic urethane color to match the car or engine bay. Very important for that stock look. Acrylic urethane is easy to spray and provides a very durable surface. Don't forget to follow the paint manufacturer's safety procedures and wear the correct respirator. Epoxy primers and urethane paints don't mix well with humans.

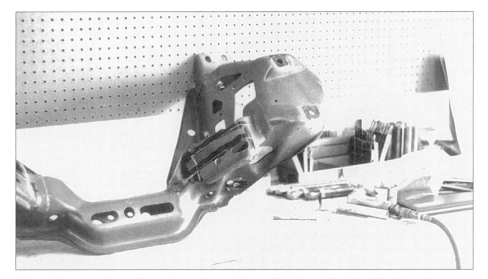

Pictured here are the scribe marks to be used as guides for cutting the left-side engine mount apart. The rectangular box as scribed by the lines will be removed and discarded.

With the engine mounts cut apart you can see the remaining pieces that will be dressed and welded in the open slots.

After the mounts on the crossmember and the remaining pieces have been dressed, they are clamped together along the long vertical edge and welded together.

Step 9: Crossmember Installation

Bolt the crossmember on the car. Before tightening the crossmember's eight mounting bolts, push it as far forward as it will go. This should be 5/8" (1/2" for high–performance street) forward of the original location. Check against the original location you marked on the frame before you removed the crossmember. If it will not slide forward 5/8" (1/2" for high–performance street),

then remove it and check your work on the mounting holes and correct as necessary before re–installing.

Check the car to ensure that it is level, using a carpenter level on the rocker panels, both laterally and longitudinally. With a plumb bob, mark the exact location on the floor for the rear lower trailing arm mounting bolt holes (on the frame), and the rearmost control arm mounting bolt holes on the crossmember (see Fig. 5-9, p. 99). Measure these distances along the length of the car and

diagonally. Tap the crossmember to adjust one side to match the other, all the while trying to maintain the desired additional forward relocation (1/2" or 5/8"). This will square the crossmember in the frame in relation to the rear axle.

If your floor is not level enough for this procedure, then hang a plumb bob by a wire hook in each of the two holes with a mark on the each of the strings the same distance from the holes. Measure the distances between the strings at the marks. Do this for both sides and

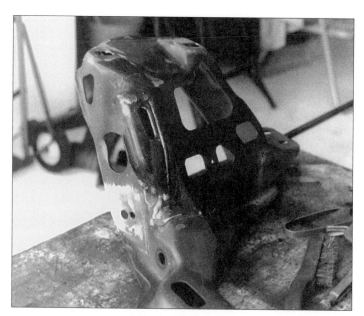

This photo shows the reassembled right-side engine mount before the welds have been smoothed.

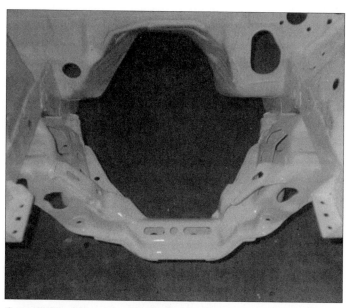

Smooth the welds with a high-speed disc sander. After painting to match the car, the modified crossmember looks factory stock.

The 1993 SCCA American Sedan champion Mustang from Steeda Autosports shows what a well-balanced front end does through a tight turn. The outside tire is firmly planted and the car demonstrates little body roll.

diagonally. Adjust until you have exact matches.

After you have completed the alignment of the crossmember, torque the eight mounting bolts to 80 ft-lbs for the large bolts and 50 ft-lbs for the smaller rear bolts. Upon completion of the modifications, and after you have had the crossmember alignment set on a laser alignment machine, MIG-weld a 1" bead along the rear edge of the lower crossmember mounts where they mate with the frame. This will ensure the crossmember will not shift under severe braking or racing conditions.

Step 10: Control Arm Gussets

In this step you will be welding gussets on the control arms to prevent distortion during severe cornering. Because the control arm pickup points have been relocated inboard it will be necessary and advantageous to use the '87-'88 Thunderbird/Cougar V8 control arms. These are 3/4" longer than the stock Mustang units and will reduce negative camber loss in the corners. An additional benefit to the longer control arms is a reduction in the vertical oscillation of the roll center as the suspension cycles.

If your car is an '87 or older non-SVO model you must use the longer rack & pinion inner socket assemblies found on the SVO or post-'87 Mustangs. This assembly is designed to work with the 1" longer Continental control arms or wider track width found on the '88 or newer Mustangs. To ensure a strong relationship between the tie–rod and socket assembly, it is necessary to use the longer socket assemblies, which will compensate for the longer adjusted length for proper toe settings. If you intend to use the

T–Bird's longer control arms without the longer inner socket assembly, be sure to check for sufficient thread contact on the tie–rods before you start racing. If one of these pulls out in a hard corner you'll probably trash a fine car. Check closely!

In order to gain additional Ackermann steering, it is necessary to install SVO/Continental spindles. Since these spindles fit the larger shank of the Lincoln Continental ball joint, it is necessary to install a reducer bushing. Shown here is the bushing set sold by Central Coast Mustang.

You can not go fast without race-quality dampeners. There are many choices available for the Mustang, however it is hard to beat the adjustable struts and shocks offered by Koni.

Step 11

The next step is to install polyurethane bushings in the freshly painted control arms. Follow the instructions found in Step 5 of Chapter 4, p. 56.

Step 12

If you are using anything but the Monroe GP or Koni competition struts you will need to modify the strut-to-spindle mounting holes for better strut action. Follow Step 4 in Chapter 4, p. 55.

Step 13: Ackermann Steering

In order to provide a few additional degrees of Ackermann steering it will be necessary to mill the rear mounting bosses on the rack housing. Essentially you will be moving the rack rearward to create a better angle with the steering knuckle. When this modification is combined with the use of the '82-'83 Lincoln Continental spindle, Ackermann steering improves to about 6°. Not a lot, but all things being equal, it's the little things that win races. Because the '94 spindle has 13° of steering axis inclination, it would be a better choice if available.

Remove the hoses from the rack and pinion and plug off the open fittings with screw-in plugs or tape. If you are using tape be sure the surface is clean and oil-free, as it is very important that the tape sticks firmly to keep metal shavings out during the machining process. Also, make every effort to avoid losing fluid and allowing air to enter the rack. It can be very difficult and time-consuming to get the air out. Generally, your steering will shudder when you attempt to turn the wheel if air has been introduced into the system. This is the pits!

If your car was equipped with the standard 20:1 power steering system, you must upgrade to the high–effort 15:1 rack and pinion and related power steering pump (E6SZ–3A674–B), as described in Chapter 4, p. 57. Read that section before proceeding.

With the correct rack in hand, press out the mounting bushings and take the rack & pinion to a competent machine shop. Have them mill .250" off the rear mounting bosses (see Fig. 5-10, p. 101).

Step 14: Offset Bushings

Clean the milled rack carefully and check the steering hydraulic line sockets for any metal shavings. Follow Step 6 in Chapter 4, p. 56, and install the offset rack and pinion mounting bushings. Generally, what you are doing is raising the rack up and moving it rearward. This will eliminate some of the bump steer associated with the lowered car and also improve Ackermann steering when used with the SVO/Continental spindles. (You may want to shorten the rack mounting bolts after you have machined the housing and installed the offset bushings.)

Step 15: Tie Rods

Either use tie rods from the '90-'93 Mustang for better bump steer control, or adapt spherical rod ends to the inner socket assemblies on your rack and modify the spindle knuckles for bolts. The '90-'93 Mustang tie rod has a longer shank than previous years and will reduce the difference between the control arm angle and the inner socket assembly angle.

Spherical Rod Ends—To adapt spherical rod ends you must fabricate a union from 7/8" diameter tubing with .188" wall thickness to connect a size 10 rod end to the 9/16–18 threads on the inner socket assembly (see Fig. 5-11,

After you have relocated the control arms, a set of solid metal offset rack & pinion housing bushings will be necessary to bring bump steer under control. Central Coast Mustang can provide you with a race-quality pair.

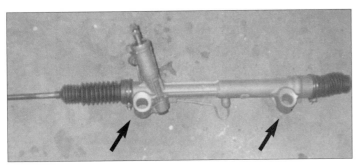

A few degrees of Ackermann steering can be gained by milling the rear mounting bosses on the rack and pinion housing .250". This modification moves the rack rearward, creating a small angle between the rack and the steering knuckle on the spindle.

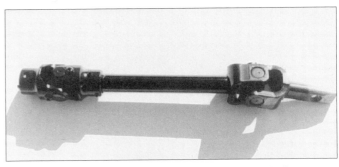

For the serious racer, replacing the spongy steering shaft insulator is a must. The optimum approach is to install a modified shaft that has been fitted with a Borgson universal joint. Shown here is the trick setup from Central Coast Mustang.

p. 100). Additionally, you must drill the tapered hole in the spindle steering knuckle out to a straight 5/8" hole in order to use a 5/8" bolt for attachment of the rod end. With this setup you will be able to insert flat washers between the rod ends and the steering knuckle to make fine adjustments in eliminating bump steer. World Challenge stuff, but not good on the street. *Warning:* Spherical rod ends have an allergic reaction to potholes and generally don't hold up well on the street.

Unless you are fitting Wilwood brakes on your car, assemble the strut and spindle. Use Loctite on the threads and torque the attaching bolts to 150, then to 175 lbs-ft. Go to Chapter 8, *Brakes,* for the procedures on the Wilwood brakes.

Step 16: Steering Shaft

I recommend that you install a Borgson universal joint steering shaft. This steering shaft is very strong as well as narrow for that additional clearance around those big-tube headers.

Step 17: Swaybar Spherical Rod Ends

In this step you will be installing the swaybar and replacing the swaybar end links with two pairs of Unibal spherical rod ends. This will significantly tighten up the swaybar action but retain some of the cushion necessary for street use. See Fig. 5-12, p. 100, for this installation. If you use this setup on the street, check

them every time you change the oil on your car. Also, always keep a spare set of the rod ends on hand.

To begin, install your swaybar using Energy Suspension swaybar mounting bushings. For this modification, you will be inserting one male rod end up through the swaybar end link hole and securing it with a standard 7/16–20 UNF lug nut and thin check nut. The Unibal end of the installed rod end will be secured to the Unibal end of a female rod end with a 3/8" grade 8 bolt and large safety washers (AN970–6) on each side. Next, the female end will be bolted to a shorter end link kit (substituting an AN6–44 bolt for the kit bolt), with the bushings, washers, and sleeve installed on the control arm by screwing a thin check nut (AN316–6) and then the female rod end on. Then the compression on the

bushings is adjusted for a normal fit. This modification, when combined with urethane swaybar mounting bushings, will reduce twist friction and provide more accurate swaybar compliance.

You will note that the factory swaybar comes stock with the lever ends (ends that attach to swaybar end links) being parallel to the frame in normal driving conditions. It is very important that you maintain that same relationship when either installing the rod ends or standard bushing end links. If you are running shorter springs it will be necessary to trim the sleeve and use a shorter bolt between the bushings to achieve this relationship. On the newer Mustangs, it will be necessary to replace the factory solid end links with the older style bolt and sleeve in order to make the necessary adjustments and fit.

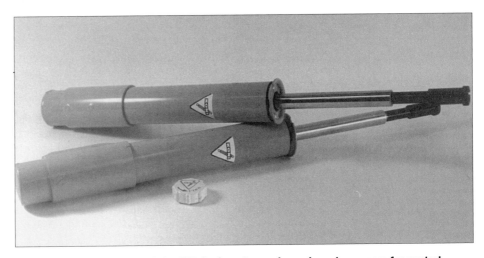

Front springs that go beyond the 750 lbs-in. rate require serious dampeners for control. Although there are several manufacturers of these, the people at Koni make a very reliable, double-adjusting strut for hard-core racing conditions. Shown here are the SPSS units that were originally developed for the SCCA's Showroom Stock class.

No front suspension is complete without fully adjustable camber plates. The Global West camber plates shown here are typical of those offered today. When installing these plates, be sure to use spacers under the top plate to raise the strut mount if your car has been lowered significantly or has the control arms relocated.

Step 18: Camber Plates

See Chapter 4, Step 9, p. 58 for how to manufacture and install camber plates. Or you can purchase the ones from Global West (1423 E. Philadelphia, Ontario, CA 91761, 909/923-6176). If this setup is for racing don't use the spring insulators (inner sleeves, coil insulators and spring perch pads). For the street, substitute the harder spring perch pads from the earlier model GT Mustangs (1982).

Step 19

As noted previously, you will need to modify the hood inner brace to clear the adjustable Koni struts when utilizing a camber plate that raises the mount 1". See Step 9 in Chapter 4, p. 59.

Step 20: Correcting Steering Shudder

If you allowed air into the steering system and are experiencing an ugly shudder when you turn the steering wheel, then jack the front of the car up, and with the engine running, have someone slowly turn the steering wheel

about a half turn each direction, while you systematically loosen and tighten the various fittings to get most of the air out. After this procedure, you must slowly turn the steering wheel about a half turn in each direction until you see air bubbles start to foam the fluid in the power steering pump reservoir. Stop, turn the engine off, wait until the bubbles have dissipated, and do it again as many times as necessary until all the air is out. Now this can be a real pain and take several hours, so do your best to minimize the fluid loss and introduction of air into the system.

If the rules of your class permit, increase the fluid capacity of your power steering pump for better cooling. Simply cut the spout from a spare or salvage power steering pump reservoir and attach to your engine's power steering reservoir. Use a neoprene or silicone hose and radiator clamps to attach the spout. This will provide a significant amount of additional fluid that could prevent it from boiling over. Optionally the Cobra R cooler will help considerably (PN F10Y-3D746-A).

Step 21: Transmission & Driveshaft

Because the engine has been relocated rearward, the transmission mount and driveshaft must be modified to fit the new location. It will be necessary to have 1" (or the amount the engine has been relocated rearward) removed from the driveshaft length. Take your driveshaft to a reputable shop that understands how to properly index the ends so they are in phase and be sure it is re-balanced. If you do not shorten the driveshaft, it will bottom out against the transmission output shaft and damage both, as well as create a very loose rear end under hard joust.

Although not recommended, I have seen cars with their engines relocated 1" or less, operating without shortening the driveshaft. Seems their owners found

sufficient play between the axle and transmission. If you attempt this, use a floor jack under the axle housing center section to cycle the rear axle completely to full bump, with the weight of the car balanced on the axle and the bump stops, without the springs and with the driveshaft installed, to determine if there is any binding. Check this closely!

Transmission Mounts—Most factory transmission mounts have enough travel left in the mounting slots to accommodate the additional 1" without modification. Check before you start. If you are using your original transmission mount, you must use a disc cutter to cut the old welds on each of the two mounting sleeves so the mount can be moved toward the rear of the car. Once you have cut the welds, relocate the mounting sleeves forward in the mount (locating the mount rearward) approximately 1" (or the amount the engine has been moved rearward). Reinstall the mount in the car using the stock rubber bushings and tack-weld the sleeves in position. Remove the crossmember and MIG-weld the bushing sleeves in the same pattern as the factory welds. If you have located your engine more than 1" rearward, it would be best to wait until the engine and transmission have been mounted in the car to determine the exact location.

Ford Double-Hump Crossmember—If your car is not equipped with factory dual exhaust, your best choice would be to purchase a Ford Motorsport "double–hump" #3 transmission crossmember. This crossmember comes without the mounting sleeves welded in place and provides clearance for dual exhaust, an absolute must for performance. By installing the engine and transmission first, you will be able to bolt up the Motorsport crossmember and slide it back and forth for the best fit. Once you have achieved the best location, tack-weld the sleeves in place, with a single

Springs that are the correct length and rate are mandatory for precision handling. The set shown here were manufactured by Eibach for Central Coast Mustang. These springs are typical of the rates used on a modified Mustang running a four-link suspension—850-1000 lbs-in. in the front and 280 lbs-in. in the rear.

And finally, the last approach is to fabricate a three–link setup. All of these setups are complex and require a complete understanding of every step before going to the next one. Setting the rear axle improperly can cause the car to be very unstable at speeds or in a turn, so take your time. Check the parts list on p. 73 and gather all of the parts you'll need for the setup you choose before you begin.

Which setup you choose to follow is a matter of personal preference and dependent on the rules for the class you will be competing in. Each type of setup has its own advantages and disadvantages. The four–link system has been around a while and consequently the parts necessary to use it are readily available. The torque arm setup can be fabricated or purchased and does not require a great deal of special items to work. However, a very large rear swaybar must be used with this setup. Although not common, the three–link setup has had significant success on the race tracks, most notably the Hal Baer World Challenge Mustang. It is, however, difficult to fabricate and install. Again, you make the call.

Bushings

Before we begin, I'd like to talk a bit about bushings in the rear suspension. The factory bushings used in the V8 cars

tack on each side, while the crossmember is still on the car. Take the crossmember off, remove the rubber bushings, and MIG-weld three 3/8" beads on each of the four sleeve/mount joints.

When reassembling the engine and transmission in the car, be sure to use Energy Suspension polyurethane transmission mount bushings. This will help stabilize the engine and provide better torque transfer to the tires.

REAR SUSPENSION

This group of modifications is directed at the most misunderstood area of the car's handling—the rear suspension. The Mustang uses a four–link system that, like the rest of the suspension, is a compromise between good handling and a comfortable ride for the grandmothers who buy the car. This compromise provides adequate handling but the rear

suspension must be improved for racing.

There are basically three approaches to choose from. The first approach is to maintain the four–link setup and utilize the stock frame-to-trailing arm attachment points. The second approach is to install or fabricate a torque arm.

In order to install polyurethane bushings, it is necessary to heat the bushing shell and press out the inner rubber or burn it away. Either way it makes a mess—but it is a necessary evil.

This photo is downright scary. Pictured here are a pair of stock upper trailing arms on a brand-new '92 GT Mustang after 15 laps at Texas World Speedway. As you can see, the soft rubber bushings overheated and slid out of the bushing shells. Driving this car into turn one at triple-digit speeds required a firm bite on the seat.

are too soft for autocrossing or road racing. Ford builds the Mustang using soft bushings in the GT/LX 5.0 cars to compensate for the stiffer springs and shocks and thereby dampen the road vibrations that could be transmitted to the passengers. Not good for the corner nut.

There are several options to correct this problem: replace your stock trailing arms with trailing arms from the base 4-cylinder Mustang, which use a much stiffer bushing; use the SVO Mustang units; use the Motorsports upper trailing arms; use the heavy-duty units from the police package option; replace your bushings with polyurethane pieces; or use a combination of spherical bearings and polyurethane bushings.

John Vermeersch of Ford SVO stated that as a production cost compromise, all the Ford replacement trailing arms come with stiffer police/taxi bushings. Although the Ford replacement units come with stiffer bushings, the aftermarket Fairmont police/taxi units that are manufactured by the original factory vendor and sold by some high–performance shops, are made of heavier gauge steel and have bushings

with higher durometer ratings than the Ford replacement units.

There are several companies that sell replacement polyurethane bushings for the trailing arms. They're fine-looking and come in colors that can match your car's paint or the urethane bushings that go in the front suspension. However, keep in mind that 100 durometer polyurethane bushings are too stiff and will not allow the twisting that is necessary for proper suspension function. Without some flex in the bushings, the trailing arms will travel in diverse and singular arcs, causing the suspension to bind up. The end result is a very high, bushing-induced roll stiffness that makes for a very loose rear end that will come around (oversteer) in the corners. I recommend bushings of 88 durometer hardness, such as those made by Energy Suspension.

Spherical Bearings—For maximum compliance, spherical bearings are the way to go. Upper trailing arms utilizing spherical rod ends can be easily fabricated from standard steel tubing. Unfortunately, having the springs nest on the lower trailing arms precludes the use

of spherical bearings on both ends of the lower trailing arms. The best approach is to fit spherical bearings on the frame end and install polyurethane bushings on the axle end.

FOUR-LINK REAR SUSPENSION

If you have not yet removed the rear axle assembly, place the car up on jackstands providing at least 18" of floor clearance. Support the axle under the center section, disconnect the flexible brake hose from the frame and remove the dampeners and shocks. Remove the coil springs, disconnect the trailing arms and remove the axle assembly. Remove the trailing arms. Finally, remove the frame mounting brackets for the dampeners as they will not be used. As with the beginning of any modification, clean everything thoroughly, including the axle assembly.

Step 22

If you have not installed a rear shock tower brace or integrated one into your roll cage, you should do so now. During severe cornering, the shock towers will flex inboard, causing less than optimum suspension compliance. See p. 33 for details.

Step 23

If you have not welded around the frame's upper trailing arm mounts it is a must for this modification. Without the cushion of the rubber bushings, any weakness in the mount attachment, when subjected to the stress of a solid spherical joint, will soon be found. Again, for this level of modification, I strongly recommend that additional inside braces be extended from the main roll bar hoop to the interior side of these mounts. Weld completely through the footing plates and the trailing arm bracket and use 3/8" aircraft grade bolts (AN6) to tie them together.

Step 24: Upper Trailing Arms

Figures 5-13, 5-14 and 5-15 on p. 101 show the construction specifications necessary to fabricate adjustable upper trailing arms. These are fabricated by threading each end of a 6" section of 1" x .219" mild steel tubing. One end of each of the fabricated trailing arms uses a left-handed thread spherical joint. If you do not have the proper left-handed tap it will be necessary to take the arms to a machine shop and have them threaded. You can use right-handed threads on both ends. However, if you do so it will be necessary to disconnect the trailing arm each time you want to make an adjustment. In addition you must make adjustments in 1/2-turn increments. This will limit fine-tuning the suspension setup.

Once you have completed the fabrication of these units, adjust their lengths to approximate the factory trailing arms (approximately 9.25"). Be sure that they are matched in length.

It will be necessary to machine upper rear axle housing bushing substitutes and side spacers. When installing the spherical trailing arm, sandwich two fabricated bushings onto the axle housing mount and secure them, along with the tubular upper trailing arm on the side closest to the frame, with a 3-3/4" x 1/2" grade 8 bolt, nut, lock washer and safety washer (AN970–8) on the rod end side. Use two AN860–8 washers between the rod end and the AN970–8 safety washer. This is necessary to provide rotating clearance for the rod ends. Use only grade 8 (aircraft quality) bolts, nuts and washers.

When attaching the trailing arm to the frame, be sure the short spacer is placed toward the exterior side of the car. Again use 3-1/2" x 1/2" grade 8 bolts, nuts and lock washers to secure these.

Using the Stock Arms—If you will not be using the adjustable upper trailing arms and will be using the stock

This is a completed pair of adjustable upper trailing arms that were built from the accompanying drawings. Using a pair of these will allow fine tuning the four-link suspension for optimum handling.

stamped-steel type, it is imperative that you replace the bushings and box in the structure with a steel plate. The stock type bushings, even the high durometer SVO/Police type, just don't provide sufficient control of the axle torque under full racing conditions. As discussed in Chapter 4, the longitudinal twisting that occurs with the stock trailing arms must also be eliminated.

Heat the bushing shells with a torch hot enough to release the rubber and just push the old bushings out. Clean any excess rubber from the bushing shells by

burning with a torch. This will reduce the rubber residue to a powder that is easily brushed out.

Fabricate reinforcement plates per Step 15 in Chapter 4, p. 62. The dimensions are in Fig. 4-12, p. 70. Follow the instructions for welding them in place.

Brush any scaling that occurs during welding and clean the trailing arm with a good grease and wax remover. Paint with two coats of epoxy paint (PPG DP90). When the paint has dried, install Energy Suspension 88 durometer bushings.

Pictured here is the correct way to attach the adjustable upper trailing arms to the axle housing. The two large spacers are sandwiched around the factory bushing mount with the tapered piece next to the rod end.

Step 25: Lower Trailing Arms

In this step you must either fabricate lower trailing arms per the instructions in Figures 5-16, 17 and 18 (pp. 102-103), or modify the stock units for racing. The 2" x 3" box steel trailing arms in the drawings are very strong and will completely eliminate the twisting that is common with the stock trailing arms. They are designed to utilize Energy Suspension polyurethane bushings.

In order to use the stock trailing arms you must follow the same procedure as specified in the previous step for the stock upper trailing arms. Just follow Step 15 in Chapter 4, p. 63, except use Figure 4-13(p. 70) for the reinforcement plates. Use the Energy Suspension 88 durometer bushings.

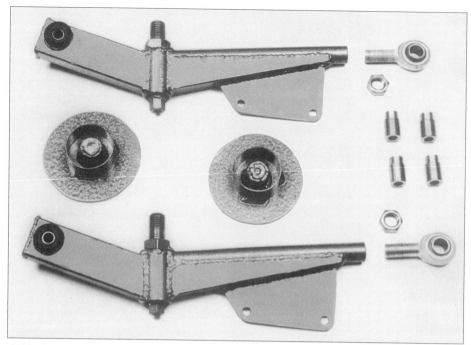

Achieving ideal corner weights is critical to optimum corner speeds. These trick lower trailing arms from Griggs Racing (MCA 2000 A) are very stout and fully adjustable. They also have interchangeable spring plates that allow the use of flat base springs.

Step 26: Anti-Squat

Everyone who is serious about road racing has had to deal with squat at the rear axle. With the four–link suspension there are two approaches to raise the anti–squat percentages. One method involves modification of the stock lower trailing arm mounting brackets on the rear axle and the other is by attaching fabricated anti–squat brackets to the rear axle assembly to relocate the pickup points. Either method accomplishes the same result. Some class rules do not permit the modification of axle brackets, so the add–on type must be used. (Anti–squat is discussed in Chapter 2, p. 15.)

Modifying Axle Brackets— This modification involves moving the pickup points for the lower trailing arm downward away from the axle centerline 1-1/2" (See Fig. 5-19, p. 103). To accomplish this you will need two 1-1/2" wide strips of 5 gauge mild steel (or 3/16") that are approximately 11" long. A much simpler option would be to use a second set of brackets from a discarded rear axle housing. Dead 7.5" housings make good donors.

To accomplish this modification, you must remove the axles and rear brakes. Balance the axle housing upside down on jackstands under the axle tubes by using a jack under the pinion part of the housing. Attach a magnetic inclinometer to the face of the yoke and adjust the jack to achieve an angle of 0° on the yoke.

Clean the exterior surface of the lower trailing arm bracket with a wire brush. Swab 1" wide vertical and horizontal strips running through the centerline of the mounting holes with layout dye. Place a level vertically on each side of the trailing arm brackets with an edge that bisects the trailing arm bolt holes. With the level resting on the axle tube and held vertically level with one edge

When modifying the lower trailing arm brackets per Step 26, it is necessary to mount the axle housing on jackstands and adjust the pinion angle to vertical. Once this is done, vertical lines can be scribed through the factory holes as references to properly align the extended bracket.

After the vertical reference lines have been scribed, the tip of the original bracket is cut off parallel to the pinion centerline as shown.

Shown here is the strip that has been welded in position to extend the bracket. By welding the rear edge first, a torch can be used to heat the corners for bending to conform to the radius of the factory bracket.

bisecting the center of the hole, scribe a line from the axle tube through the center of the hole to the edge of the bracket. Scribe a parallel line on the pinion side of the first line with a gap of .065 between the two lines.

Next, scribe a perpendicular level line for cutting. This line should pass through a point 1/4" below the upper edge of the outside hole (with the axle inverted it will be the edge closest to the axle tube), starting from the forward edge of the bracket, and proceed around the back of the bracket and through a point 11/32" above the upper edge (toward the axle tube with the axle housing inverted) of the inside hole to the forward edge of the bracket. Use the level to define the basic line location before cutting. Double-check your lines, then cut the tip of the brackets off at the perpendicular lines.

If you are using a 1-1/2" strip to extend the bracket, dress the edges of the brackets on the axle housing and the tip that was cut off with a grinder to a 45° angle for welding. Dress both long edges of the strips to a 45° angle also. Center the strip on the rear edge of the axle housing bracket and tack-weld to the bracket. Check the vertical alignment with the back of the bracket and weld the rear edge. Use a torch and heat the areas

to be bent to conform the strips to the bracket's "U" shape. Weld the two sides to the axle bracket. *Warning:* Be sure the welding ground is on the end you are welding. When the ground is on the other end the welding current passes through the bearings in the differential and can damage them. Expensive lesson.

Place the tip on the edge of the extended bracket and align the previously scribed centerline of the hole with the forward parallel line. This will move the hole forward to compensate for the rotational difference in pickup points that the new angle of the trailing arm makes. Also weld the shock mount tab hole closest to the axle tube closed. Again, check your alignment carefully then weld the tip in place. The mounting holes' new locations, as measured from the axle tube, should be 3 1/2" on the outside and 3 19/32" on the inside. Check closely before you weld.

When you are finished with both brackets, dress the welds with a high-speed sander using an 80-grit disc. Before you finish you will have to redrill the slots for the shock mount tab. This slot is 1/2" long and approximately .340" wide ("R" drill bit or 11/32"). To cut the slot, mark two points on a vertical centerline from the shock mounting

bracket hole, one being 1 3/4" above and one being 2-1/4" above. Use a center punch to define the points for drilling and drill with an "R" or 11/32" drill bit. File or grind the metal between the two holes to create a slot. Dress the surface with the high-speed sander when you are finished.

If you are using a second set of brackets cut them off two inches above the centerline of the outside holes as specified above for the axle brackets. Dress the edges of the axle bracket on the housing and the second brackets to a 45° angle for welding. Place the new pieces on the axle brackets and align the centers of the mounting holes, using a straight edge, with the parallel line closest to the pinion as explained above. Check your alignment carefully and weld the edges together.

With the alignment of the holes checked carefully, the original tip is welded in the new position.

After the brackets have been completed, painted and properly aged with a torch for that stock look, the modified axle housing is ready for reinstallation.

Anti-Squat Brackets —See Fig. 5-20 on p.104 for details on the fabrication of these brackets. You will note that the outside plate is longer than the inside plate. Also, you can either fabricate the bracket by bending a constant length of 3/16" steel plate or, as shown in the drawing, weld the two sides and the end pieces together. Be sure to tack-weld the side pieces to the end piece while bolted to the rear housing to match the factory mounts on the axle housing (distances to the shock mount vary with each housing). When you have completed the fabrication, use 12mm x 25mm bolts to attach the brackets to the factory holes, and a 1/2" x 1" bolt to attach the bracket to the factory shock mount hole. Make sure the rear plate fits snug against the shock bracket mounting surface. If your racing class permits, weld the bracket to your housing.

Springs—It is important to note that by using this method to eliminate squat, it will be necessary to use rear springs that will not drop the car more than 3/4" over the stock ride height. Because you will be moving the axles upward in relation to the spring perch on the lower trailing arm, the suspension travel will be reduced. Too short a spring and your suspension will bottom out easily. Generally a spring that has a free length of approximately 13" to 13-1/2" is necessary to provide the proper ride height.

Step 27

While you are working on the axle housing, it is very important to drill a second vent hole in the left axle tube at approximately the same distance from the center section as the factory right vent. This is best achieved by inserting a shop towel in the axle tube past the point to be drilled and standing the housing on that tube so the drill shavings will fall out. After you have drilled the new hole, pack wheel bearing grease into the threads of a 1/4" pipe tap to catch the filings, tap the housing and install a

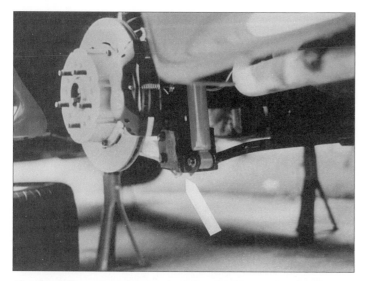

The tip of the arrow points to an anti-squat bracket that has been installed on a GT Mustang. These brackets significantly improve rear wheel traction and do not require any modification of the axle housing brackets. By relocating the lower trailing pickup points further away from the axle centerline the instantaneous center is moved up and rearward, causing the tires to plant rather than lift as is the case with the stock suspension.

Fabricating anti-squat brackets requires cutting out 7 pieces of 3/16" mild steel and drilling several holes for each bracket. Just follow the dimensions shown in Fig. 5-20 on p. 104.

To maintain proper pinion angle it is very important to get the alignment of the lower holes correct before welding the pieces together. The straight-edge in this photo shows that the lower hole is slightly in front of the upper hole. This is done to compensate for the increased arc of the lower trailing arm as it is moved away from the axle centerline.

To insure a good fit, it is best to assemble the sides and rear plates to the axle brackets they will be used on, then weld the corners together. Due to manufacturing tolerances, there is considerable variation in the factory brackets from one axle housing to another. The photo is for demonstration purposes only—don't cut your brackets off.

standard 3/8" x 1/4" pipe fuel nipple with a 3/8" fuel hose for venting purposes. Modify the fuel nipple prior to installation by brazing the nipple hole closed and then drilling a 3/32" hole for venting. The installation of a second vent is very important to prevent premature seal failure. Under racing conditions, the pressures inside the axle housing generated by the off-gassing and deteriorating axle grease can blow the seals out.

Step 28: Installing 9" Axles

The use of disc brakes on the rear requires a stable, unmoving rotor to operate properly. The best cure is to modify a set of 9" Ford housing ends and substitute them for the ends on your 8.8" housing along with a pair of quality axles (see Fig. 5-21, p. 104).

Moser Engineering Kit—As another option, you can purchase a kit from Moser Engineering that provides

the modified housing pieces and a pair of racing axles. Moser's kit provides two strong axles splined to fit either the 28- or 31-spline differentials, and two bearing carriers that are from a large bearing 9" Ford housing. This axle/bearing carrier has proven itself in millions of miles of racing.

To install this kit, cut off the ends of the axle tubes just inside the brake backing plate flange on your 8.8" housing. Insert a shop towel into each

This is what a completed set of brackets should look like. As with any modification in this book, take your time and the brackets will actually fit.

Fitting tough 9" Ford axles to the 8.8 housing requires specific bearings and seals (Timken/BCA A-20 and Federal Mogul 3195) as well as specially machined 9" housing ends. These pieces can be acquired from Greg Moser Engineering or, if you are industrious, follow the instructions in Fig. 5-21 and machine the ends yourself.

Before the machined 9" bearing carriers can be installed on the 8.8 housing, the bearing ends must be cut off. Use a Saws-all or cut-off saw and cut the ends of the 8.8 axle housing off at approximately where the axle tube expands to full size.

tube to prevent filings from contaminating the differential center section and dress the ends smooth and even. Install the axle bearing carriers on the new axles and slip over the ends of the axle tubes. Check the axle tips through the rear inspection cover to ensure they are inserted the proper depth. (The axle splines must extend completely through the drive gears in the differential.) Twist the bearing carrier flanges to achieve the proper index on the brake caliper brackets. Check your work a couple of dozen times, then tack-weld the bearing carriers to the housing in four places. Don't forget about having the welding ground on the end you are welding.

Remove the axles and weld the bearing carriers completely around the axle tubes. Dress the welds with a high-speed sander using an 80-grit disc. Clean up any scaling that may have formed inside the axle tubes. This stuff is generally pretty hard and will ruin a carrier bearing or trash a ring and pinion. Check carefully.

Before final assembly, tack-weld the bearing retainer to the axle. This will prevent the axle from pulling out under severe cornering loads. Seems impossible, but it has happened.

The aluminum Moser Engineering C–Clip Eliminator Kit is not strong enough to withstand the abuses of road racing. Essentially the stock axles are the major culprit. They bend and flex so badly that the rotors will actually rub the caliper mounting brackets. With this much bending they just don't have a very reliable life. When you are running this setup be sure to check the centers of the axles on the flange end before every race. If you see a circle forming in the center, especially if it is starting to concave, replace the axle. Breaking an axle generally occurs at the most inopportune time, so pay close attention to this.

Step 29: Replacing Upper Trailing Arm Bushings

Follow Step 13 in Chapter 4, p. 60 and remove the axle bushings from the axle housing. Do not reinstall a bushing since you will be utilizing spacers to clamp around the bushing tang for installation of the adjustable upper trailing arms. If you are using the stock type trailing arms instead of the adjustable tubular types, do not remove the bushing shells from the axle housing. Instead, burn the rubber out and install Energy Suspension 88 durometer polyurethane bushings.

Step 30: Panhard Bar

There are several Panhard bars on the market today. However, at this writing, the only ones strong enough to withstand the rigors of racing are made by Central Coast Mustang, Griggs Racing, Baer Racing and Saleen Performance. These are well made pieces, with the Griggs Racing and Baer Racing being the

Mount the axle housing on jackstands and level the pinion yoke before aligning the bearing carriers.

When you have leveled the pinion yoke, install the axle, retainer, brake backing plate or disc caliper bracket and bearing carrier onto the modified 8.8 housing. Check the axle tips for full insertion in the carrier gears. Then, twist the bearing carrier until a level reading is achieved for the caliper bracket or brake backing plate.

After rechecking the pinion level and the bearing carrier index a couple of dozen times, MIG- or TIG-weld the bearing carriers to the axle tubes. Note that it is very important to ground the welder to the lower trailing arm bracket on the end you are welding to prevent potential damage to the bearings.

strongest. They are an expensive but necessary evil. Because these are all reputable manufacturers, I recommend that you purchase a bar rather than go through the masochistic exercise of fabricating your own.

Installation — To install a prefabricated bar, remove the gas tank and re–assemble the rear suspension. Do not torque the trailing arm or shock bolts at this time. Next, reinstall all brakes, all interior, wheels and tires, and the engine and transmission if you have not done so already. Leave the driveshaft out. The car should be in race condition except for

the fuel tank. Place approximately 60 lbs. of weights over the spare tire well to compensate for the weight of 1/2 tank of gas. On a level floor, jack the car up and insert car ramps of equal height under each wheel. Place weights in the driver's seat equal to the weight of the normal driver and joust the suspension several times to settle the springs.

Carefully align the location of the Panhard bar as noted in the manufacturer's instructions accompanying the bar. Take considerable care in making this fit. Be sure you have aligned the brackets so as not to cause

interference with the normal rotation of the axle. The axle housing flange must be mounted so the rotating Panhard bar is on a parallel line with the centerline of the axles. If this is not the case you will bias the suspension. Recheck the attachment points and be sure you are correct. When you are certain of the mounting locations, MIG-weld the mounting plates to the frame. Before welding the bracket to the axle, joust the suspension one last time. Set the alignment on the axle bracket to achieve a parallel bar and weld in position.

It is critical that you follow the steps outlined here. If you improperly align the Panhard bar you will cause the arc on the rear axle to be less than optimum and consequently bias the suspension, which will cause some strange handling problems.

Step 31

At this point you should remove the axle assembly, brush the welds clean and paint the entire axle housing with an epoxy primer (PPG DP 90) or a red oxide primer.

Step 32

Reassemble the rear suspension as noted above. Be sure to joust the suspension several times to settle the

A completed 8.8 axle housing that has been fitted for the wider SVO Mustang width is ready to be cleaned and repainted.

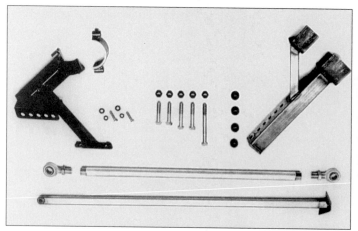

Pictured here is one of the toughest Panhard bars on the market today. This kit (MTA 1200 R) from Griggs Racing is the hot setup. It's tough and fully adjustable.

When installing a Panhard bar, it is imperative that the bar be parallel to the centerline of the axle to prevent biasing the suspension. Check this with the weight of the car on the axle, 1/2 tank of fuel and the driver behind the wheel.

springs, then torque the trailing arm and shock bolts to factory specifications.

Place an inclinometer on the pinion yoke and adjust the upper trailing arms to achieve a 1° down setting as a starting point. Be sure to adjust both trailing arms exactly the same amount. Generally both trailing arms should be in tension when set correctly. If one is taut and the other rotates freely, recheck the lengths. Once you have adjusted the trailing arms tighten the jam nuts.

Step 33

Bleed the brakes according to the instructions in Chapter 8, p. 139. This completes the four–link rear suspension modifications.

TORQUE ARM SUSPENSION

There are several torque arms on the market that all basically attach to the axle housing through the inspection cover bolts and the harmonic dampener attachment holes. These setups generally work great for road racing but lack the strength for high-horsepower applications. They are especially susceptible to breakage when subjected to the occasional drag race start. Keep this in mind if you are installing one of these kits.

Included are drawings (figures 5-22

through 5-27, pp. 104-105) showing how to fabricate a very strong torque arm. You can either weld brackets to the housing or fabricate the ends to bolt on. Study the drawings carefully before you begin. Essentially you will be fabricating a long lever arm that attaches firmly to the axle housing and pivots on the forward end on a bracket attached to the subframes. How you attach the arm to the housing is dependent on your class rules. Obviously welding brackets to the axle tubes would be the strongest. However, some classes don't permit this, so check the rules first.

Step 34: Rear Shock Tower Brace

Again, if you have not installed a rear shock tower brace or integrated one into your roll cage, you should do so before you start this modification. See p. 32.

Step 35

At this time the car should be mounted on jackstands placed under the rocker panel seams at the jacking notches. Remember to provide at least 18" of ground clearance for minimum working room. It is very important the car be level for doing the fitting of a fabricated

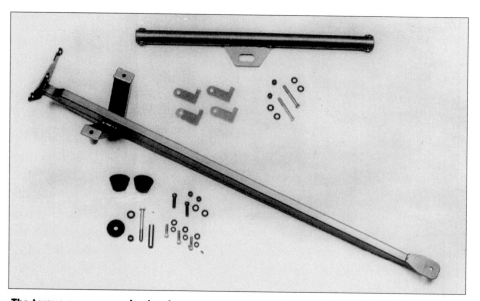

The torque arm suspension has become popular with the Mustang crowd, primarily due to the Griggs Racing kit (PN MTA 1000 F). These things really make the rear end hook up. Installation is simple but does require a mega-strong Panhard bar and rear springs in the 350 to 450 lbs-in. rate.

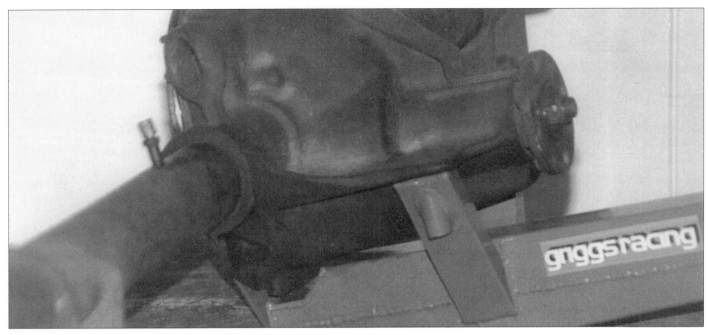

If you have your axle assembly out, trial-fit the torque arm to your housing and make adjustments as necessary. Manufacturing tolerances in the 8.8 housing can send you looking for the Tylenol when fitting one of these to your car.

torque arm. Use a large carpenter level and shim the jackstands as necessary to level the car.

Step 36: Lower Trailing Arms

Build new lower trailing arms per figures 5-16, 5-17 and 5-18 or modify your stock trailing arms per the instructions in Step 15 in Chapter 4, p. 63.

Step 37: Torque Arm

Follow the specs in figures 5-22 to 5-27 and fabricate the long lever arm of the torque arm. Select the method you will be using to attach the torque arm to the subframe crossbrace (spherical rod end or polyurethane bushings) and build the tip accordingly.

Fabricate the brackets to attach the rear tip of the torque arm to the housing. Again select the approach you will be using, either welding or clamping the brackets to the axle tubes. Once you have fabricated the rear mounting bracket, remove the axles and rear brakes from the axle assembly.

On a large flat surface, balance the axle housing upside down on jackstands under the axle tubes. Attach a magnetic

inclinometer to the face of the yoke and place a jack under the pinion part of the housing. Adjust the jack to achieve an angle of 0° on the yoke.

Bolt the torque arm to the harmonic dampener holes on the housing. Obviously this assumes that you have already discarded the anchor that comes on these housings from the factory. Bolt the rear mounting bracket to the torque arm and carefully align it. Use a tape measure and measure from the end of the axle tubes to the center of the mounting pivot on the forward tip of the torque arm. Square the torque arm by adjusting side-to-side distances until both measurements are equal. With a level placed on the torque arm, adjust the pitch until it is perfectly level. Tack-weld the bracket to the housing or the torque arm, depending on which approach you have chosen. *Warning:* Be sure the welding ground is on the end of the housing you are welding. When the ground is on the other end the welding current passes through the bearings in the differential and will damage them. Expensive lesson.

Remove the torque arm and weld the brackets completely. If you welded the

brackets to the axle tubes be sure to clean the scaling from inside the tubes as noted in Step 28 above.

Attach the torque arm to the housing and recheck the alignment carefully. Again the torque arm must be square from the tip to the end of the axle tubes, and level with the pinion set at 0°. If it is off, cut the bracket loose and try again.

Install the lower trailing arms and connect the axle housing with the torque arm to the trailing arms. Use a jack placed under the center of the housing to support it correctly. Jack the axle housing up until the trailing arms are level. Attach the fabricated forward cross-mount to the torque tube and adjust the pitch with a carpenter level until it hangs level. With the cross-mount level and centered, tack-weld the mounting brackets in position. Disassemble everything, then MIG-weld the brackets to the subframe connectors.

Springs & Swaybars

A torque arm suspension demands a high rear roll stiffness to function correctly. This can be accomplished by using a large rear swaybar, typically at least 1" in diameter, and very stiff rear

To secure the forward tip of the torque arm, the crossmember must be attached to the subframes on each side. Griggs Racing's torque arm can be purchased to fit the stock subframes, or you can add on a round or square subframe connector as shown here.

springs. Currently, the quick setup seems to be using the stock GT rear swaybar while using some very stiff rear springs. When using the torque arm without a rear swaybar, you will generally need to use rear springs that have a minimum rate of 450 lbs-in.

Step 38

To prevent seal blowout, drill a second vent hole in the left axle. Follow the instructions in Step 27, p. 89.

Step 39

Follow Step 28 on p. 90 and install the 9" axles and bearing carrier to your 8.8" axle. Follow Fig. 5-21 on p.104 or purchase a Moser Engineering kits.

Step 40: Locating Device

Since upper trailing arms will not be used, a Panhard bar, Watt's Link or Jacob's Ladder must be installed to secure the axle squarely in the car. I

strongly suggest you purchase a Panhard bar from the manufacturer's I recommended on p. 91.

Follow Step 30 above and fit the Panhard bar to the axle assembly. After you have welded the brackets to the frame and axle housing, adjust the bar length to center the axle in the car. Use a tape measure and adjust the bar length until the diagonal distance between the trailing arm brackets and the rear mount on the front control arm on the opposite side is identical.

Step 41

Remove the axle assembly, brush the welds clean and paint the entire axle housing, torque arm and forward cross mount with an epoxy (PPG DP 90) or red oxide primer.

Step 42

Reassemble the rear suspension, with wheels. Relocate the jackstands under the control arms and axle tubes or place car ramps under the wheels. Joust the suspension several times to settle the springs, then torque the lower trailing arm and shock bolts to factory specifications.

The CP Mustang of Doug Wille is equipped with a Griggs Racing torque arm. Like many torque arm-equipped Mustangs, the lack of sufficient rear roll stiffness causes the inside tire to lift in a hard turn.

Step 43

Go to Chapter 8, p. 139 and follow the procedures for bleeding the brakes. This completes the torque arm rear suspension modifications.

THREE-LINK REAR SUSPENSION

Baer Racing is the only company currently producing a three-link suspension kit for your Mustang. This type of suspension provides for more freedom of axle movement than the four–link but, like the torque arm, it does require an axle locating device such as the Panhard bar. The installation of this setup is a little more difficult than the other two. However, the success of the Baer Mustang in World Challenge racing clearly demonstrates that it works. For more information on this kit, see p. 126.

BUMPERS

Step 44

Weight saving is always important to the racer. Since bumpers are mandatory on a road-race car, considerable weight savings can be had by substituting your stock steel rear bumper reinforcement with an aluminum one from the early

The three-link suspension from Baer Racing is arguably the best rear suspension system for the Mustang on the market today. This setup enabled the lowly Mustang to defeat some very expensive and exotic race cars in the World Challenge Series in 1993. Shown here is the prototype for the current kit.

Turbo 4 Mustangs. These aluminum reinforcements look identical to the stock steel ones but weigh substantially less.

For the pre-'87 Mustang, the front bumper reinforcement should be replaced with the plastic unit found on the '87 or newer cars. You will need to fabricate aluminum impact absorbers that are 1" longer than those used on the plastic bumpers or place 1" spacers between the plastic reinforcement and the impact

absorber that goes with it. For the serious competitor, impact absorbers should be made from 6061–T6 aluminum.

If your class rules allow, fabricate an aluminum front bumper reinforcement from 4" wide 6061–T6 channel–formed aluminum (see Fig. 5-28) Notch the ends 12" from center and bend to an 8° angle. Heli–arc the notches. Fabricate the impact absorber substitution tubes. Use a square to align the tubes vertical and heli–arc in place. The best approach is to install the tubes on the car, then fit the aluminum channel. Heli–arc the channel to the tubes while bolted to the car.

Step 45

If your car no longer has the rear tie–down plates used for shipping, you will need to scrounge one side from a salvage yard and attach to your car. On the front, if you have not done so already, you should weld a 3" eyelet to the front edge of the crossmember to provide a place to attach a tow hook. If you have fabricated an aluminum front reinforcement, then heli–arc a tow tab to the back of it that extends to the lower air opening in the nose piece. ■

On pre-'87 Mustangs, the front bumper reinforcement is made of heavy steel. Considerable weight can be removed by fitting the plastic bumper from one of the post-'86 cars. Use the impact absorber from the '87-'89 Mustang (E7ZZ-17754-A) and aluminum spacers approximately 1" thick.

Mustang Crossmembers

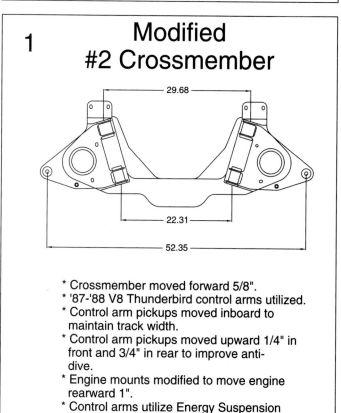

Pre '88

30.125
22.75
16.5°
51.37

'88 - '93

31.125
23.75
16.5°
52.37

SVO

29.5
23
14.5°
53.36

Fig. 5-1

Control Arms

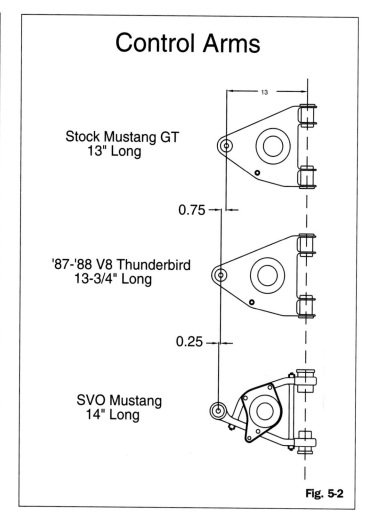

Stock Mustang GT
13" Long

13

0.75

'87-'88 V8 Thunderbird
13-3/4" Long

0.25

SVO Mustang
14" Long

Fig. 5-2

1 Modified #2 Crossmember

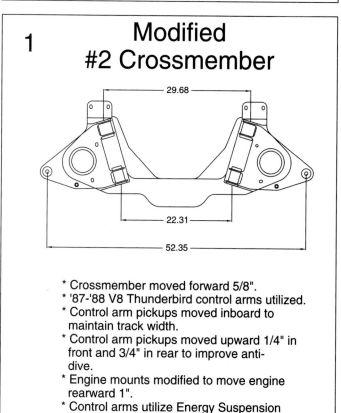

29.68

22.31

52.35

* Crossmember moved forward 5/8".
* '87-'88 V8 Thunderbird control arms utilized.
* Control arm pickups moved inboard to maintain track width.
* Control arm pickups moved upward 1/4" in front and 3/4" in rear to improve anti-dive.
* Engine mounts modified to move engine rearward 1".
* Control arms utilize Energy Suspension Polyurethane bushing, Part No. 4-3123.

Fig. 5-3

2 Modified #2 Crossmember

Relocating Front Mounting Holes

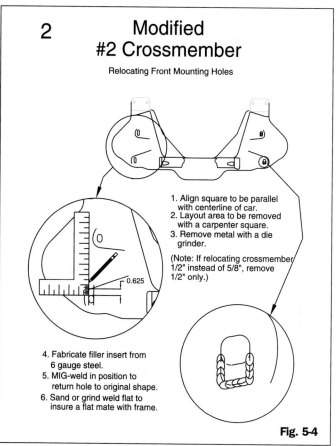

0.625

1. Align square to be parallel with centerline of car.
2. Layout area to be removed with a carpenter square.
3. Remove metal with a die grinder.

(Note: If relocating crossmember 1/2" instead of 5/8", remove 1/2" only.)

4. Fabricate filler insert from 6 gauge steel.
5. MIG-weld in position to return hole to original shape.
6. Sand or grind weld flat to insure a flat mate with frame.

Fig. 5-4

3

Modified
#2 Crossmember

Modifying Rear Mounting Holes

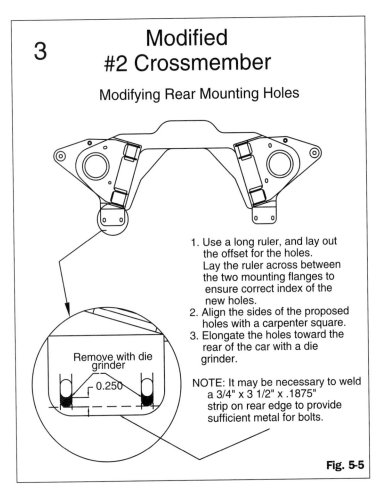

1. Use a long ruler, and lay out the offset for the holes.
   Lay the ruler across between the two mounting flanges to ensure correct index of the new holes.
2. Align the sides of the proposed holes with a carpenter square.
3. Elongate the holes toward the rear of the car with a die grinder.

NOTE: It may be necessary to weld a 3/4" x 3 1/2" x .1875" strip on rear edge to provide sufficient metal for bolts.

Remove with die grinder
0.250

Fig. 5-5

4

Modified
#2 Crossmember

Relocating Control Arm Outer Mounting Holes

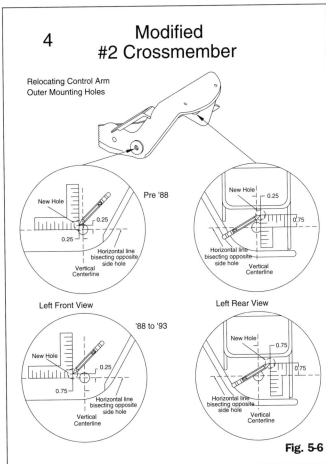

New Hole
0.25
0.25
Horizontal line bisecting opposite side hole
Vertical Centerline
Pre '88

New Hole
0.25
0.75
Horizontal line bisecting opposite side hole
Vertical Centerline

Left Front View

Left Rear View

New Hole
0.25
0.75
Horizontal line bisecting opposite side hole
Vertical Centerline
'88 to '93

New Hole
0.75
0.75
Horizontal line bisecting opposite side hole
Vertical Centerline

Fig. 5-6

5

Modified
#2 Crossmember

Relocating Inner Control Arm Bracket

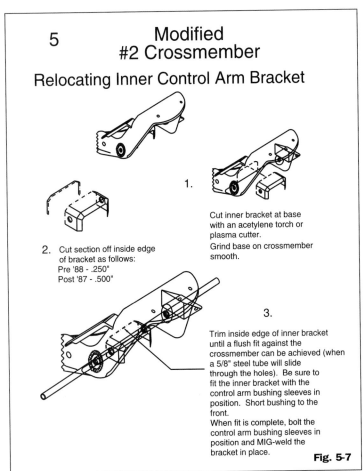

1. Cut inner bracket at base with an acetylene torch or plasma cutter.
   Grind base on crossmember smooth.

2. Cut section off inside edge of bracket as follows:
   Pre '88 - .250"
   Post '87 - .500"

3. Trim inside edge of inner bracket until a flush fit against the crossmember can be achieved (when a 5/8" steel tube will slide through the holes). Be sure to fit the inner bracket with the control arm bushing sleeves in position. Short bushing to the front.
   When fit is complete, bolt the control arm bushing sleeves in position and MIG-weld the bracket in place.

Fig. 5-7

6

Modified
#2 Crossmember

Relocating Engine Rearward

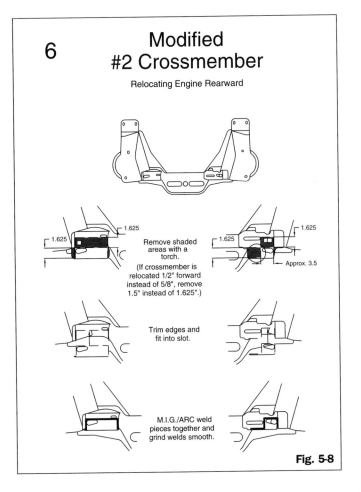

1.625   1.625

1.625   1.625

Approx. 3.5

Remove shaded areas with a torch.
(If crossmember is relocated 1/2" forward instead of 5/8", remove 1.5" instead of 1.625".)

Trim edges and fit into slot.

M.I.G./ARC weld pieces together and grind welds smooth.

Fig. 5-8

#2 Crossmember Alignment

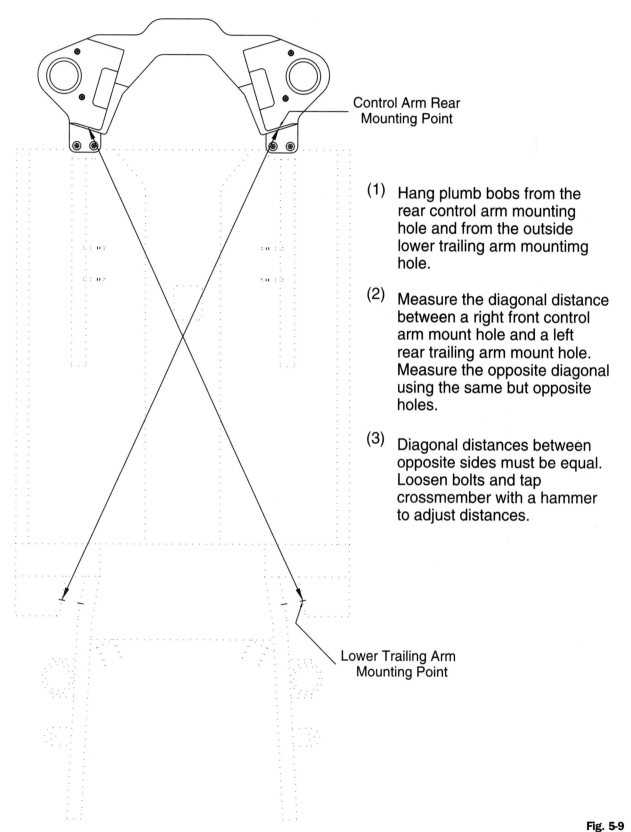

Control Arm Rear
Mounting Point

(1) Hang plumb bobs from the rear control arm mounting hole and from the outside lower trailing arm mountimg hole.

(2) Measure the diagonal distance between a right front control arm mount hole and a left rear trailing arm mount hole. Measure the opposite diagonal using the same but opposite holes.

(3) Diagonal distances between opposite sides must be equal. Loosen bolts and tap crossmember with a hammer to adjust distances.

Lower Trailing Arm
Mounting Point

Fig. 5-9

Rack and Pinion Modification

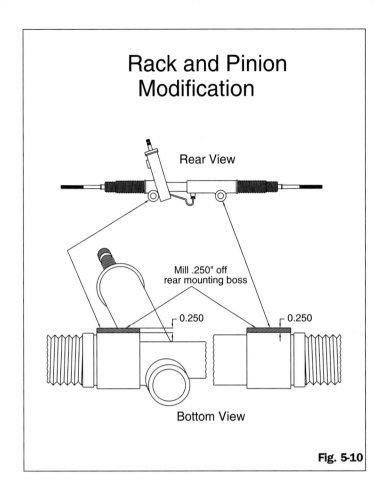

Rear View

Mill .250" off
rear mounting boss

0.250   0.250

Bottom View

Fig. 5-10

Spherical Rod End

Tie Rods

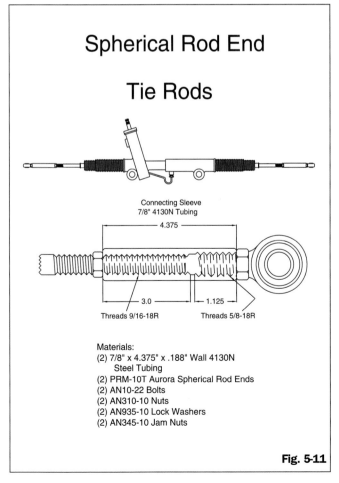

Connecting Sleeve
7/8" 4130N Tubing

4.375

3.0   1.125

Threads 9/16-18R   Threads 5/8-18R

Materials:
(2) 7/8" x 4.375" x .188" Wall 4130N
    Steel Tubing
(2) PRM-10T Aurora Spherical Rod Ends
(2) AN10-22 Bolts
(2) AN310-10 Nuts
(2) AN935-10 Lock Washers
(2) AN345-10 Jam Nuts

Fig. 5-11

Spherical Rod End
Swaybar Attachment

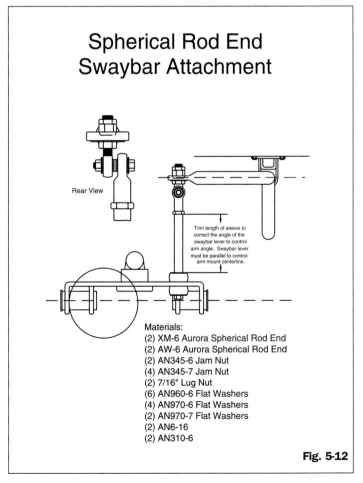

Rear View

Trim length of sleeve to
correct the angle of the
swaybar lever to control
arm angle. Swaybar lever
must be parallel to control
arm mount centerline.

Materials:
(2) XM-6 Aurora Spherical Rod End
(2) AW-6 Aurora Spherical Rod End
(2) AN345-6 Jam Nut
(4) AN345-7 Jam Nut
(2) 7/16" Lug Nut
(6) AN960-6 Flat Washers
(4) AN970-6 Flat Washers
(2) AN970-7 Flat Washers
(2) AN6-16
(2) AN310-6

Fig. 5-12

1 Adjustable Upper Trailing Arm

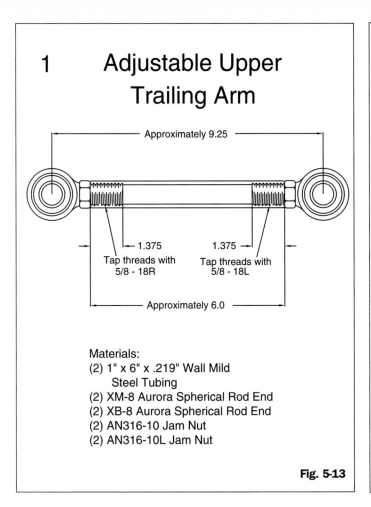

Approximately 9.25

1.375   1.375

Tap threads with
5/8 - 18R

Tap threads with
5/8 - 18L

Approximately 6.0

Materials:
(2) 1" x 6" x .219" Wall Mild
     Steel Tubing
(2) XM-8 Aurora Spherical Rod End
(2) XB-8 Aurora Spherical Rod End
(2) AN316-10 Jam Nut
(2) AN316-10L Jam Nut

Fig. 5-13

2 Upper Trailing Arm Spacers

for use with adjustable trailing arms

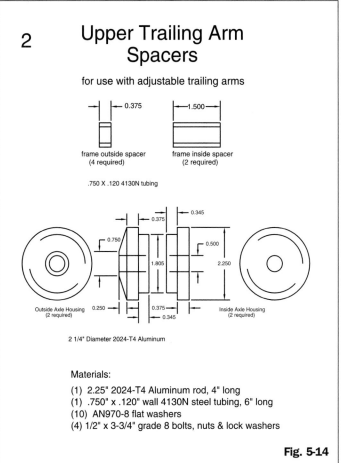

0.375

1.500

frame outside spacer
(4 required)

frame inside spacer
(2 required)

.750 X .120 4130N tubing

0.375   0.345

0.750   0.500

1.805   2.250

0.250   0.375

0.345

Outside Axle Housing
(2 required)

Inside Axle Housing
(2 required)

2 1/4" Diameter 2024-T4 Aluminum

Materials:

(1) 2.25" 2024-T4 Aluminum rod, 4" long
(1) .750" x .120" wall 4130N steel tubing, 6" long
(10) AN970-8 flat washers
(4) 1/2" x 3-3/4" grade 8 bolts, nuts & lock washers

Fig. 5-14

3 Adjustable Upper Trailing Arm Installation

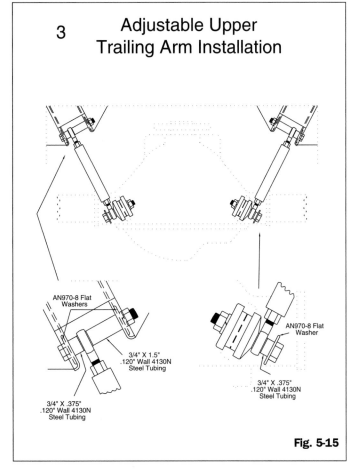

AN970-8 Flat
Washers

3/4" X 1.5"
.120" Wall 4130N
Steel Tubing

3/4" X .375"
.120" Wall 4130N
Steel Tubing

AN970-8 Flat
Washer

3/4" X .375"
.120" Wall 4130N
Steel Tubing

Fig. 5-15

Tubular Lower Trailing Arm

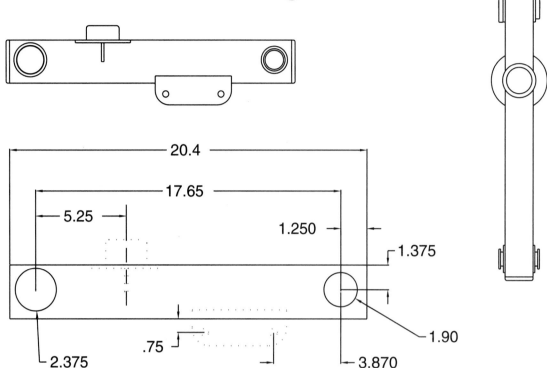

Main Bar
2" x 3" Rectangular Tubing
(2 req'd)

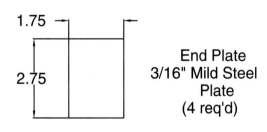

End Plate
3/16" Mild Steel
Plate
(4 req'd)

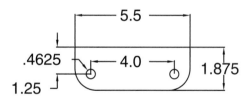

Swaybar Attachment
3/16" Mild Steel Plate
(2 req'd)

Materials:
(1) 2" x 3" x 42" .1875" Wall
Mild Steel Rectangular Tubing
(1) 2" (2.375" O.D.) Steel Pipe
10" long, Schedule 80
(1) 1-1/2" (1.900 O.D.) Steel Pipe
5" long, Schedule 160
(1) 1-1/4" (1.660" O.D.) Steel Pipe
2" long, Schedule 80
(2) HAB-12T Aurora Spherical Bearing

(1) 1.250" 1018 Cold Roll Steel
7" long
(1) 8" X 10" x .1875" Mild Steel
Plate
(2) 1/2" x 3 1/2" Bolts, Nuts
& Lock Washers, Grade 8
(2) 1/2" x 4" Bolts, Nuts
& Lock Washers, Grade 8
(1) 4-3114 Energy Suspension Bushing Set

Fig. 5-16

2 Tubular Lower Trailing Arm

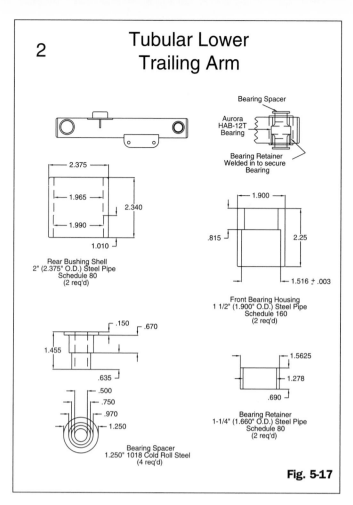

Bearing Spacer

Aurora HAB-12T Bearing

Bearing Retainer Welded in to secure Bearing

2.375
1.965
1.990
2.340
1.010

Rear Bushing Shell
2" (2.375" O.D.) Steel Pipe
Schedule 80
(2 req'd)

1.900
.815
2.25
1.516 ± .003

Front Bearing Housing
1 1/2" (1.900" O.D.) Steel Pipe
Schedule 160
(2 req'd)

.150 .670
1.455
.635

.500
.750
.970
1.250

Bearing Spacer
1.250" 1018 Cold Roll Steel
(4 req'd)

1.5625
1.278
.690

Bearing Retainer
1-1/4" (1.660" O.D.) Steel Pipe
Schedule 80
(2 req'd)

Fig. 5-17

3 Tubular Lower Trailing Arm

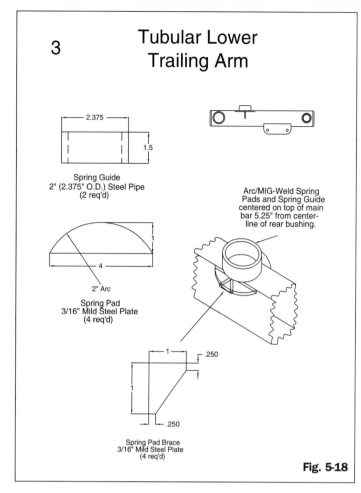

2.375
1.5

Spring Guide
2" (2.375" O.D.) Steel Pipe
(2 req'd)

4
2" Arc

Spring Pad
3/16" Mild Steel Plate
(4 req'd)

Arc/MIG-Weld Spring Pads and Spring Guide centered on top of main bar 5.25" from center-line of rear bushing.

1 .250
1
.250

Spring Pad Brace
3/16" Mild Steel Plate
(4 req'd)

Fig. 5-18

Adjustable Lower Trailing Arm

For Use With Coil-Over Shocks

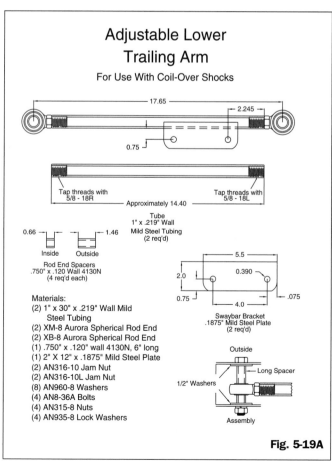

17.65
2.245
0.75

Tap threads with 5/8 - 18R
Tap threads with 5/8 - 18L
Approximately 14.40

Tube
1" x .219" Wall
Mild Steel Tubing
(2 req'd)

0.66 1.46

Inside Outside

Rod End Spacers
.750" x .120 Wall 4130N
(4 req'd each)

5.5
0.390
2.0
0.75
4.0
.075

Swaybar Bracket
.1875" Mild Steel Plate
(2 req'd)

Outside

Long Spacer
1/2" Washers

Assembly

Materials:
(2) 1" x 30" x .219" Wall Mild
    Steel Tubing
(2) XM-8 Aurora Spherical Rod End
(2) XB-8 Aurora Spherical Rod End
(1) .750" x .120" wall 4130N, 6" long
(1) 2" X 12" x .1875" Mild Steel Plate
(2) AN316-10 Jam Nut
(2) AN316-10L Jam Nut
(8) AN960-8 Washers
(4) AN8-36A Bolts
(4) AN315-8 Nuts
(4) AN935-8 Lock Washers

Fig. 5-19A

Anti-Squat Axle Bracket Modification

Road Racing

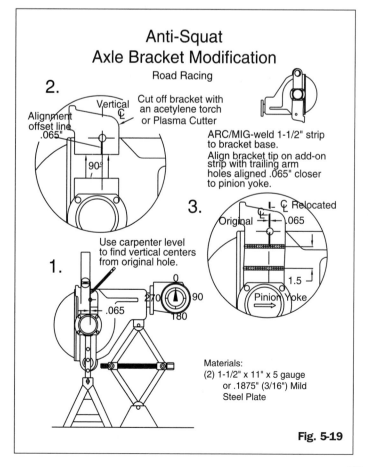

2.

Alignment offset line .065"

Vertical

90°

Cut off bracket with an acetylene torch or Plasma Cutter

ARC/MIG-weld 1-1/2" strip to bracket base.
Align bracket tip on add-on strip with trailing arm holes aligned .065" closer to pinion yoke.

1.

Use carpenter level to find vertical centers from original hole.

.065

270 90
180

3.

Original

Relocated
.065

1.5

Pinion Yoke

Materials:
(2) 1-1/2" x 11" x 5 gauge
    or .1875" (3/16") Mild
    Steel Plate

Fig. 5-19

Anti-Squat Bracket
Road Racing

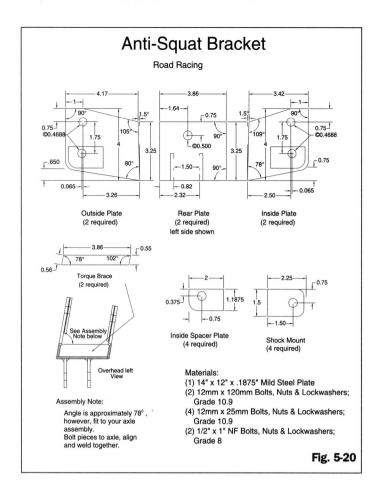

Outside Plate
(2 required)

Rear Plate
(2 required)
left side shown

Inside Plate
(2 required)

Torque Brace
(2 required)

Overhead left View

See Assembly Note below

Inside Spacer Plate
(4 required)

Shock Mount
(4 required)

Assembly Note:

Angle is approximately 78°, however, fit to your axle assembly.
Bolt pieces to axle, align and weld together.

Materials:
- (1) 14" x 12" x .1875" Mild Steel Plate
- (2) 12mm x 120mm Bolts, Nuts & Lockwashers; Grade 10.9
- (4) 12mm x 25mm Bolts, Nuts & Lockwashers; Grade 10.9
- (2) 1/2" x 1" NF Bolts, Nuts & Lockwashers; Grade 8

Fig. 5-20

Installing 9" Axles in 8.8 Housing

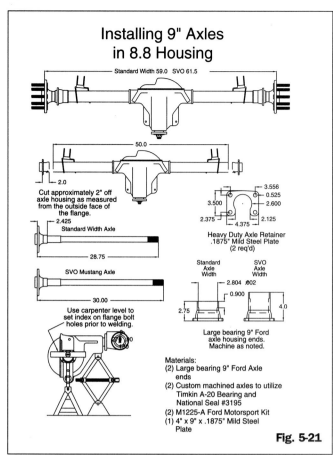

Standard Width 59.0   SVO 61.5

Cut approximately 2" off axle housing as measured from the outside face of the flange.

Standard Width Axle

SVO Mustang Axle

Use carpenter level to set index on flange bolt holes prior to welding.

Heavy Duty Axle Retainer .1875" Mild Steel Plate (2 req'd)

Standard Axle Width   SVO Axle Width

Large bearing 9" Ford axle housing ends. Machine as noted.

Materials:
- (2) Large bearing 9" Ford Axle ends
- (2) Custom machined axles to utilize Timkin A-20 Bearing and National Seal #3195
- (2) M1225-A Ford Motorsport Kit
- (1) 4" x 9" x .1875" Mild Steel Plate

Fig. 5-21

1 Torque-Arm Suspension

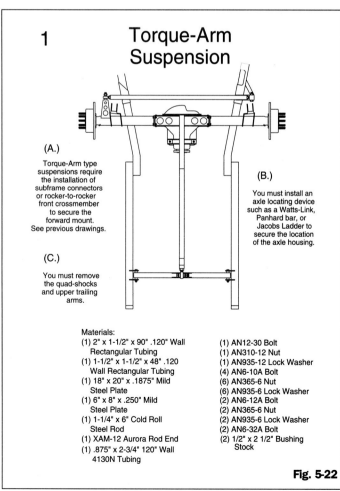

(A.)

Torque-Arm type suspensions require the installation of subframe connectors or rocker-to-rocker front crossmember to secure the forward mount.
See previous drawings.

(B.)

You must install an axle locating device such as a Watts-Link, Panhard bar, or Jacobs Ladder to secure the location of the axle housing.

(C.)

You must remove the quad-shocks and upper trailing arms.

Materials:
- (1) 2" x 1-1/2" x 90" .120" Wall Rectangular Tubing
- (1) 1-1/2" x 1-1/2" x 48" .120 Wall Rectangular Tubing
- (1) 18" x 20" x .1875" Mild Steel Plate
- (1) 6" x 8" x .250" Mild Steel Plate
- (1) 1-1/4" x 6" Cold Roll Steel Rod
- (1) XAM-12 Aurora Rod End
- (1) .875" x 2-3/4" 120" Wall 4130N Tubing

- (1) AN12-30 Bolt
- (1) AN310-12 Nut
- (1) AN935-12 Lock Washer
- (4) AN6-10A Bolt
- (6) AN365-6 Nut
- (6) AN935-6 Lock Washer
- (2) AN6-12A Bolt
- (2) AN365-6 Nut
- (2) AN935-6 Lock Washer
- (2) AN6-32A Bolt
- (2) 1/2" x 2 1/2" Bushing Stock

Fig. 5-22

2 Torque-Arm Suspension

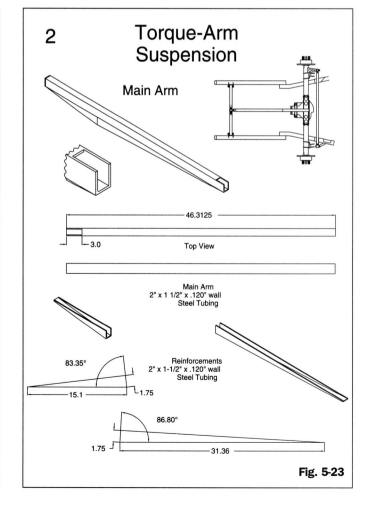

Main Arm

Top View

Main Arm
2" x 1 1/2" x .120" wall Steel Tubing

Reinforcements
2" x 1-1/2" x .120" wall Steel Tubing

Fig. 5-23

3 Torque-Arm Suspension

Main Arm Fittings

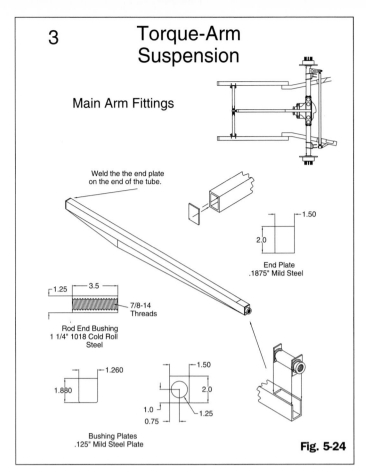

Weld the end plate on the end of the tube.

End Plate
.1875" Mild Steel

1.50
2.0

Rod End Bushing
1 1/4" 1018 Cold Roll Steel

1.25
3.5
7/8-14 Threads

Bushing Plates
.125" Mild Steel Plate

1.260
1.880
1.50
2.0
1.0
0.75
1.25

Fig. 5-24

4 Torque-Arm Suspension

Axle Attach Brackets

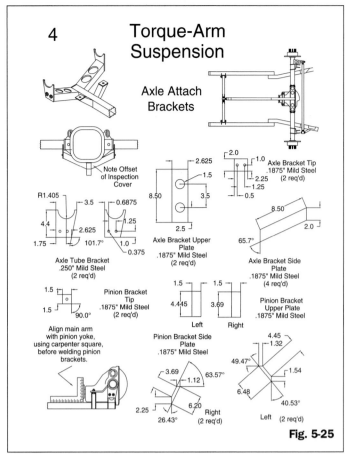

Note Offset of Inspection Cover

Axle Tube Bracket
.250" Mild Steel
(2 req'd)

R1.405
3.5
0.6875
4.4
2.625
1.25
1.75
101.7°
1.0
0.375

Axle Bracket Upper Plate
.1875" Mild Steel
(2 req'd)

2.625
1.5
8.50
3.5
2.5

Axle Bracket Tip
.1875" Mild Steel
(2 req'd)

2.0
1.0
2.25
1.25
0.5

Axle Bracket Side Plate
.1875" Mild Steel
(4 req'd)

8.50
2.0
65.7°

Pinion Bracket Tip
.1875" Mild Steel
(2 req'd)

1.5
1.5
90.0°

Pinion Bracket Upper Plate
.1875" Mild Steel

1.5
1.5
4.445
3.69
Left   Right

Align main arm with pinion yoke, using carpenter square, before welding pinion brackets.

Pinion Bracket Side Plate
.1875" Mild Steel

3.69
1.12
63.57°
2.25
6.20
26.43°
Right (2 req'd)

4.45
1.32
49.47°
1.54
6.48
40.53°
Left (2 req'd)

Fig. 5-25

5 Torque-Arm Suspension

Front Crossmember

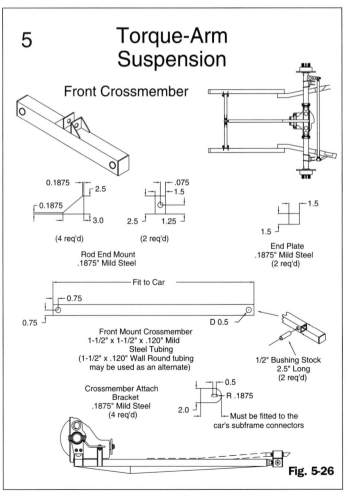

0.1875
2.5
0.1875
3.0
(4 req'd)

.075
1.5
2.5
1.25
(2 req'd)

Rod End Mount
.1875" Mild Steel

End Plate
.1875" Mild Steel
(2 req'd)

1.5
1.5
1.5

Fit to Car
0.75
0.75
D 0.5

Front Mount Crossmember
1-1/2" x 1-1/2" x .120" Mild Steel Tubing
(1-1/2" x .120" Wall Round tubing may be used as an alternate)

1/2" Bushing Stock
2.5" Long
(2 req'd)

Crossmember Attach Bracket
.1875" Mild Steel
(4 req'd)

0.5
R .1875
2.0

Must be fitted to the car's subframe connectors

Fig. 5-26

6 Torque-Arm Suspension

Alternate Mounts

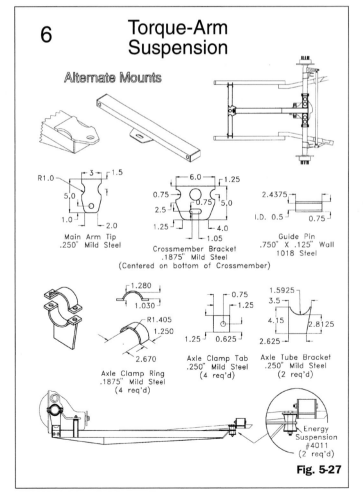

R1.0
3
1.5
5.0
1.0
2.0

Main Arm Tip
.250" Mild Steel

6.0
1.25
0.75
0.75
5.0
2.5
1.25
4.0
1.05

Crossmember Bracket
.1875" Mild Steel
(Centered on bottom of Crossmember)

2.4375
I.D. 0.5
0.75

Guide Pin
.750" X .125" Wall
1018 Steel

1.280
1.030
R1.405
1.250
2.670

Axle Clamp Ring
.1875" Mild Steel
(4 req'd)

0.75
1.25
1.25
0.625

Axle Clamp Tab
.250" Mild Steel
(4 req'd)

1.5925
3.5
4.15
2.8125
2.625

Axle Tube Bracket
.250" Mild Steel
(2 req'd)

Energy Suspension
#4011
(2 req'd)

Fig. 5-27

Front Bumper Reinforcement

Racing Only

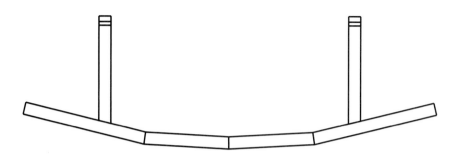

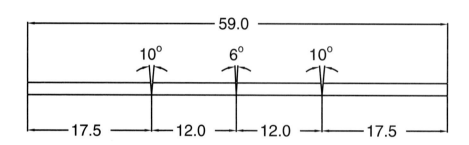

Aluminum Structural Channel
4" x 1.647" x .247"
6061-T6

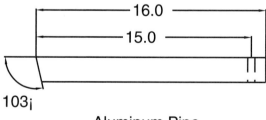

103ᵢ

Aluminum Pipe
1-1/4" Sch 80
6061-T6

Materials:
(1) 4" x 1.647" x .247"
   Aluminum Structural
   Channel
(1) 1-1/4" Sch 80 Aluminum
   Pipe

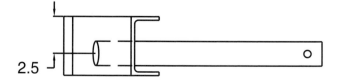

Left Side View

Fig. 5-28

DRAG RACING SUSPENSIONS

6

If you are a quarter-mile leadfoot and have waded through the previous chapters you probably found it hard to believe anyone could find this stuff useful. However, you should have picked up on the potential gains to be derived by some of the madness, such as relocating the front crossmember and engine. Better weight distribution, as in better bite and launch, is the result of these two modifications. The benefits derived from the modifications that follow will not be as noticeable as the addition of a Vortech supercharger, however, it could make the difference in a close race.

The modifications presented in this chapter will establish a solid baseline for a competitive drag racing car. Obviously, an Alston suspension and deep wheel tubs would be the trick setup. However, a slow pass through the pits at a 5.0 meet will provide ample support for using the stock platform. Numerous machines running in the 10's and even a few in the 9's use the same basic setup as provided in this chapter. The success of your car is dependent on the quality of work you do. The important thing to remember is to pay attention to detail. Take your time and keep good records of what you did.

FRONT SUSPENSION

Step 1

Mount your car on jackstands placed

One of the nation's fastest small-block Mustangs is the Central Coast Mustang machine with Dennis Hillaird at the wheel. Shown here on its way to a 9.63 run, this Mustang is equipped with a Griggs Racing Torque Arm, Koni drag racing dampeners and CCM drag springs in conjunction with an Air Lift bag inside the right rear spring. Talent and muscle keep this horse in the sub-1.40-second 60-ft. zone.

PARTS REQUIRED:

Koni SPA–1 Drag Struts

Koni SPA–1 Drag Shocks

4-cylinder Mustang Front Springs

GT Mustang Rear Springs

Air Lift Bags

4-cylinder Mustang/Capri Front Swaybar (street cars)

Pre–'86 Cars: '87 Mustang Front Crossmember

Manual Steering Rack & Pinion (TRW 15508R)

Double–hump #3 Crossmember

Polyurethane #3 Crossmember Bushings

'93 GT Engine Mounts

Traction Bars

Polyurethane Trailing Arm Bushings (100 Durometer)

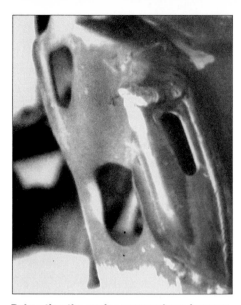

Relocating the engine rearward can improve your launch by putting the weight where it counts. Just follow the instructions provided in Chapter 5.

under the rocker panel jack notches. Either remove the engine and transmission or use a hoist to suspend the engine while the crossmember is out. Disassemble the front suspension, being sure to remove the springs, struts, spindle/rotors, swaybar, rack & pinion and control arms. Use wire or bungee cords to suspend the calipers while the crossmember is out. Scribe a line at the rear edge of the lower crossmember mounts for reference, then remove the crossmember.

If your car is a pre-'87, then swapping your heavy crossmember for the '87 version would shave several pounds off the front end. On the '90 and newer cars, the more narrow track width of this crossmember would allow camber to be set at 0° or slightly positive to reduce rolling friction.

Step 2

Clean the crossmember, control arms and spindles before beginning. Follow Step 4 in Chapter 5, p. 74 and relocate the crossmember forward.

Step 3

Modify the engine mounts to relocate the engine rearward, as instructed in Step 6 in Chapter 5, p. 77. Remember: When calculating the amount to remove from the engine mount, add to the distance you are moving the engine rearward the amount you moved the crossmember forward. Also, add extra bracing around the left engine mount using 3/16" steel plate. Basically, you will be boxing in the open area of the mount as much as possible, as well as adding more braces to the top sides (reinforcements added to the top of the mount move the engine up with the center of gravity and help weight transfer). This mount takes considerable stress from the shock loading when the car is launched, and should be checked after every weekend of racing, especially if your engine is turbo or supercharged. Most of the popular headers will fit without interference if you limit the relocation to 1". Beyond that and you'll probably have to do some major fabrication for everything to clear.

Step 4

Once you have completed these modifications, clean the crossmember with a good grease and wax remover (PPG DX–330), prime with a good epoxy paint (PPG DP–48), and paint with an acrylic urethane color to match the car or engine bay. Very important for that stock look. Acrylic urethane is easy to spray and provides a very durable surface. Don't forget to follow the paint manufacturer's safety procedures and wear the correct respirator. Epoxy primers and urethane paints don't mix well with humans.

Step 5

Follow Step 9 in Chapter 5, p. 79 and reinstall the crossmember.

Step 6: Shortening Header Pipes

If yours is a street car or you are running a required exhaust system under class rules, don't forget to shorten the header-to-muffler extension pipes by the distance the engine has been moved rearward. Make sure you do not remove an amount that includes the distance the crossmember was moved forward.

Aerodynamic drag can slow a car down significantly and hurt elapsed times. The S/G Mustang of Chester Andrews shows the best setup with the entire car lower and a slight rake (about 1 degree).

Step 7: Convert Steering

To reduce parasitic loss and drop about 15 lbs. of useless weight, convert your power steering to manual. The only unit that is a direct bolt-in replacement is from the '82–'87 Mustang or Capri. When making the conversion on an '88 or newer car, you should swap the inner socket assemblies from your power steering rack to provide the correct thread contact in the tie rods when the toe is set. When removing your power steering unit, don't forget to delete the oil cooler bolted in front of the A/C condenser.

Since this manual rack can be difficult to find in a salvage yard, a new or rebuilt unit can be purchased from most major auto parts stores. Just specify one for a 1987 Mustang when ordering (TRW 15508R).

Step 8: Struts

Using the correct strut can make the difference between a competitive 60-foot

time and a win light in the other lane. If your car is trailered and will not be driven on the street, then the new Koni "SPA-1" drag struts are the way to go. Most shocks/struts are built with a 1:3 ratio of resistance to compression and extension. Basically, this means your stock strut will resist extension three times greater than compression. This is

to allow the average car to drive over potholes without jamming the wheel into the hole before the car passes it. Since the object of drag racing is to achieve sufficient weight transfer for the slicks to bite properly, a strut that resists extension obviously is not the way to go.

These Koni drag struts have replaced the old 90/10 shocks that once ruled drag

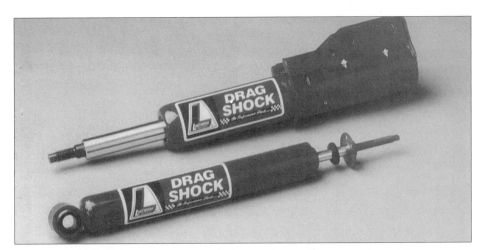

Optimum bite off the line requires a good balance between the suspension and the dampeners. Controlling the weight transfer is critical and the sole job of the struts and shocks. Pictured here are the new Lakewood shocks and struts that are designed to be both street and strip compatible.

Setting up your front end for drag racing requires a spring that will allow full extension of the lower control arms to maximize the use of the triggering lights. The short road racing spring on the left would be a poor choice for drag racing.

racing. The special valving found in the SPA–1 series struts provides a variable rebound rate that is "velocity sensitive," and has virtually no bump (compression) resistance. What this translates to is a strut that slows down the weight transfer as the bite improves, while at the same time allowing the front end to settle quickly to avoid catching air under the car, thereby improving aerodynamics. Great stuff for drag racing.

Dual-Purpose Struts—Just as wonderful as these are for drag racing they are equally unpleasant on the street. These struts and the matching rear shocks will make your car very unstable and dangerous on the street. The special valving will not control your car when negotiating a turn, much less a sudden lane change. If you have a street car that is also set up for drag racing, replace your struts with a set from a non-GT/5.0 Mustang. The softer valving in these will provide better weight transfer while providing a streetable vehicle.

When re–assembling your front end, place large-radius 1/8" washers on the three bolts for the upper strut mounts. This will place the strut mount slightly lower, allowing for more suspension

travel and of course a wider reaction window at the lights.

Step 9: Springs

As you reassemble the front suspension, replace your stock springs with those from a four-cylinder Mustang. These units are noticeably lighter and will permit the front end of your car to sit lower without sacrificing spring length and suspension travel. This change permits more effective utilization of the suspension by providing more usable suspension travel. This allows the driver a little bit quicker reaction window before tripping the lights.

Step 10: Swaybar

To increase weight transfer, drag racers commonly eliminate their front swaybar. Not only does this eliminate 25 lbs. of useless weight, but it also allows the control arms to extend fully, giving extra reaction time before tripping the lights. Unfortunately, eliminating the front swaybar reduces your car's ability to negotiate turns and lane changes in a level attitude.

If you want to reduce weight but still have some suspension control on the street, use the four-cylinder Mustang swaybar and fabricate longer stabilizer end links to allow full extension of the front suspension. A 1" to 1-1/2" longer link should provide sufficient suspension travel. To fabricate these, purchase (2) 3/8" x 11" NF bolts with self-locking nuts and 13" of 1/2" O.D. x .060" wall tubing. Also purchase (8) of the old-style soft rubber insulators. Cut two 6" pieces of the tubing and reassemble the end links, using your factory washers and nuts, with the long bolt passing from the bottom of the control arm up to the swaybar. This makes for a screwy swaybar-to-control arm relationship that would freak out any self–respecting road racer, but works well for the straight-line fans.

Step 11: Transmission

Since the engine has been relocated you must modify the transmission mount and driveshaft to accommodate this change. Follow Step 21 in Chapter 5, p. 83 for this procedure.

If your Mustang trips the clocks in the 11.99 and under category, NHRA and IHRA will require a door net for the safety of the driver. These things are available from several manufacturers, including Simpson and Racer's Components.

For the serious drag racer, a front driveshaft hoop is mandatory. Most drag strips will not allow you to race a modified car without one, so plan on the expense.

REAR SUSPENSION

Setting up the Mustang's rear suspension for drag racing mostly involves relocating the instantaneous center to generate a high anti–squat percentage or rise rate. Because the Mustang is nose-heavy with a forward center of gravity, it is necessary to create a setup that will allow the car to transfer that weight to the slicks. This is accomplished by relocating the lower trailing arm mounts at the axle housing 2-1/2" lower. This moves the instantaneous center up to approximately 13" on a 26" slick and 40-1/2" forward of the axle centerline. What this translates to is a rise rate that equals approximately 102%. If you observe a car with this type of setup launching from the lights, the car seems to rise on all four wheels. That effect causes all of the car's weight to be levered at the rear slicks. The modifications in this section are provided to achieve this effect.

Traction Bars—The simplest approach to traction bars would be to purchase a set of the South Side Machine (259 E. Main Street, Smithville, OH 44677, 216/669-3556) or Texas Turbo (9703 Plainfield, Houston, TX 77036, 714/988-0541) traction bar kits. They

work well and are simple to install. However, for the industrious I have provided drawings (Figures 6-1, 6-2, 6-3, p. 119) to fabricate a set of traction bars that operate on this same principle.

Anti-Squat Brackets—Additionally you can fabricate a set of anti–squat brackets (Fig. 6-4, p. 119) that have the trailing arm holes relocated 1-1/2" and 2-1/2". These brackets, when used in

conjunction with fabricated or modified lower trailing arms, provide the same effect as traction bars but also allow the ability to relocate the trailing arms for highway driving. Unfortunately the polyurethane bushings will flex considerably when subjected to 400+ horsepower launches, generally causing the lower trailing arms to permanently twist or bend. If you are in the mega-horsepower crowd stick with the traction bars. Again, you make the call.

Step 12

If you have not yet removed the rear axle assembly, do so now. Support the axle under the center section, disconnect the flexible brake hose from the frame and remove the dampeners and shocks. If you do not wish to disconnect the brakes, simply pull the axles and detach the brake lines and backing plates from the housing. Then hang them with wire or bungee cords. Remove the shocks, coil springs and swaybar, then disconnect the trailing arms and remove the axle assembly. Remove the trailing arms. Finally, remove the frame mounting brackets for the dampeners, as they will

The popular Southside Machine Co. traction bars move the lower trailing arm pickup approximately 2–1/2" out from the stock location. Moving the pickup points alters the instantaneous center location, which creates a lifting action that plants the slicks firmly to the track for a much improved launch. (Yes, those 28.5" x 10.5" slicks, on 10" wheels, do fit in the fender wells.)

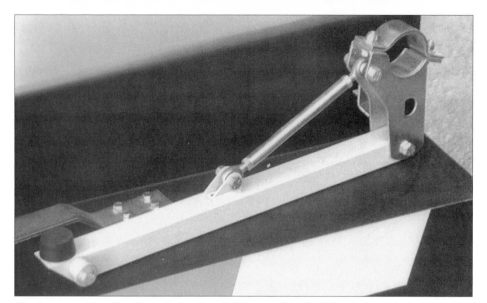

The Lakewood traction bar bolts to the axle tubes and the lower trailing arm bolt. These bars are basically old technology compared to the replacement lower trailing arm types. However, they will provide a marked improvement over the stock suspension. See the sidebar on p. 116 for installation details.

not be used. As with the beginning of any modification, clean everything thoroughly, including the axle assembly.

Step 13

If you have not welded around the frame's upper trailing arm mounts, it is a must for this modification. Without the cushion of the rubber bushings, any weakness in the mount attachment, when subjected to the stress of a solid spherical joint, will soon be found. Again, for this modification I strongly recommend that additional inside braces be extended from the main roll bar hoop to the interior side of these mounts. Weld completely through the footing plates and the trailing arm bracket and use 3/8" aircraft grade bolts (AN6–14) to tie them together.

Step 14: Axles

Although the stock Mustang housing equipped with the 31-spline axles is quite strong, the most reliable approach is to install the 9" axles and large bearing carriers to your 8.8" axle assembly. See Figure 5-21 on p. 104 for construction or purchase one of the Moser Engineering kits. Obviously, another alternative would be to install one of the many converted 9" housings. Equally obvious

is the considerable cost. Many 10-second cars run the stock 8.8" without trouble so there must be something to it.

If your car is equipped with the 7.5" axle assembly, give it a good send-off and drop it in the river. These axle assemblies can't take the torque of a stock, no-traction Mustang, much less one that hooks up. Replacement is a must. Check the various salvage yards

for an 8.8 or purchase a take–off from one of the many suppliers listed in the various Ford-themed magazines.

To install the Moser kit, follow the instructions provided in Step 28 of Chapter 5, p. 90.

Step 15: Adjustable Upper Trailing Arms

Follow Step 24 in Chapter 5, p. 86 and fabricate adjustable upper trailing arms or modify your stock units. If you are modifying your stock upper trailing arms, use 100 durometer Energy Suspension bushings.

Step 16: Axle Bushings

Follow Step 13 in Chapter 4, p. 60 and remove the axle bushings from the axle housing. Do not reinstall a bushing if you will be using the adjustable upper trailing arms. If you are using the stock-type upper trailing arms instead of the adjustable tubular types, do not remove the bushing shells from the axle housing. Instead, burn the rubber out and install Energy Suspension 100 durometer polyurethane bushings.

Another popular traction bar that is marketed by Texas Turbo has a unique urethane/aluminum bushing that allows squeak-free street operation. The bushings are designed to function like any other urethane bushing, however under load the urethane compresses, forcing the aluminum inner sleeve against the outer bushing shell for a solid bearing effect.

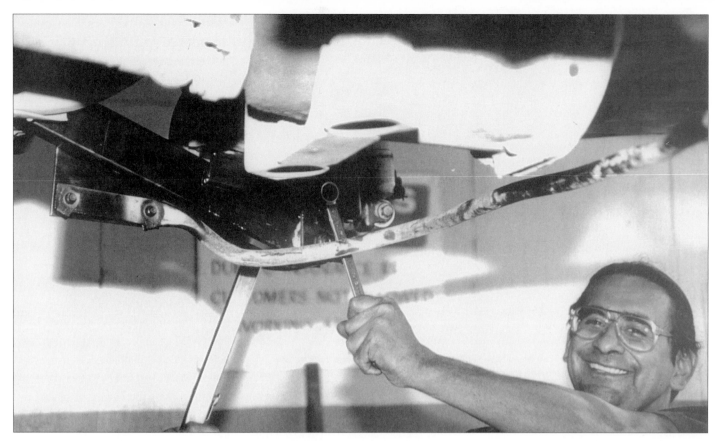

When installing a replacement lower trailing arm type traction bar (Southside Machine, Texas Turbo or per the accompanying drawings), it is very important to adjust the angle of the attachment plate to achieve the correct pinion angle. Joe Rivera, owner of EFI Hyperformance in Houston, Texas, is seen here torquing the plates in position before drilling the brackets for the additional safety bolts.

Step 17

At this point you should brush the welds clean and paint the entire axle housing with an epoxy (PPG DP 90) or a red oxide primer.

Step 18: Installing Traction Bars

In this step you must install traction bars, either aftermarket or fabricated units, per figures 6-1, 6-2, and 6-3.

With the fabricated or purchased traction bars, reassemble the rear suspension using a set of Mustang GT rear springs with Air Lift bags fitted to the centers. Replace the spring pads with the harder ones from an early model GT Mustang upper spring if you're going to run this car on the street. If you are using the tubular adjustable upper trailing arms, be sure to observe the assembly as noted in the drawings, p. 119. Relocate the rear jackstands under the axle housing tubes

Traction can be improved and better controlled on most drag racing Mustangs with the installation of Air Lift air bags inside the rear coil springs.

If you find the traction bars are too restrictive for street, modifying the lower trailing arm brackets (see Chapter 5) can provide excellent weight transfer and traction for a hot street machine.

and joust the suspension several times to settle the springs.

Place a magnetic inclinometer on the pinion yoke and adjust the mounting brackets on the lower trailing arms to achieve a 1-1/2° down setting when using the tubular trailing arms, and 2-1/2° with the stock upper trailing arms. It is very important to adjust both brackets exactly the same amount. Adjusting the right upper trailing arm can be used to fine-tune the traction bias later on. Use a tape measure and check the diagonal distance between the lower inside edge of the axle brackets to the rear bolt on the front control arms. This is important to ensure your car will track straight. When you are satisfied they are square, torque the attaching bolts. Drill a 7/16" hole through the outside of the factory brackets through the traction bar brackets approximately 1" above the factory bolt and install 7/16" x 1" grade 8 bolts, nuts and lock washers. This will prevent the bracket from rotating. (The best approach would be to weld these in place). If you have not done so already, tighten the jam nuts (if used) on the adjustable upper trailing arms if you're

using them.

As mentioned, an alternative to traction bars is to fabricate the anti–squat brackets and lower trailing arms per the accompanying drawings and/or modify the stock lower trailing arms for racing. The 2" x 3" box steel control arms are very strong and will completely eliminate the twisting that is common with the

stock lower trailing arms. They are designed to utilize Energy Suspension polyurethane bushings.

In order to use the stock lower trailing arms, you must follow Step 15 in Chapter 4, p. 62. Use Energy Suspension 100 durometer bushings instead of the 88s.

Anti-Squat Brackets—Just follow the instructions in Figure 6-4 for details on the fabrication of these brackets. Be sure to bolt the side pieces and rear piece to the trailing arm mounting brackets on the axle housing to achieve a proper fit. Once the plates are aligned correctly, tack-weld the corners, then remove and weld completely. When you have completed the fabrication, use the factory bolts to attach the brackets to the factory holes (insert a spacer the width of the bushings inside the factory brackets), and a 1" x 1/2" bolt to attach the bracket to the factory shock mount hole.

This setup works best when using adjustable upper trailing arms. Pinion angle can be adjusted properly to prevent potential driveshaft bending or breakage. Just follow the same basic procedure for setting the traction bars with the inclinometer, listed above. Adjust the

The simplest approach to improving traction is to fabricate a set of the dual purpose anti-squat brackets per Fig. 6-4. These brackets have two lower trailing arm pickup points that allow the racer to go from street/cornering geometry to a high-lift drag racing setup. (The second set of holes have not been drilled in the brackets shown so don't freak out.)

upper trailing arms equally to create a 1-1/2° down setting for starters. This completes the drag racing rear suspension modifications.

Step 19: Bumpers

Follow the recommendations in Step 44 of Chapter 5, p. 96 and replace your bumpers. If yours is a trailered car and your class rules do not require bumpers, spray the bumper reinforcement cavity inside of the nose-piece with the insulating foam used by plumbers and carpenters to seal around pipes and exterior wall sections. This stuff is virtually weightless. It will expand to fill the void and will provide significant structural rigidity to the nose-piece. This is important to maintain the aerodynamic shape of the nose-piece at speeds. ■

Mustangs equipped with the 10" slicks will require the axles be upgraded to the tougher 9" type. The stock 28-spline axles are just not adequate. Installing a Greg Moser Engineering kit or fabricating one as specified in Chapter 5 is the best approach.

In order to run the big 10" slicks on your Mustang, you will have to use a wheel with a 6" backspacing (alternately a 6-1/4" backspacing, long studs and a 1/4" spacer) and perform some heavy-duty pounding of the inner fender panel. Rework the areas noted by the arrows, paying particular attention at the spring perch area.

HOOKING UP
with
LAKEWOOD TRACTION BARS

text & photography by Michael Lutfy

Having more power than the guy next to you means nothing unless it's transferred to the ground. And, the rear suspension on a stock Mustang GT or LX is well-equipped to handle the 300 lbs-ft. torque of a stock 5.0 liter as long as it's applied with a relatively steady and even throttle. But if you're the type who likes to drop the hammer now and then (preferably on a drag strip under safe conditions), then you'll quickly realize that the only place you may be going is nowhere—fast. This is especially true when you begin adding superchargers, cams, heads and any other SVO or aftermarket product that raises the stock torque output.

The stock bushings in the Mustang's rear lower control arms are very flexible, designed so to allow the rear axle assembly vertical travel to eliminate bone-jarring rides during daily driving. But when subject to a sudden torque rush, the bushings flex, allowing the rear axle assembly to twist upward, taking the rear wheels with it. The result is *wheel hop* and a loss of traction—which doesn't do much for straightline acceleration times. This is especially evident with slicks added.

The problem can be solved with a set of traction bars from Lakewood Industries (PN#20161). Lakewood traction bars are designed to fit all '79-'93 Mustangs, including rear quad shock applications. The bars are designed with an adjustable link for a more precise snubber adjustment for preloading of the chassis to fine tune handling for various street or track conditions.

The traction bars are mounted directly to the rear end, on the axle housings, at the same level as the pinion gear. When the rear axle housing twists upward during hard acceleration, the rubber snubbers on the front of the bars contact the frame rails, which effectively redirects the torque to the rear and levers the axle downward, planting the rear tires on the ground. Traction is obviously enhanced, and you're out of the hole with plenty of grip.

Traction bars work best on the strip with slicks, although they can be left on the car for daily driving. However, speed bumps, potholes and frost heaves will cause the traction bars to thump the frame repeatedly, so you might want to tie them down. The other option is to install them for drag strip runs, then remove them for street driving. This is less of a problem than it seems, because they are easily installed, as demonstrated in the accompanying photos.

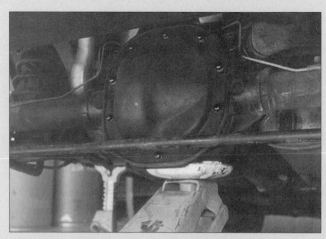

1. Support the car on jackstands on the frame rails. Then support the axle with a hydraulic floor jack to remove the weight from the lower control arms.

2. Remove the four sway bar bolts (two on each side) in the lower control arms and remove the sway bar.

3. After removing the sway bar, support the lower control arm with a floor jack or jackstand, underneath the spring seat, to keep the rear spring under pressure so it doesn't suddenly pop out, which can be harmful.

4. Remove the lower control arm bolt (arrow). This may require a little jockeying around with the jack to relieve pressure on the axle. You may need to tap it with a rubber mallet.

5. Next connect the lower traction bar bracket by reattaching the lower control arm bolt. You may need a friend to push in on the axle to line up the hole.

6. Connect the upper half of the bracket and make sure you go *under* the brake line. To fit, you may need to bend the brake line slightly, very carefully. This is extremely important, because if the bracket goes over the line, it could shear the line under acceleration. Attach the upper bracket to the lower with the two 5/8" bolts provided.

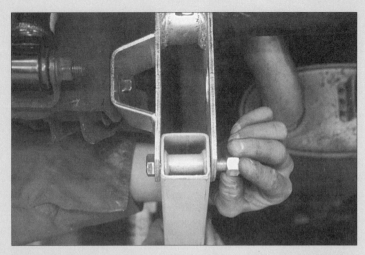

8. The Heim joints are next. On the upper part of the Heim joint, you'll need to add two bushings, one on either side of the joint, inside the bracket. Do not attach the lower Heim joint yet. Lower the car to the ground and make sure it's level.

7. Attach the rubber snubber to the end of the traction bar, then attach the traction bar to the lower bracket. Then, before you go any further, attach the other traction bar to the other side of the car. When both traction bars are on the car, reattach the rear sway bar. You need to do this before attaching the Heim joints, otherwise the sway bar won't go in.

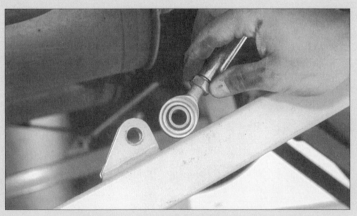

10. Set the height of the rubber snubber by adjusting the lower Heim joint. The clearances should be 1/2 inch on the passenger side, 5/8 inch on the driver's side.

9. The lower Heim joint is where you'll adjust the ride height of the traction bar, by turning this nut. Hold up the traction bar, and set the Heim joint length.

Remember that traction bars don't take kindly to potholes, speed bumps and frost heaves. If you're only going to the drag strip occasionally, you might want to remove and install the bars just before you go racing. If you're going to keep them on the street, then you may want to tie them down so they don't rap the frame rails every time you go over a bump.

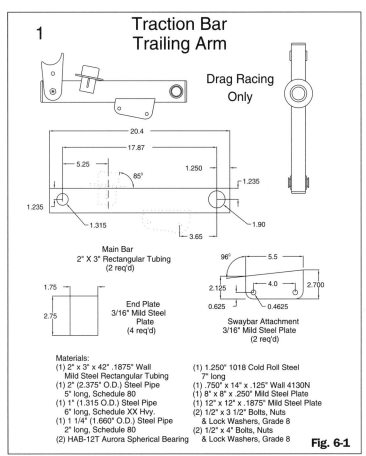

1   Traction Bar Trailing Arm

Drag Racing Only

20.4
17.87
5.25
1.250
85°
1.235
1.235
1.315
1.90
3.65

Main Bar
2" X 3" Rectangular Tubing
(2 req'd)

1.75
2.75

End Plate
3/16" Mild Steel Plate
(4 req'd)

96°
5.5
2.125
4.0
2.700
0.625
0.4625

Swaybar Attachment
3/16" Mild Steel Plate
(2 req'd)

Materials:
(1) 2" x 3" x 42" .1875" Wall
   Mild Steel Rectangular Tubing
(1) 2" (2.375" O.D.) Steel Pipe
   5" long, Schedule 80
(1) 1" (1.315 O.D.) Steel Pipe
   6" long, Schedule XX Hvy.
(1) 1 1/4" (1.660" O.D.) Steel Pipe
   2" long, Schedule 80
(2) HAB-12T Aurora Spherical Bearing

(1) 1.250" 1018 Cold Roll Steel
   7" long
(1) .750" x 14" x .125" Wall 4130N
(1) 8" x 8" x .250" Mild Steel Plate
(1) 12" x 12" x .1875" Mild Steel Plate
(2) 1/2" x 3 1/2" Bolts, Nuts
   & Lock Washers, Grade 8
(2) 1/2" x 4" Bolts, Nuts
   & Lock Washers, Grade 8

Fig. 6-1

2   Traction Bar Trailing Arm

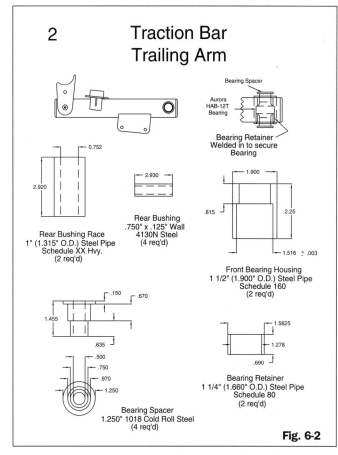

Bearing Spacer

Aurora
HAB-12T
Bearing

Bearing Retainer
Welded in to secure
Bearing

0.752
2.920

Rear Bushing Race
1" (1.315" O.D.) Steel Pipe
Schedule XX Hvy.
(2 req'd)

2.930

Rear Bushing
.750" x .125" Wall
4130N Steel
(4 req'd)

1.900
.815
2.25
1.516 ± .003

Front Bearing Housing
1 1/2" (1.900" O.D.) Steel Pipe
Schedule 160
(2 req'd)

.150
.670
1.455
.635
.500
.750
.970
1.250

Bearing Spacer
1.250" 1018 Cold Roll Steel
(4 req'd)

1.5625
1.278
.690

Bearing Retainer
1 1/4" (1.660" O.D.) Steel Pipe
Schedule 80
(2 req'd)

Fig. 6-2

3   Traction Bar Trailing Arm

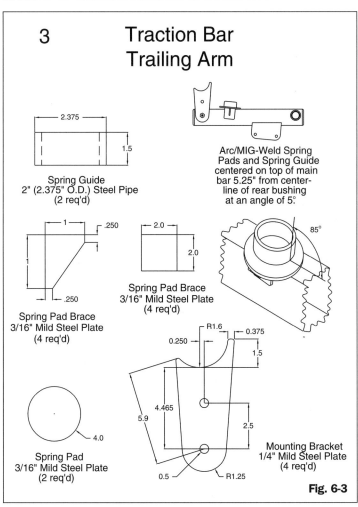

2.375
1.5

Spring Guide
2" (2.375" O.D.) Steel Pipe
(2 req'd)

Arc/MIG-Weld Spring
Pads and Spring Guide
centered on top of main
bar 5.25" from center-
line of rear bushing
at an angle of 5°

1
.250
.250

Spring Pad Brace
3/16" Mild Steel Plate
(4 req'd)

2.0
2.0

Spring Pad Brace
3/16" Mild Steel Plate
(4 req'd)

85°

4.0

Spring Pad
3/16" Mild Steel Plate
(2 req'd)

R1.6
0.375
0.250
1.5
4.465
5.9
2.5
0.5
R1.25

Mounting Bracket
1/4" Mild Steel Plate
(4 req'd)

Fig. 6-3

Anti-Squat Bracket

Dual Purpose

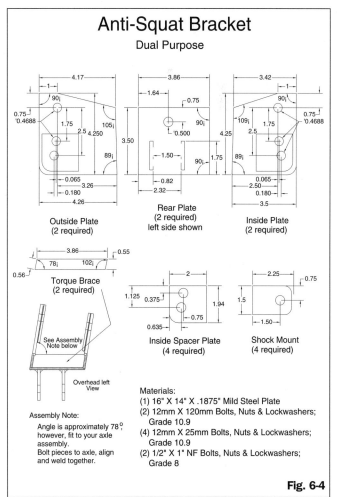

4.17
1
90°
0.75
0.4688
1.75
2.5
4.250
105°
89°
0.065
3.26
0.180
4.26

Outside Plate
(2 required)

3.86
1.64
0.75
90°
3.50
0.500
1.50
90°
1.75
0.82
2.32

Rear Plate
(2 required)
left side shown

3.42
1
90°
0.75
0.4688
109°
1.75
4.25
2.5
89°
0.065
2.50
0.180
3.5

Inside Plate
(2 required)

3.86
0.55
78°
102°
0.56

Torque Brace
(2 required)

See Assembly
Note below

Overhead left
View

2
1.125
0.375
1.94
0.75
0.635

Inside Spacer Plate
(4 required)

2.25
0.75
1.5
1.50

Shock Mount
(4 required)

Assembly Note:
Angle is approximately 78°,
however, fit to your axle
assembly.
Bolt pieces to axle, align
and weld together.

Materials:
(1) 16" X 14" X .1875" Mild Steel Plate
(2) 12mm X 120mm Bolts, Nuts & Lockwashers;
   Grade 10.9
(4) 12mm X 25mm Bolts, Nuts & Lockwashers;
   Grade 10.9
(2) 1/2" X 1" NF Bolts, Nuts & Lockwashers;
   Grade 8

Fig. 6-4

BOLT-ON SUSPENSION KITS

7

MIG–welders, acetylene torches, drill presses, grinders, etc. are not always available to the average car enthusiast. The vast majority of Mustangers do not want race car handling and prefer to improve the handling of their cars with basic tools and bolt-on type pieces that can be installed in their driveways. There are numerous companies that will sell you suspension packages. These packages go from simple swaybar and bushing changes to completely modified front crossmember and axle assemblies. Selecting a suspension upgrade is dependent on your bank account and the effort you are willing to make. This chapter is designed to help you make an informed decision and to provide you with a view of what to expect from each of the selected manufacturer's packages.

It is important to realize before you evaluate the available packages, that properly assembled with the correct spring rates and dampeners, any of the top suspension setups will significantly improve the handling of your Mustang and can put you on the front row at any track. Other than a properly built three-link rear suspension, there is not a noticeable difference in lap times between any of them, especially for the bolt-on crowd. The individual's driving style will dictate which type of suspension fits best. Every weekend new

Improving the handling on your Mustang requires a balanced package of suspension changes that will work in harmony with each other. The Kenny Brown XS Outlaw Mustang is one of the best examples of what can be done to a poor-handling convertible with the right combination. (Photo courtesy Kenny Brown Performance Products)

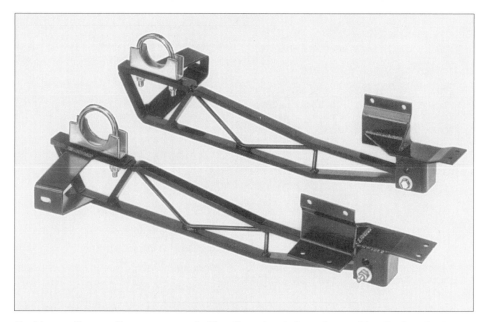

Hooking up the rear tires means controlling the axle windup. Competition Engineering's bolt-on ladder bars are quick and easy to install. These bars are lightweight and well engineered. (Photo courtesy Competition Engineering)

drag racing, so help in assembling a package is just a phone call away.

Probably the most commonly used bolt-on component by the Mustang drag racer is the traction bar. Competition Engineering's ladder bar-type traction bar is well engineered and the workmanship is excellent. The bolt-on ladder bar is simple to install and requires the usual hand tools and drill. It is attached to the axle by clamps on the axle tubes and the lower trailing arm bolt. The forward bracket is bolted to the frame next to the lower trailing arm mount. Using this type traction device will generally require a little more effort to dial in your launch than the replacement lower trailing arm traction bar (Southside Machine). The changes to the instantaneous center with a ladder bar traction bar will tend to make the car rotate on the rear axle, causing the front end to wheelie. Correct springs and dampeners become critical to the management of this characteristic to achieve a consistent and quick launch.

innovations appear and unknown fabricators become the hot item. In reality, unless you are a serious competitor in an SCCA or IMSA class, go for the best service and price.

COMPETITION ENGINEERING
80 Carter Drive
Guilford, CT 06437
(203) 453-5200

Geared strictly for the drag racing crowd, Competition Engineering builds first-class chassis components. Bolt-on ladder bar-type traction bars, subframe connectors, bolt-in roll bars and cages, strut tower braces, front chassis underbody crossbraces and drag race specific springs and shocks are available for your Mustang. Competition Engineering does not offer packaged kits, so you will have to piece the parts together. Fortunately the people with Competition Engineering really know

SUSPENSION TECHNIQUES
13546 Vintage Place
Chino, CA 91710
(714) 465-1020

The suspension package from

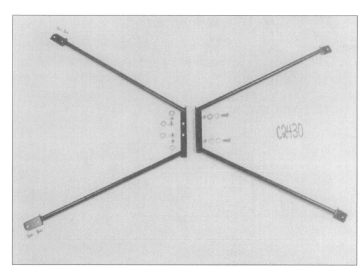

Anything that improves the structural rigidity of your Mustang will enhance its cornering capability. The front underbody braces from Competition Engineering are an inexpensive bolt-on kit that will reduce some of the twisting action of the stock chassis. (Photo courtesy of Competition Engineering)

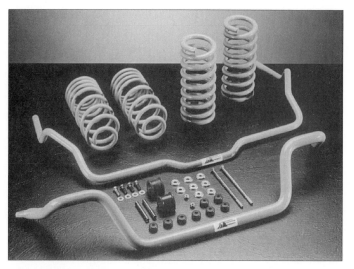

The spring and swaybar package from Suspension Techniques will provide a firm ride with much-improved cornering speeds. These springs and swaybars form the basis for several of the major chassis kits from other manufacturers. They are well made and they bolt in cleanly. (Photo courtesy Suspension Techniques)

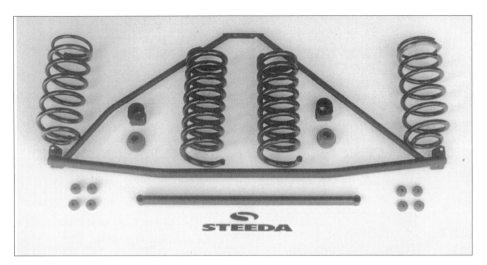

The Steeda Autosports G-Trac I kit shown provides a good foundation to improve the stock Mustang suspension. The package installs with basic tools and is designed to work with the stock swaybars. (Photo courtesy Steeda Autosports)

Suspension Techniques includes larger front and rear swaybars, stiffer springs, and urethane swaybar bushings. This is a balanced package that will provide a substantial improvement in handling over a stock GT Mustang setup. Other than a rented coil spring compressor, no special tools are necessary for installation.

There are three items that must be considered when purchasing this package. First, the rear springs and swaybar are pretty stiff, therefore directional stability can suffer on rough roads at slower speeds, especially if your car is a coupe. Second, stiffer springs require upgraded struts and shocks for control, so plan for this. Finally, as with any stiffer suspension, sticky tires are necessary to realize the intended gain. Make no mistake, this is a well-balanced package; however, it is definitely for the aggressive driver.

STEEDA AUTOSPORTS
2241 Hammondville Rd.
Pompano Beach, FL 33069
(305) 960-0774

Anyone who has followed the American Sedan class in SCCA knows of the success of the Steeda Mustangs. Steeda races what it sells and sells what it races. The suspension packages from Steeda come in three levels, from the

basic G-Trac I kit (springs, strut tower brace, and G/Trac bar) to the complete G-Trac III package, which includes all pieces in the G-Trac I kit plus Tokico Illumina adjustable struts and shocks, Steeda adjustable rear swaybar, Steeda HD upper trailing arms, chrome-moly subframe connectors and a four-point roll bar. These kits are well made, the fit is excellent and the spring-to-swaybar balance provides a .9+ *g* capability on a street car.

Other than a drill and coil spring compressor, no special tools are needed to install the Steeda kits. The installation of the adjustable rear swaybar brackets

can be a pain but otherwise the kit installation is pretty much a remove-and-replace drill. The performance improvement is significant but will require the usual fat, sticky tires to realize the gains.

GLOBAL WEST
1423 E. Philadelphia
Ontario, CA 91761
(909) 923-6176

One of the oldest and most diversified suspension component manufacturers in America is Global West. Their products are extremely well crafted and the fit is factory perfect. Included in their vast array of suspension pieces are several components for the Fox Mustang. Global West does not offer a complete package but can sell you the requisite strut tower brace, subframe connectors, serious lower trailing arms, offset rack bushings, solid aluminum offset control arm bushings (Del-A-Lum™), camber plates (McCaster™), springs, Konis, and the new rear axle Traction Separator kit. If you own an SVO Mustang, Global West is the only supplier of high-performance replacement control arm bushings for these cars.

With the exception of the solid aluminum Del-A-Lum™ bushings, the Global West components install with the

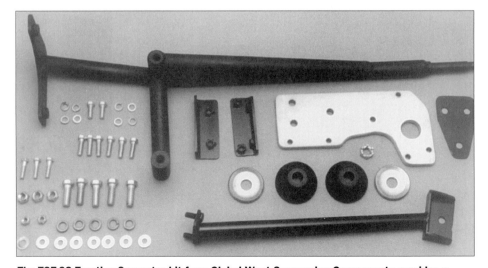

The TSF-93 Traction Separator kit from Global West Suspension Components provides a more neutral feel to the rear axle for a high-performance street machine. The kit requires no special skills and installs with hand tools and a drill. It is also offered in the Ford Motorsports catalog (PN M5478-G).

Global West was one of the first companies to produce a camber/caster plate. Called McCaster Kit™, the plate allows complete adjustment of caster and camber. (Photo courtesy Global West Suspension Components)

usual tools and drill. The aluminum bushings are a challenge to install since you must remove the factory bushing shells before fitting the machined bushings. These bushings cost several times the price of the urethane bushings, but are the finest thing short of spherical rod end. They do not squeak or deflect and they come with a replacement warranty.

The new Traction Separator kit (TSF-93) provides a fifth link to stabilize the rear axle under braking and acceleration. A noticeable reduction in brake dive and a more predicable rear axle breakaway are the selling points of this device. Similar to the Griggs torque arm, the link bolts to the axle housing inspection cover bolts and harmonic weight flanges. It is attached to a bracket that bolts to the rear seat bulkhead with a brace that runs to the driver's inside seat belt anchor bolt. The link pivots in a bushing and socket arrangement on the bulkhead bracket that is similar to the early Mustang strut rod bushings. The axle windup control of the Traction Separator eliminates the quad dampeners, allowing the use of wider wheels and tires. Most aftermarket, large-tube exhaust systems will have to

be modified to clear the bulkhead bracket and link. This is a good alternative to a torque arm and it does not require a Panhard bar for street duty. It is also available from Ford Motorsport (PN M5478-G).

GRIGGS RACING
285 Prado Street #A
San Luis Obispo, CA 93401
(800) 655-0336

Getting power to the ground has always been the Fox Mustang's biggest nemesis. Bruce Griggs' solution to the problem is the Torque Arm rear suspension kit. Sold as a weld-in or bolt-on package, this device connects to the lower inspection cover and harmonic weight flanges on the axle housing. It is secured at the front tip to a tubular crossmember that serves as the pivot point. Griggs also sells the correct springs and Panhard bar necessary to make it work. Because this device controls axle rotation, the upper trailing arms are disconnected and removed. This thing is one of the best rear traction devices that money can buy. It really plants the tires and makes them hook up. Dennis Hillaird of Central Coast Mustang uses one of Griggs', Torque-Arms on his 351-powered drag racing Mustang that runs in the 9.60s. Pretty good testimonial.

Installation of the bolt-on version does not require special tools or skills. The biggest problem in the installation of the torque arm is fitting it to the axle housing. Factory machining tolerances on the axle housing will typically require a little hand fitting with a rat-tail file. No big deal, but plan on it.

There are two other points you should be aware of before buying a torque arm.

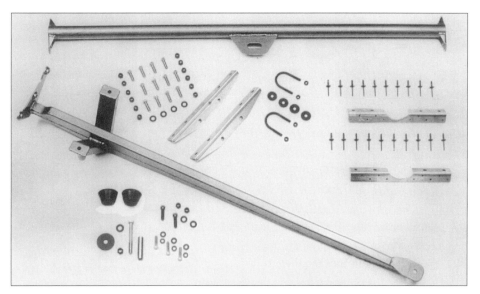

The Griggs Racing bolt-on torque arm kit has gained considerable popularity with the autocross and road racing crowd. It is relatively easy to install and provides much improved rear traction when used with the correct springs. (Photo courtesy Griggs Racing)

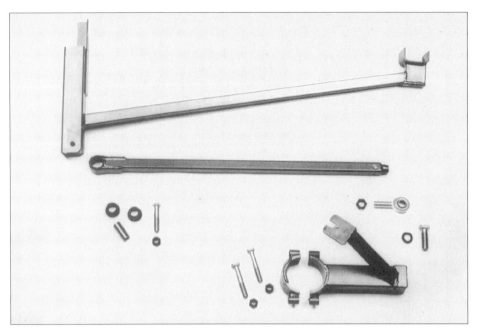

Installation of a torque arm or three-link type rear suspension will require a strong Panhard bar. The Griggs Racing kit is very sturdy and fits well. However, it must be welded in place. (Photo courtesy Griggs Racing)

CENTRAL COAST MUSTANG
708 W. Betterravia
Santa Maria, CA 93455
(805) 925-8848

Dennis Hillaird's Central Coast Mustang is one of the top Mustang performance shops in the nation. Dennis sells what works rather than what is popular. Complete and well-balanced suspension packages that are backed by constant testing in real races are what make the Central Coast kits work so well.

Depending on what you want, Central Coast Mustang offers complete conventional four-link packages with matching springs, swaybars and bushings, balanced torque arm setups, modified crossmembers and a drag racing package as well. I have used and tested all of the Central Coast components and found them to fit properly and work well when used in the recommended combinations.

The best street/race camber plates on the market are sold by Central Coast Mustang. Their camber plates provide a quick-change street or racing setting that takes the headache out of the alignment process. The Central Coast Mustang

First, the torque arm requires the removal of the upper trailing arms, and consequently a Panhard bar must be installed to locate the axle housing. If you are doing this in your driveway without the benefit of a welding machine, you will need to install either a Central Coast Mustang or Saleen bolt-on Panhard bar. Although I do not recommend a bolt-on Panhard bar, it will work. Breaking a Panhard bar on a torque arm type suspension can be pretty disconcerting on a race track, but on the street it can be a lot worse. If you bolt yours on, I suggest you spend the extra bucks and drive your car to a competent welder and have it welded in place. The need for a Panhard bar obviously will raise the cost of this type of suspension setup.

The second point you should consider is the need for high-rate rear springs. With a stock swaybar, you will need a minimum-rate spring of 350 lbs-in. for the street with 450 lbs-in. on the track. Without the correct springs to provide the required roll stiffness, the extremely low rear axle roll center will cause the inside front wheel to lift and upset the front and

rear suspension geometry. Obviously, if you have high-rate rear springs, you will have a noticeable deterioration in directional control over rough surfaces. Since race tracks are generally smooth this is not a problem. For street use however, you will need to adjust your driving style to compensate for the slow-speed rear axle dance that will occur over washboard roads.

The best camber plate for the street/competition enthusiast is one that allows simple adjustment and quick change from a street setting to a race application. The Central Coast Mustang camber plate shown has two positions for indexing the strut mount that provide ideal caster in streetable trim as well as the racing position. (Photo courtesy Central Coast Mustang)

There are numerous bolt-in Panhard bars on the market. One of the best and easiest to install is from Central Coast Mustang. The bar is well made and very lightweight. (Photo courtesy Central Coast Mustang)

Panhard bar is a good street piece that can be bolted on or welded in. When using this Panhard bar in competition, it is imperative that the horizontal alignment be correct or the bolt-on axle bracket will be overstressed and break. Fabrication of an axle bracket that provides accurate horizontal alignment (at racing weight and ride height) is a given. This is not unique to this bar. High-performance components from all manufacturers that are designed for the general public as "one size fits all" are always a compromise. It is a good piece. Just understand the limitations.

with either stock, Koni or Monroe shocks and struts, and lower the car 1-1/2 inches. Recent testing of their package produced a ride that was substantially smooth and comfortable, with exceptional cornering ability for the street.

J. BITTLE PERFORMANCE
7149-C Mission Gorge Rd.
San Diego, CA 92120
(619) 560-2030

One of the first companies to develop high-performance chassis components

for the Fox Mustangs was J. Bittle American (now called J. Bittle Performance). Bittle's background racing the Shelby and Boss 302 Mustangs has been applied to the development of their late-model suspension packages. Like most high-performance chassis shops, Bittle's packages are the standard struts, springs, swaybars, bushings and braces that provide relief for the highly compromised Mustang chassis.

Bittle uses national brand components or has them manufactured to his specifications. With the exception of weld-on subframe connectors, no special tools are required to install the Bittle suspension packages. Custom racing applications can be ordered in pre-assembled packages that will bolt in without special skills, but of course the cost is substantially higher.

SALEEN PERFORMANCE PARTS
3080 29th Street
Long Beach, CA 90806
(800) 888-8945

Unless you were born last night, you have heard about or seen a Saleen Mustang. These cars are the modern-day Shelby Mustang. Saleen Performance Parts sells complete Saleen Mustang suspension, brake and aero packages that are home-garage friendly. Until recently,

BBK PERFORMANCE
1611 Railroad Street
Corona, CA 91720
(909) 735-8880

BBK has gained quite a following with the bolt-on performance street crowd. Their subframe connectors, strut tower brace, g-load brace and Panhard bar are easy to install, designed to be either bolted or welded in. No special tools are required. They also manufacture their own specific and progressive rate coil springs, which are well-tuned for streetable high-performance handling

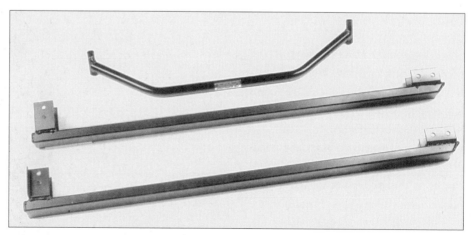

BBK Performance makes their own braces and connectors on-site. All kits are easy to bolt-in or weld in place, and like others, improve chassis stiffness considerably. The g-load brace shown here has been replaced with a newer, four-point unit. (Photo courtesy BBK Performance)

the Saleen suspension packages were just too stiff for anything but Daytona International Speedway. Fortunately, the newer kits have springs that are better suited for the average driver on normal streets.

The quality of the Saleen components is as good as it gets and the fit is excellent. The downside is the cost. There's an added premium for the name, but the quality is there, so you'll be getting what you pay for.

KENNY BROWN PERFORMANCE
8549 Lake Street
Omaha, NE 68134
(402) 391-3558

Kenny Brown is a legend among chassis freaks. He has drawn on his extensive racing experience and developed some of the most well-balanced suspension packages available for the Fox Mustang. The Trackit Plus II Panhard Kit is the only Panhard bar sold that actually addresses the anti-squat problem of the Mustang. Sold in staged packages, Kenny Brown's AGS Systems (Advanced Geometry Suspension) can change your car from mild to wild.

If you are looking for racing suspension geometry, Kenny Brown will be more than happy to assemble one of his modified front crossmembers and racing rear chassis sets for you. Going fast cost big bucks, so don't forget the trunk full of money.

Sold as separate components or complete packages, the Kenny Brown Performance Parts kits are well engineered. No special skills are required to install the kits and the standard Craftsman 102-piece tool set and hand-drill will get you there. The only hassle can be in the installation of the Trackit Panhard bar. Due to the manufacturing tolerances of the stock axle housing, the axle housing/trailing arm brackets will generally require hand fitting with a big mill file and a lot of patience.

If you intend to race your Mustang, you will want to fabricate an additional brace for the Trackit Panhard bar. Under racing conditions, the brace to the trunk floor has a tendency to tear out. The kit works pretty well on the street but the floorpan mount is not adequate for racing type side loads. A 1.25" x .090" wall 4130N tube brace should be welded to the frame bracket, just above the horizontal bar attachment point, up to the frame on the opposite side. This modification goes beyond the bolt-on criteria of this chapter. However, unless you are using a purchased or fabricated anti-squat bracket, this Panhard bar will significantly improve the rear suspension geometry and tire bite, so this ounce of prevention is worth it.

BAER RACING
3108 W. Thomas Rd., Ste. 1201
Phoenix, AZ 85017
(602) 233-1411

Not since the days of rented Shelby Mustangs has anyone accomplished so much on a shoestring budget. If you are a road racing Mustang enthusiast, the sight of the Baer Racing Mustang sitting on the pole of a World Challenge race (with factory-backed ZR-1 Corvettes, twin-turbo Nissans and turbo Porsches gridded behind it) is a religious experience. This Mustang really handles. Fortunately, Baer Racing has developed some excellent suspension packages for the serious "g" junkie. Complete modified crossmembers, shortened struts, and a very trick three-link rear suspension setup are available from Baer as well as mega-brake systems. Make no mistake about it, Baer's components are for serious use only. In addition, Baer Racing has complete racing suspension packages that will make your Mustang handle well beyond the 1 g threshold.

Installation of the Baer Racing kits is on par with all the major performance chassis sets. Simple hand tools and a coil spring compressor will complete the job. The new three-link suspension is a very slick setup that is also a bolt-in affair. This is the best handling system available for the Fox Mustang, bar none. Unlike the racing version used on their World Challenge Mustang, it does not eliminate the rear seat. The three-link kit comes with a very stout Panhard bar and the price is very reasonable. The improvement over the four-link system is well worth the cost for the individual wanting "white knuckle" handling.

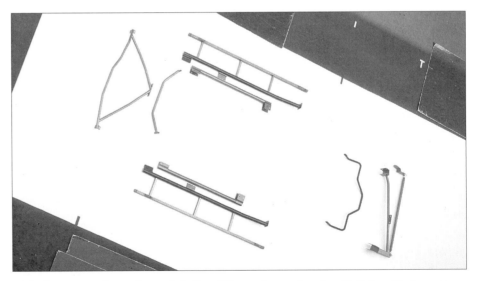

Major improvements can be made in the stiffness of your chassis with Saleen Performance Parts. Shown here are various individual components (no complete kits are available) that comprise the Saleen chassis bracing system. (Photo courtesy Saleen Performance Parts)

The Kenny Brown Performance Products AGS System 4.1 shown is a well-crafted, balanced kit that provides the bolt-on enthusiast with corrected rear suspension geometry and near race car performance. (Photo courtesy Kenny Brown Performance Products)

SVO FORD MOTORSPORT
Tech Line: (313) 337-1356

A complete suspension package is not available from Ford Motor Co. The Ford purist can combine the following Ford and Motorsports parts to achieve a reasonably well-handling Mustang. The parts listed are necessary to upgrade a typical 1979 to 1993 Mustang. Obviously if your car is equipped with a part that is listed, replacement will not be necessary.

1993 Cobra-R Springs or Ford Motorsport Super Sport for a softer ride M5300-C

1993 Cobra-R swaybars or stock GT 1.31" front bar and 1987/88 Lincoln LSC rear bar E4LY-5A772-D

1985–'86 GT Mustang #2 Crossmember

1987–'88 V8 T-Bird control arms (1994 GT Mustang) E7SZ-3078-A & E7SZ-3079-A

1994 GT Mustang spindles

1984–'86 SVO Mustang lower rear trailing arms, E2BZ-5A649-A

Ford Motorsport upper trailing arms, M5500-A

Ford Motorsport Koni struts, M18124-G606

Ford Motorsport Koni shocks, M18125-G603

1984–'86 SVO Mustang onion head strut mounts, D8BZ-18A161-B

1990–'93 tie rods, F0ZZ-3A130-A

Ford Motorsport subframe connectors, M5478-B

Ford Motorsport strut tower brace, M20201-A50

1987–'93 convertible rocker panel reinforcements E6ZZ-66102B66-A, E6ZZ-66102B67-A

Ford Motorsport underbody brace kit M5024-A

With the exception of the convertible rocker panel reinforcements, all the parts listed are bolt-on and require no special skills. The installation of the rocker reinforcements will require you to rent a

Marson "Big Daddy Riveter" and drill about a million 1/4" holes for the rivets. Although it is a time-consuming process, these braces will dramatically improve the structural rigidity of your Mustang.

The 1985-'86 #2 crossmember is used to allow the use of the longer T-Bird or '94 Mustang control arms. On the pre-'87 Mustangs, this will increase the front track width 1.5" and may cause some tire-to-fender interference with tires that are larger than 24.5" in diameter. Use the hammer. It's worth it. On the '87-'93 Mustangs, this setup will increase the front track width .5" and should present no problems in clearance, especially on the '90-'93 Mustang with the wider fenders.

SUMMARY

Improving the handling of your Mustang can be accomplished in your driveway over a weekend with a package from any of the companies discussed. Generally the thickness of your wallet will be the deciding factor. Everyone

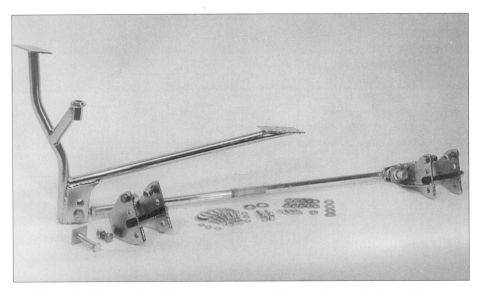

For those individuals wanting to improve rear suspension compliance, the Kenny Brown Trackit Plus II kit is an ideal choice. This kit not only includes a Panhard bar, but it also lowers the bottom trailing arm pickup to provide much needed anti-squat. (Photo courtesy Kenny Brown Performance Products)

claims to have the ultimate setup. The truth of the matter is, they are all compromises when it comes to bolt-on stuff. For the handling enthusiast going the bolt-on route, the less expensive approach is to upgrade your stock suspension with springs, dampeners and braces. More aggressive handling means torque arm, anti-squat rear geometry or a three-link and modified crossmembers. Obviously, the skill level for installation increases and more bucks will be required.

Regardless of which package you decide on, your car will not show appreciable improvement in handling without good tires. Fat, sticky tires mounted on the correct width wheels will make a dramatic difference even on ill-handling cars, so plan for them in your budget.

If you are upgrading your suspension in stages, do it in the following sequence:

1. Stiffen the chassis. Strut tower brace, g-load brace and subframe connectors are the minimum. Rocker panel braces and a four-point roll bar should be considered.

2. Upgrade the suspension bushings. Urethane or aluminum, control arm,

swaybar, strut and trailing arm bushings are a must.

3. Fat, sticky tires and wheels should go on next.

4. Springs, swaybars and dampeners. Do not make the mistake of installing stiff springs without upgrading your struts and shocks. Without the valving to

dampen the stronger springs your car's handling will be unpredictable and you will probably ruin your front tires. The same holds true for installing racing type dampeners on soft springs. Too aggressive dampening will not allow the suspension to rebound correctly.

5. Modified crossmember and rear suspension kits. This is for the person wanting to build a silk purse from the sow's ear.

The most important point to remember when modifying your car with bolt-on suspension kits is *balance*. The handling improvements to your car will be far more satisfying if you stick to the recommended combinations of the company you have chosen. Recognize your limitations, both skill and budgetary. The suspension combinations that are packaged by the major shops have been developed and tested to work in harmony. Combining bits and pieces from various shops without the skill to select the correct combinations can be disastrous. ∎

The Ford Motor Co. convertible rocker panel braces are an adequate substitute for the street/autocross enthusiast who does not have access to a welder or cannot install subframe connectors due to class rules. These braces are glued on with structural adhesive and then riveted with a crate full of 1/4" pop rivets.

BRAKES

8

Whether you are a corner racer or a straight-line addict, brakes are very important to a successful run. If you cannot brake hard enough to control your speed at the end of a straight, you'll have to lift sooner to negotiate the turn. Obviously your lap times will suffer. To the drag racer, being able to stop at the end of the quarter on some tracks can mean the difference between clean underwear and a smelly situation. The increasing popularity of clubs renting race tracks to allow their members and guests to test their machines has made the need for better brakes even more critical. A typical Sunday at Texas World Speedway harassing the Porsche Club will clearly demonstrate the limits of the stock brakes on your 'Stang. Lastly, there is a need for superior, safe braking capability on the street, especially if your Mustang has been modified.

STOCK BRAKE SYSTEMS

The stock brakes on the Mustang fall into five groups: 10" rotor systems, post-'86 11" rotors, the four-wheel discs on the 1993 Cobra Mustang, the four-wheel disc system found on the SVO Mustang, and the four-wheel disc system found on the 1994 Mustang. The Mustangs with the 10" rotors are a joke for autocrossing or road racing. The pre-'87 Mustangs and non-GT/LX 5.0 cars

In 1993, Ford's SVT (Special Vehicle Team) group released the 1993 Cobra Mustang, utilizing the standard 11" front brakes in conjunction with the Motorsport M2300-C 10" rear disc setup. This is a well-balanced braking system that, when combined with quality pads, will provide good brakes for street and autocrossing action.

Is this scary or what? This is a graphic example of why the stock Mustang brakes are inadequate for high-performance use. Those cracks are an accident waiting to happen.

with 10" rotors in the front and the microscopic drums and shoes in the rear are adequate for stopping a VW Beetle at best. Experience in Showroom Stock racing and a deafening outcry from performance buffs convinced Ford to upgrade the front rotors to approximately 11" in 1987. This was a major improvement.

Four-Wheel Discs

Four–wheel disc systems first appeared on the 1984 SVO Mustang. This system, with 11" rotors, was transplanted from the '82-'83 Lincoln Continental. Prior to the 1994 Mustang, these brakes were the best factory system available for the Mustang. In 1993, Ford's SVT (Special Vehicle Team) group released the 1993 Cobra Mustang, utilizing the standard 11" front brakes in conjunction with the Motorsport M2300–C 10" rear disc setup. This is a well-balanced braking system that, when combined with quality pads, will provide good brakes for street and autocrossing action.

The long-awaited 1994 Mustang is built with standard 11" rotors and solid disc 10" rear rotors. Ford engineers say these brakes are mounted to a new spindle that has been designed to reduce

steering axis inclination to 13.5°. Basically, these brakes are the same as the post-'86 front brakes, and the rears are a new solid disc type. But the best brakes can be found on the '93 Cobra R model and perhaps the proposed 13.5" front, 12" rear brakes on the '94 version. This four-wheel disc setup includes 13.1" radial cooled fronts with newly designed 10.58" rears. These are absolutely outstanding brakes that can be bolted on to older Mustangs.

For the drag racer, the stock brakes will

be adequate to slow your car, even on a 9-second run. Just upgrade your disc pads to one of the high-quality sets such as those manufactured by Porterfield. For those with 10" rotors wanting a little more stopping power, upgrade your brakes to the post-'86 11" brakes as instructed in this chapter.

If you are a serious Conehead, road racer, or plan to run The Nevada Silver State Classic, then forget the stock brakes. The Mustang is capable of reaching speeds of 200 mph with the modified engine combinations currently available. When combined with a rolling weight in excess of 3,000 lbs., the stock brakes will vaporize almost instantly when subjected to speeds over 150 mph. In 1991, Richard Holdener, driving an '88 Mustang coupe, won the fall Nevada Silver State Classic. At that time his car had the best factory brakes available for the Mustang—the SVO four–wheel disc brakes and racing brake pads. When Rick tried to stop at the end of his run (while traveling 175 mph) the pads caught fire and were completely fried— and that was just one stop. The moral of the story is, if you intend to go real fast, save your nickels and buy a set of the Wilwood 12" brakes, '93-'94 Cobra R brakes or Baer Racing 13" brakes.

If improving your stock disc/drum braking capability is your goal (without the expense and hassle of the racing brake systems), then step up to the larger 73mm calipers from the SVO/Lincoln LSC brakes. Kenny Brown Performance Parts has made the job easy by offering a Club/Sport Brake Kit which includes the larger calipers, correct master cylinder, heavy-duty pads and an adjustable proportioning valve.

FRONT BRAKE UPGRADE

Parts Required:

Calipers:
'87–'93 Mustang or

'82–'83 Continental (73mm), or

'87–'88 Lincoln Mk VII LSC (73mm)

Rotors:
'87–'93 Mustang (4–lug), or

'87–'88 T–Bird (4–lug), or

'82–'83 Continental (5–lug), or

'87–'88 Lincoln Mk VII LSC (5–lug)

Spindles:
'87–'93 V8 Mustang or '94 GT Mustang if available

Brake Hoses:
'87–'93 V8 Mustang

Caliper

Bushings:
Steeda SS04

HIGH-PERFORMANCE BRAKE UPGRADES

The following procedures will guide you through the correct combinations for upgrading your brakes for high-performance use other than hard competition road racing.

Front Brake Upgrade

To upgrade a pre–'87 V8 Mustang or any of the non-V8 cars with the smaller 10" rotors to the post-'86 11" brakes, you will need the components listed in the chart above. The post–'86 brakes can be enhanced by using the larger 73mm caliper from the '82-'83 Continental, Lincoln Mark VII, or SVO Mustang. It is important to note that when upgrading your car to 11" brakes, the spindles are thinner at the strut mount on the 11" brakes and consequently require a different strut.

There are several companies that sell new take–offs of 4–lug rotors and calipers for very reasonable prices. These are generally advertised in the various Ford-themed magazines. You can also improve the heel–to–toe feel by utilizing the brake pedal from an automatic transmission-equipped Mustang.

The misalignment of the caliper to the rotor causes the disc pads to wear unevenly. You should replace your soft stock pieces with the stainless steel bushings sold by Steeda. They will significantly improve the feel and function of the stock calipers. Or, if you have the necessary fabricating skills and equipment, you can make your own (see Fig. 8-1, p. 140).

Rear Disc Brake Upgrade

Installing rear disc brakes can be achieved by installing one of the Ford M2300–C (4–lug) or M2300–F (5–lug) kits on your Mustang. However, calling around to the salvage yards for the rear disc brakes from an '82–'83 Lincoln Continental (11"), T–Bird Turbo Coupe, '87–'88 Lincoln Mark VII LSC, or the rare SVO can provide brakes at a reduced cost. You will need the parts listed in the chart on p. 132 to make the installation complete.

When buying disc brake systems from a salvage yard, always check the thickness of the rotors with a vernier caliper or micrometer. Be sure it is within the factory minimum standard as noted on the inside of the rotor. Also check the rotational play on the axles and the axle splines carefully. Worn or twisted splines means they will have to be replaced soon.

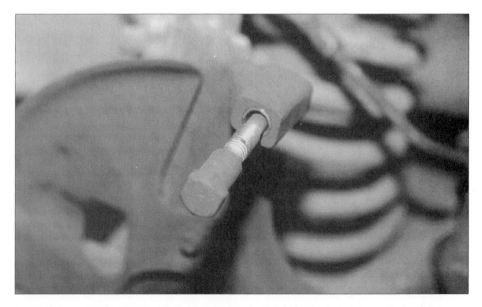

A mandatory modification to stock front brakes is the replacement of the rubber caliper guides with a set of stainless steel bushings. The factory rubber bushings have a tendency to allow the caliper to cock sideways under heavy braking reducing their efficiency. These bushings are available from several sources or can be machined from Fig. 8-1.

Upgrading to rear disc brakes can be achieved with one of the Stainless Steel Brake kits. Pictured here is a nearly complete installation being fitted to Curt Rich's National Rally Champion Mustang. The rigid stainless steel line to the caliper makes caliper service a real pain.

If you can't pony up the money for a rear disc swap, then SVO's five-lug rotors and axle/drum kits will add strength and increase your choice of wheels. The kit uses the stock brakes and installs with no special tools. (Photo courtesy BBK Performance)

Rear Disc Brake Upgrade

Parts Required:

Calipers

Caliper Mounting Brackets

Rotors

Axles

All brake lines and hoses attached to the axle housing

Emergency Brake Cables

Master Cylinder (E25Y–2140–A)

SVO Proportioning Valve (E4ZZ–2B257–A) or:

Motorsport M2328–A or M2328–C Adjustable Proportioning Valve

Rear Axle lube, Motorsport Friction Modifier M19546–A, and silicone sealer

Optional:
    SVO or Automatic Transmission Brake Pedal (E4ZZ–2455–A), and Automatic Transmission Brake Pedal Pad (E1BZ–2457–B)

The old and the new. Pictured here is a comparison of the SVO Mustang stamped-steel rear caliper bracket and the current factory bracket.

Under severe braking conditions the caliper brackets will bend and twist, especially the stamped steel brackets. This affects braking efficiency considerably. The best thing to do is fabricate braces from strips of 3/16" steel that weld to the axle housing tube. The strip should have a bolt hole on the other end and extend to the caliper bracket where it is sandwiched between the caliper mounting bolt and the bracket (see Fig. 8-2, p. 142).

RACING BRAKES

The quality of brakes on your Mustang is directly proportional to the size of your bank account. Adequate brakes can be assembled using factory parts for high–performance street or autocrossing. However, no matter how hard you drive on the street or at an autocross event, there is no comparison to the demands made on your brakes on a road racing course. With the exception of the new Cobra-R model brakes, nothing the factory offers, not even the excellent SVO brakes, will hold up under the abuses of a race track. High-quality pads and brake fluid will allow you to run hard briefly before the calipers and rotors are burned up. The only cure is the Wilwood or Baer Racing Kits. Although JFZ makes excellent calipers and rotors, they do not offer bolt-on bracketry for the Mustang.

The process of upgrading to the Baer Racing or the Wilwood brakes is not a simple bolt-on job. You can expect to spend the better part of a weekend installing these kits. Even if you buy the complete brake line and hose kit, it is still a very involved procedure. On the front you will have to cut the factory caliper mounting tangs off and drill out the backing plate holes and tap them to accept the new caliper mounting bracket

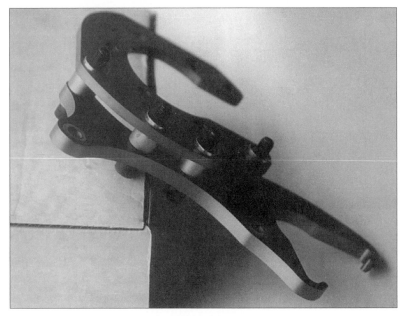

Aluminum rear caliper brackets or the stamped-steel SVO Mustang units flex considerably under severe use. If you are experiencing this problem follow Fig. 8-2 and fabricate braces to eliminate the flex.

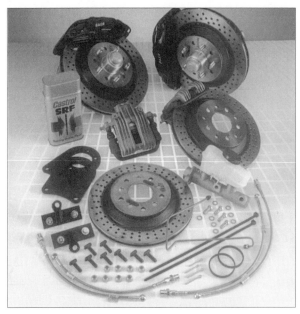

The Baer Racing 13" front brake kits are absolutely outstanding. These kits come completely assembled on the spindles incorporating very rigid caliper mounts that are welded to the spindles. Stopping your Mustang with a set of these is truly a religious experience.

when installing the Wilwood kit. Since the Mustang spindle is 4000 series steel, cutting and tapping are very difficult. Most inexperienced mechanics will break at least one tap off in a spindle and immediately go to a full Defcon 5 panic. If you cannot fish it out the safest thing to do is take it to a professional machine shop and have them tap it out or remove it with a torch.

On the rear you must install some sort of C–Clip eliminator to stabilize the axles. The in-and-out movement associated with the C–clip secured axle will drive the pads back into the caliper, preventing proper braking action or even causing the rotors to rub against the caliper body. In this state, essentially you end up with expensive non-functioning rear brakes.

The easiest method to get a set of double throw-down brakes is to install the 13" brakes from the '93-'94 Cobra R Mustang. These are super brakes and the '94 spindle has only 13.5° of steering axis inclination compared to the older models. Unfortunately, it may take a while to find one in salvage, and I'm sure the cost of purchasing them from a Ford dealer is prohibitive. It is also pretty unlikely the production pieces will be as light as the Wilwood or Baer aluminum calipers and rotors with the aluminum hats.

One of the great advancements in technology that has come from the space program is the hard surfacing process for friction surfaces. This process involves bombarding a spinning brake rotor with particles of tungsten, chromium or titanium to create a surface so hard and resistant to wear (90c Rockwell hardness) it must be machined with a diamond cutting wheel. Essentially the process involves spraying these particles,

Wilwood Engineering offers everything from a street package kit that maintains the basic factory wheelbase to the custom assembled and exotic setups for the serious drag or road racer. Shown here is the heavy-duty rear disc street package with the emergency brake caliper to keep it legal.

The Wilwood front brakes (12.19" rotors shown) are outstanding brakes for stopping your Mustang. If you are installing this setup with the heavy-duty hubs, you will find your wheels are offset outboard an additional 3/4" over the stock width. This can require a different offset wheel if you are running the 8+" widths.

The difficulty of a non-factory front brake upgrade has always been how to mount the front caliper. When installing the Wilwood 12" or 13" brakes, the factory caliper mounts must be cut off and the shield retainer bolt holes drilled and tapped for larger bolts. Ford spindles are made from 4000 series steel (chrome-moly), so expect this modification to take quite a while.

at about Mach 6, using a high-velocity oxygen-feed nozzle at a temperature of 4,000°F. The end result is a rotor that will outlive conventional racing pads and significantly extend the period between replacement. This is the trick deal for metal rotors. Turbine Metal Technologies in Burbank, California, is where to get them.

Brake Pads

There are a couple thousand brake pad and shoe manufacturers in the world. Every auto parts store and brake shop sells national name-brand sets as well as house brands. Generally speaking, the house brands are unreliable for road racing use. Stay with nationally known brands like Raybestos, Porterfield, Braketech, Ford Motorsport, etc. If, however, you are driving a hot street machine that sees duty on the drag strip or autocross circuit, the less expensive house brand metallic or semi–metallic sets will generally provide good service and are very reasonably priced. Typically you can buy five sets of the house brands for what a set of the competition pads go for.

Selection—When selecting a pad, it is important to recognize the balance between hardness, average stopping speeds and rotor life. The less expensive national brand semi–metallic replacement pads sold by most auto parts stores will generally have good stopping ability without significant wear on the rotors. But the pads themselves wear quickly, so keep a close eye on them.

The metallic pads sold under the "Heavy Duty" label are generally excellent pads for serious street and

If stopping your Mustang from triple-digit speeds is part of your driving experience, then 13" rotors are the only way to go. Shown here is the Baer Racing installation of "real brakes," which utilize huge 12.95" drilled rotors and the famous PBR calipers.

When installing a rear disc kit you will save yourself the pleasure of pulling an axle again (replacing the seal you cut) by taking your time. Always handle the axle with a firm grip, gliding it slowly from the tube, carefully avoiding contact between the axle and the seal, especially the axle splines.

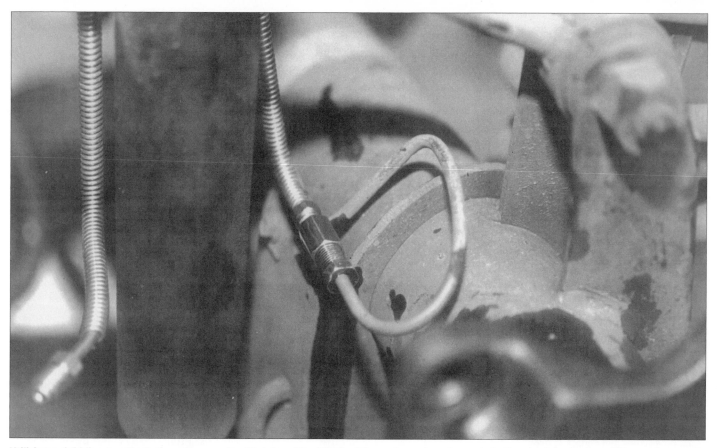

Utilizing a rigid line to attach the caliper on the Stainless Steel Brake kit requires a loop be made in the stock brake line. This can be a real pain for an amateur. Again, use the correct tubing bender and take your time.

autocross competition. They do wear the rotors much faster but have better fade resistance. Some of the competition metallic pads provide outstanding stopping ability from warp speeds;

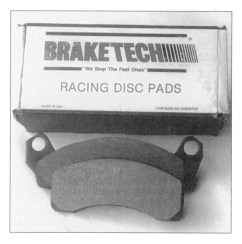

If you are using stock brakes, the effectiveness of your brakes under racing conditions boils down to quality of the brake pads. High-quality pads, like the BrakeTech pieces shown here, can dramatically improve the stopping ability of the factory brakes.

however, they will wear the rotors out very quickly. We tested a set of hard carbon metallic pads from a top brake kit manufacturer on the *Slot Car Mustang* in an open track event at Texas World Speedway. The pads offered excellent stopping ability when brought up to temperature with no fade whatsoever. However, after 40 laps the Wilwood rotors were worn so thin the brakes were unsafe. Very expensive lesson.

The point is to know the parameters of your driving needs. Hard racing-type pads provide impressive fade resistance when properly bedded in. However, given the average racer's budget and the common use of standard cast-iron rotors, these pads just don't make sense. If you are an autocrosser stick with the faster-wearing metallic or semi–metallic pads. They will come up to temperature quickly and provide good stopping power in the short span of a typical run. They will also prolong the life of your

rotors. By far the best approach is to install a complete set of good metallic pads already bedded in the night before you go racing and remove them when it's over for the next event.

Running stock brakes on a road racing car limits your choice to the harder pads. Without pads that can provide quick deceleration you will spend longer periods on the brakes, which means slower lap times. You will also transfer more heat to the calipers and consequently you may boil the brake fluid. The obvious trade-off is the excessive wear on the rotors. Unfortunately this is one of the costs of racing. Obviously learning to manage the brakes is one of the keys to being a successful driver.

Tempering Pads—Before installing pads it is important to heat-temper them. This is best done in the outback (they smell bad) with an old toaster oven. Put the pads in face up and leave them for at

135

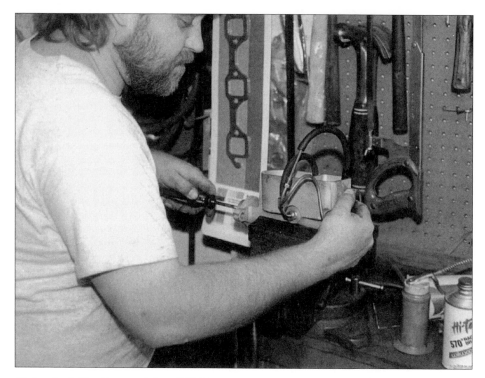

Before installing the mandatory SVO Mustang master cylinder for rear disc installation, bench bleed it. To do this rig lines from the outlets of the master cylinder to the reservoir, then slowly and repeatedly depress the piston until all of the air has been purged. Howard Duffy of Heavy Duty Racing demonstrates this procedure with a simple arrangement rigged from brake lines and neoprene hoses.

least 30 minutes, preferably one hour, and let cool. Be sure your toaster is not within several feet of anything flammable as it will get pretty hot. Also, if you're smart, don't use your wife's toaster—not unless you prefer sleeping on the couch.

Bedding Pads—If you are installing new pads on new rotors, it is important that the rotors be bedded in with the pads to be used. Never install a set of heat-tempered or previously bedded pads on new rotors. They will eat right through the new rotors before they are heat-tempered and you'll be spending bucks for a new set.

The proper way to bed new pads and rotors is to make a series of high-speed hard stops, preferably in a safe, controlled environment like a race track (your local Main Street is not a good place). When the pedal begins to fade, stop and let the brakes cool. The brakes should be ready for action after they have completely cooled.

Brake Components

Pushrod—Check the adjustment on the pushrod protruding from the brake booster before installing the SVO type master cylinder on a newer model Mustang. Adjust the length as necessary to achieve approximately a .010" clearance. Too much clearance and the brake pedal will have excessive travel before engaging the master cylinder piston. If the pushrod is adjusted too long, the brakes will drag and lock up. This is a pain but necessary when installing the master cylinder for four–wheel discs. Always check your fit with the engine running. You should be able to feel a small amount of movement at the pedal before the pushrod contacts the master cylinder piston, when everything is cold.

Master Cylinder—Before installing the master cylinder, always *bench-bleed* it before installing it on the car. This is done by running brake lines from the outlets on the master cylinder to the fluid

chambers on top. These lines should be well into the chambers so they will remain below the fluid level at all times. Clamp the master cylinder in a vise and fill the chambers with fluid. Slowly pump and release the piston with a long punch until air no longer exits the lines as you pump. This will ensure there is no air trapped between the pistons that could make it impossible to bleed properly.

Brake Lines—If you are competing in a road racing class, substitute steel-braided Teflon lines for the factory brake hoses to improve pedal feel and feedback. Oftentimes the driver will complain of a long or spongy pedal, especially in a fast autocross event. Everyone scrambles to bleed the air that somehow managed to get in the system at the last second only to find the sponge gremlin returns again toward the end of the next run. Many times the problem is caused by expansion of the stock brake hoses under intense braking pressure after being softened by hot brake fluid. The average Mustang will lock up ordinary tires with about 600 lbs-in. of line pressure on the street. However, it is not uncommon to see brake pressures upwards of 1,600 lbs-in. under severe racing conditions. With these kinds of pressures the stock hoses will not function properly. The steel-braided Teflon pieces are the only way to go. Always use #3 lines. Using incorrect I.D. lines screws up the hydraulics and the differential braking.

Be sure you remove the rubber dust shields on the calipers for severe competition. These things will catch fire under racing conditions or melt around the piston, causing it to drag or freeze up. Not good.

Brake Valve—An adjustable brake proportioning valve should be installed on any car that is competing in autocross or road racing. The best location is on the driveshaft tunnel inside the car within easy reach of the driver. This is done by either running lines through the driveshaft tunnel from the proportioning valve and splicing into the brake line running to the rear axle, or preferably, by fabricating new one-piece lines from the proportioning valve to the factory proportioning valve and rear axle flexible line. Drill 5/16" holes through the tunnel or floorpan to pass the brake lines through, then fit MS35489-4 (AN931-3-5) synthetic rubber grommets to prevent chafing. Certain racing classes do not permit brake bias to be adjusted from the cockpit. If this is your situation, just install the adjustable proportioning valve in place of the brass coupling located just above the A/C dryer on the right side of the engine compartment.

Fluid Recirculators—Brake fluid recirculators are an excellent way to manage fluid boiling problems in a road-race car. These systems constantly circulate the fluid that is normally trapped in the calipers, back to the brake reservoirs to improve cooling. Because of the improved cooling, the brake pedal is constantly firm. These systems are trick, but expensive and will increase the cost of your braking system. However, this is the future for racing and it's available now.

When installing a non-stock master cylinder, particularly an SVO Mustang unit, it is necessary to adjust the length of the power brake booster rod to provide about .010" end play. Failure to do this will result in the brakes dragging with ugly results.

Brake Pedal—If you are a corner racer, then you should replace your brake pedal with the SVO pedal. This is an automatic transmission-equipped Mustang brake pedal with a wide foot pad. This not only allows better heel–toe action, but the wide pedal spreads the contact pressure of your foot over a larger area so it doesn't get sore during a long race. If you have to modify this pedal to better suit your driving style, always cold bend it. Heating with a torch will destroy the temper of the steel and the pedal will bend under hard usage. Generally this happens when you get carried away while attempting to outbrake one of your competitors and find yourself in way too deep.

Rotor Runout—It is important to check the runout on all rotors with a dial indicator, whether new or used (especially new), before racing. Although a couple of thousandths runout will keep the pads from dragging, anything over .005" will generally cause a noticeable pulsation at the pedal and a very definite reduction in braking efficiency. This becomes particularly noticeable at speeds when your brakes are working the hardest.

When having your rotors or drums turned, it is very important that the operator of the turning lathe check the runout on the mounting shaft. These shafts have two tapered races that must seat squarely to run true. Unfortunately, when these shafts are swapped for different rotor applications, metal shavings from the previous rotors can get caught between the race and seat on these shafts and cause them to run out of round. What you end up with is a rotor that is nice and smooth but with a

Plagued by that low-speed squeak in the rear brakes? Check the axle-to-rotor fit for the telltale bright interference circle inside your rotor. Oftentimes there is not enough chamfer on the edge of the axle to allow for a flat fit.

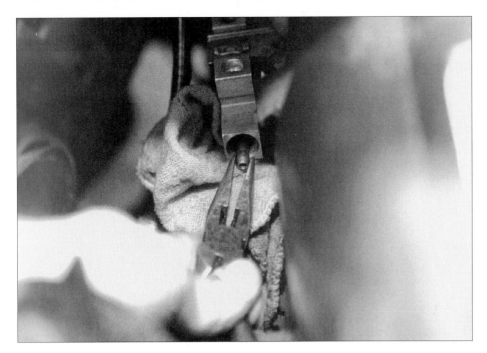

Unless you are using the factory SVO Mustang proportioning valve (E4ZZ-2B257-A) with your rear disc conversion, it will be necessary to remove the spring, spring cup and seal from your stock proportioning valve for proper braking bias.

distinctive wobble, requiring more turning to correct. Additionally, on most rotor-turning lathes, there is a small set-screw that adjusts the side–to–side tension on the mount for the rotor cutting head. If that screw is not snug the cutting heads can shift around, causing the cut surface to be out of true. Also not good. These are small things that can cause a pretty unpleasant brake pedal feel, not to mention the hassle and expense of removing the rotors and having them turned again.

Cutting Pads & Shoes—The brake pads and shoes, if applicable, should have slots cut perpendicular to the direction of the rotor or drum rotation. This is to allow the hot gases generated by the friction material under severe braking conditions to escape quickly. Without these the pads can actually be held away from the rotor or drum by a thick layer of gas. Obviously, braking efficiency goes in the toilet. Generally, a hacksaw is used to cut these grooves to a depth of about 2/3 of the way through the pad or shoe's friction material. Spacing these grooves about 1-1/2" apart is sufficient.

Fluid Boiling—If you are having brake fluid boiling problems and the brake fluid recirculator system is out of your budget, you can reduce the heat transferred to the brake fluid by fitting stainless steel shields inside the calipers. These will provide a reflective surface to radiate heat away from the caliper. Make a pattern that will fit inside your calipers, behind the pads, with a hole for the pistons. Trace the pattern onto a piece of 304 stainless steel. Cut the shields out

and polish any signs of cutting marks as well as the exterior surface. This will reduce cracking and provide a more reflective surface. Fit the shields inside the calipers and re–install the pads. (These shields are standard issue on many Japanese cars and trucks.)

Front brake cooling ducts that fit the GT Mustang can be purchased from the Shelby American Auto Club. These are well-designed, molded plastic ducts that fit inside the fog light holes.

Fluid—Finally, unless you have the mega-dollars to flush the system completely every time the car goes to the track, do not use silicone brake fluid, and definitely do not use it on the street. This stuff sucks moisture like regular fluid but does not keep it suspended. Instead, moisture in silicone brake fluid pools and vaporizes into a large spongy steam pocket as the temperature of the fluid passes water's boiling point. Brake pedal feel becomes spongy and the differential braking gets weird. Then, when the race car sits for a couple of weeks until the next race, that pooled water creates a nice rusty pit inside the brake line, caliper or master cylinder where it happens to settle. Again a most uncool situation. Stay with the Ford Heavy Duty brake fluid.

To ensure a proper fit between the axle and rotor, use a mill file or high-speed sander to increase the chamfer on the edge of the axle.

BLEEDING BRAKES

It is imperative that you bleed any air that may have entered your brake system. This is particularly important if you have disconnected any lines for any installation or repairs. It is also recommended that you bleed them prior to any competitive event. The following is a basic brake bleeding procedure.

1. Acquire one quart of Ford's Heavy Duty Brake Fluid.

2. Remove the master cylinder's lid and use a suction bulb to remove all the residual brake fluid.

3. Clean any yuk remaining in the master cylinder with Brake–Kleen.

4. Refill the master cylinder with the Ford Heavy Duty brake fluid and return the lid immediately. Always screw the cap on the brake fluid can tightly when closing. Brake fluid acts like a sponge and draws moisture from the air. Moisture is very uncool in brake systems.

5. Fill a glass quart jar with 1/2" of brake fluid.

6. Attach a 3/16" vacuum hose to the bleeder screw, starting with the wheel farthest from the master cylinder (the rear wheel opposite the side with the brake line splitting block on the housing) and emerge the open end in the brake fluid in the jar.

7. Have someone slowly pump the pedal to build pressure and hold.

8. Open the bleeder screw and release air and fluid into the jar. Close the bleeder screw when the pedal has been depressed to the floor and before the pedal is released. Be sure to keep the hose firmly attached to the bleeder screw to reduce the possibility of compromising the system.

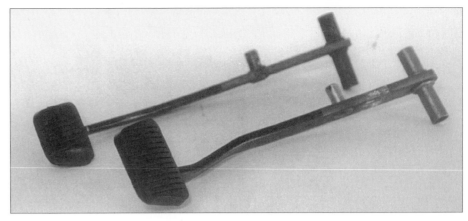

Installing an SVO Mustang brake pedal, shown here below the stock unit, is one of the simplest and least expensive improvements you can make to your Mustang's stock braking system. This pedal is manufactured using the larger automatic transmission foot pad with a placement that provides better heel-toe brake control.

9. Repeat this process twice and move to the other rear wheel, then the right front and finally the left front, following the same procedure each time. Refill the master cylinder before and after bleeding the front brakes.

10. Empty the spent brake fluid from the jar and refill with 1/2" of new fluid.

11. Start the process over, except this time bleed each wheel until there are no more air bubbles and only clear fluid emerges. Don't forget to keep a watchful eye on the fluid level in the master cylinder. If you let it run dry you'll have to start over.

12. When you have completed the process, fill and close the master cylinder and clean any brake fluid spill on the floor or tires before proceeding. This stuff will ruin tires and sneakers, so clean well.

13. Discard any brake fluid that was not used. Once you open a can of brake fluid it must be used immediately or discarded. ■

Drag racing brakes slow the car down over a longer distance than a road-race car. Consequently, calipers and rotors can be substantially lighter when limited to this purpose.

Caliper Bushing

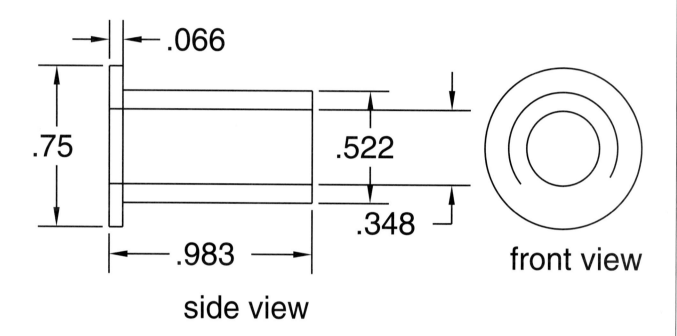

.066

.75

.522

.348

.983

side view

front view

Materials:
(4) .75" Stainless steel rod, 1" long   45° view

Fig. 8-1

Rear Caliper Mount
Reinforcement

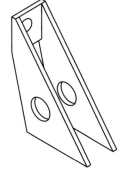

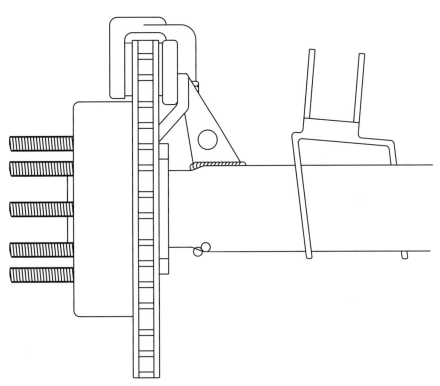

O.D.+0.010" of Caliper
Mounting Bolt

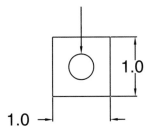

1.0

1.0

Bolt Flange
.125" Mild Steel
(2 req'd)

Offset to clear
axle flange and
bolts

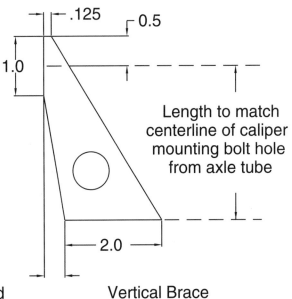

.125

0.5

1.0

Length to match
centerline of caliper
mounting bolt hole
from axle tube

2.0

Vertical Brace
.125" Mild Steel
(4 req'd)

Fig. 8-2

WHEELS & TIRES

9

The correct selection and combination of wheels and tires are vital to the success of your Mustang. Obvious, right? Unfortunately, the combinations that are typically seen on the Mustang just don't get the job done. The proper matching of wheel width, size and offset to the tire is absolutely necessary. A fat, sticky tire mounted on a narrow wheel will provide significantly less usable tire contact than a narrow tire on the correct wheel width. To the corner racer, a tire with a section width that is too wide for the wheel being used not only means less usable tire patch on the track, but also considerable sidewall flex. That excessive sidewall flex translates into overheated tires, understeer and the need to run excessive negative camber to compensate for the tire rolling under. The results are less than optimum handling.

The same principle applies to the drag racer trying to run a slick that is too wide for the wheel being used. If the wheel is narrow, there will be excessive sidewall deflection, and the tire could spin on the rim, even when screwed down. The real problem, however, is the tendency of the slick to concave in the middle during the launch as weight is transferred, reducing the contact patch. Couple this with the unstable launch that can occur as the sidewalls flex laterally, and things can go bad quickly. The resulting excessive

Running tires that are the correct width for the wheels you are using is critical to optimum performance. Faster lap times will result when running a smaller tire that fits the wheel rather than a larger tire that flexes too much and rolls under. (Photo by John Hafemeister)

This set of M&H Streetmasters demonstrates how not to get the maximum benefit from your tires. These 275-15 tires are mounted on wheels that are too narrow, requiring abnormally low air pressure to correct the footprint. You'll get poor traction at best.

lateral flexing can cause unequal weight distribution and consequently left-to-right traction. The end result is a tendency to move out of the groove to the sides where no rubber has been laid down. This exaggerates the left-to-right traction differential and the car heads sideways. As previously mentioned, running into your competitor's lane or the concrete retaining wall is considered most uncool.

TIRE BASICS

Before we address the specific limits of the Mustang, it is important to understand how a tire is defined and how to calculate its minimum requirements. Every tire has a minimum recommended rim width to function adequately. Generally that is defined as a percentage of the section width. As a general rule of thumb, the 60 or 50 series tire will

Wheel Width
vs.
Tread Width

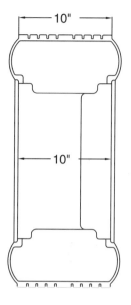

For near optimum performance, the wheel width should be at least as wide as the tire's tread. In the example above, the tire, a 275-50/16 has a tread width of approximately, 10". The wheel, a 16 x 10, provides excellent sidewall stabilization by matching the width of the tread.

Fig. 9-1

typically require a minimum rim width that is 70% of the section width, with the lower profile tires requiring about 85%. As an example, the 225/60–15 tire would require a minimum rim of 6.2" or a standard 6" to 6-1/2" wide wheel ([225 x .70]/25.4), where the 245/45–16 would require approximately an 8" rim.

To the road-racing crowd, the minimums just don't cut it. For a tire to function properly under racing conditions, it must have a minimum rim width that is equal to the width of the thread. This is a minimum. For optimum performance, the rim should be approximately 1" wider than the tread width and/or at least within 1/2" of the

Selecting a wheel for your big drag slick or road racing tire will require a width that is at least as wide as the tread for road racing and as wide as the tread for drag racing. This '85 Mustang had to be modified with tubs and a four-link Alston suspension to fit these huge 32 x 16" Goodyear slicks.

The fast 1986 CP Mustang of Doug Wille runs short but wide Goodyear road-racing slicks. The key to getting the most from these tires is the correct 10" wide wheel. Obviously some front fender modification was required to clear the lower front fender lip.

manufacturer's recommended maximum. Different tires require different sizes. Some work best with rims that are as much as 2" wider than the tread width. The wider rim is necessary to stabilize the sidewall under the severe cornering loads and maintain a flat footprint.

If you are unable to replace your wheels with the width to maximize your suspension, it is best to run the smallest diameter competition tire that fits your rim. The smaller diameter will have less sidewall flex on the small rim and therefore maintain a wider footprint on the track.

Drag racing slicks also follow the same basic principles. However, drag slicks generally have a much wider latitude than road-racing tires. For the optimum traction and launch, it is generally believed that a slick should be run on a rim as wide as the tread width. Try not to run anything less than 1" smaller than the tread width. Too narrow a rim and the footprint is not optimized, translating into slower E.T.'s.

Fitting Tires

The Mustang's narrow overall width severely limits the size of wheel and tire you can wedge in. There are three dimensions that must be considered

before determining the maximum usable tire. First, you must determine the maximum width that will fit in the fender without using a big hammer. Generally you must have at least 1/2" clearance on the sidewalls when the rim width equals the tread width. Anything less and the gap must be widened, especially on the inside at the strut. Second, the diameter of the tire is limited and will restrict the width of the tire that is usable, with the rear wheelwell being the most difficult. Finally, the scrub radius in the front will limit both diameter and width. As the centerline of the wheel moves outboard from the steering axis intersection with the road, the wider the arc the outside edge of the tread swings. When the wheel swings, it moves toward the fender lower lips. This is most prevalent along the front edge. All of these things are further complicated by the model year of the car. All cars prior to 1990 have a more narrow lower front wheel opening. Consequently, it is more difficult to use the fat series of tires on these cars without modifying the fenders.

Tire Size

Calculating the size of a tire is very straightforward. The nomenclature on modern tires provides either 5 or 6 items

of data about the tire. This can best be understood by examining a typical high-performance tire, such as the Yokohama P275/40ZR17. If you break down each of the components of the nomenclature the following information is provided:

P: This letter is for passenger car use. Had an "LT" been used it would have designated a *Light Truck* tire. Many high-performance tires don't include this at the start of their numbers.

275: The next three positions define the section width of the tire in millimeters. To convert this to inches, divide this number by the number of millimeters per inch, 25.4.

40: The next two numbers express the percentage that the height of the tire is of the section width. In this case 40%, a very low-profile tire.

Z: This position designates the speed rating of the tire. A "Z" rating is currently the highest rating accorded to a D.O.T.-approved street tire. If your car is capable of speeds in excess of 145 mph, a Z-rated tire is mandatory.

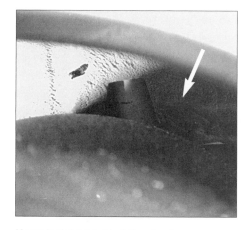

If you look just behind the shock you can see why correct wheel offset, a Panhard bar and a big hammer are necessary ingredients for achieving tire clearance. The tire rubbing may be acceptable in an autocross event but will probably cause a tire failure in a typical road race. Always correct this before running any race.

R: The eighth position tells whether the tire is Bias Belted or Radial in construction. The "R" specifies radial construction and is the standard for high–performance tires today.

17: The last two positions specify the diameter of the wheel that must be used with the tire. In this case a 17" diameter wheel.

Taking the information provided by this tire's nomenclature, the width and diameter can easily be determined. First, the section width is 275 millimeters which, when divided by the number of millimeters per inch or 25.4, converts to 10.83". Since you know from the previous discussion that the height of the tire is defined as a percentage of its section width, you simply multiply the 10.83" by 40% (positions 5 & 6 in the nomenclature), which works out to 4.33". With this information, the overall diameter of the tire can be calculated by multiplying the section height by 2 and adding the wheel diameter specified (last two positions in nomenclature). In the current example, that calculation would be (4.33" x 2) + 17 or 25.66".

Front Tires

A stock LX/GT will generally have about 16" to 16-1/2" from the frame behind the strut to the edge of the tire section, before it starts to rub on the front fender under full compression. With yellow Koni struts there is about 11" from the strut to the vertical edge of the fender. Given a minimum of 1/2" clearance between strut and fender and tire sidewall, theoretically the largest tire that would clear could not have a section width greater than 10" or 255 (on a rim of sufficient width). Ignoring the potential problem of scrub radius and given a typical tread width of 9" on a 255 tire, the maximum diameter tire that will clear from lock-to-lock is about 26" on a '90 or newer fender. The pre-'90 cars are generally limited to a 24-1/2" or 25" diameter. Given this information, you only need to calculate the section width and/or wheel diameter that is necessary to fall within the diameter restriction.

Given the limitation of the stock front fenders of the Mustang, the example Yokohama tire explained above will not clear without rubbing somewhere. Although the diameter is within the limitation of 26" on the '90 or newer LX/GT Mustang, the section width is .83" too wide. This will leave only .17" of clearance to split between both sides of the tire. Even if a 10" wheel was used, some sidewall flex will occur and the tire will contact the strut or fender. This tire is the current size allowed the Mustangs in World Challenge Professional Racing. Obviously, a big hammer has to be used on the fenders. It is also pretty common to see large gaps between the fenders and the hood where the fenders have been moved outboard to provide additional clearance. This increases aerodynamic drag, but it is a necessary evil under the rules.

Obviously, if scrub radius is excessive, the widths and diameters you can use will be limited.

Rear Tires

The rear wheelwell is about 11-3/4" to the fender lip from the inside wall. Given the minimum clearance requirement of 1/2" on each side, the maximum tire that would clear is 10.75" or a 275 section width on a 10" wide rim. The diameter that can be used on the rear without major modifications is also determined by the section width. The Mustang's inner rear fender panels have a large radius in each corner and dramatically limit the utilization of the space. With the 275 section width tire, a maximum overall diameter of approximately 25-1/2" can be used without major modifications under the

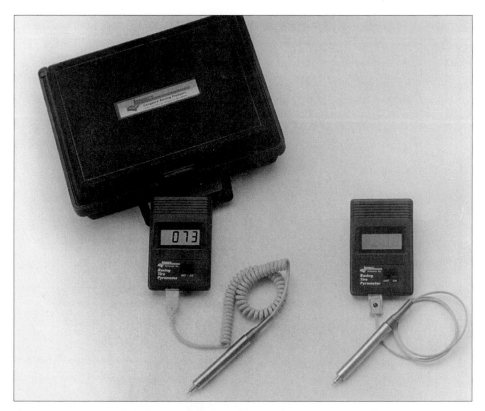

If you want to go fast it is important to have the correct suspension settings and tire pressures. The easiest way to fine tune your suspension is with a pyrometer. By reading the temperature of the tire's contact area at the inside, middle and outside you can determine if the air pressure is correct and how your suspension is working. The Longacre digital pyrometers shown here are the best direct reading units available. (Photo courtesy Longacre Racing Products)

The largest slick you can generally run under the rear fender of your Mustang without modifying the wheelwell opening is the 26 x 10-15 shown here. This size slick will require a 10" wide wheel with a 6" backspacing.

right circumstances. The Yokohama P275/40ZR17 used in the previous example could probably be used if it was mounted on a 10" wide wheel with the correct offset (5-3/4" backspacing) on a drum brake car sporting a Panhard bar, with some slight hammer work on the front and rear inner radiuses, and no dampeners or frame brackets. The most important point to catch is the mandatory wide wheel. Sidewall flex in a hard turn that causes the carcass of the tire to move away from center can only be controlled by the proper width rim. This is especially critical on the rear of the Mustang.

Unfortunately, the rear tire selection is complicated by the type of suspension used. If there is no axle locating device, such as a Panhard bar, the axle will move considerably in a hard turn, mandating at least an additional inch on the inside and probably an extra 1/2" to 3/4" on the outside. Under racing conditions, the axle can move over 1" inboard on cars without axle locating devices. Combine this with a tire mounted on the incorrect width rim and you have a disaster. This

translates into a limitation of a 245 or 235 section width tire without an axle locating device.

WHEEL OFFSETS & BACKSPACING

Now that you know how to figure the maximum usable section width and tire size, the question of offsets becomes critical. The offset of a wheel is defined as the distance the axle mounting face, as viewed through the edge, is from the parallel centerline of the wheel (see Fig. 9-2). If a wheel has its centerline behind the axle mounting face (toward the longitudinal centerline of the car) it is said to have a negative offset with the reverse being positive offset. For example, an 8" wheel would have a centerline at 4". If that centerline is 1-1/2" behind the axle mounting face, the wheel would have a 1-1/2" negative offset.

To most Mustang racers, the offset of the wheel is more clearly reflected when expressed in terms of backspacing. Unlike offset, backspacing defines the distance from the outside mounting bead to the axle mounting face. This provides real world numbers on just how far in the

wheel must go to properly fit and clear. A stock LX/GT wheel has a backspacing of approximately 4-1/4" (110mm), with the SVO wheel having a 5-1/4" (135mm) backspacing.

The SVO crossmember and long control arm provide a special front track width when measured at the wheel mounting surface on the rotors. Although 2" wider than the other Mustangs of the same model year, the SVO wheel–to–wheel mounting surface width on the rotors is only 1" wider than the post-'87 Mustangs. In order to utilize the longer Continental control arm and spindle/brakes on the SVO, Ford moved the control arm front pickup points outboard 1/8" on each side and moved the rear pickup points inboard 3/8" on each side. This reduced the control arm–to–centerline angle from 16-1/2° to 14-1/2°. The result was to swing the ball joint rearward and slightly inboard to produce the same basic spindle location as a stock GT. However, since the SVO utilizes the '82-'83 Continental spindle and rotor, the wheel mounting flange is 1/2" more outboard on each side than the '88 or newer Mustang. Had Ford not done this, it would have required a

One of the best wheels available for your Mustang is the 17" x 10" Borbet wheel from Kenny Brown Performance Products. This wheel has the correct offset and is very strong. (Photo courtesy Kenny Brown Performance Products)

Wheel Offset & Backspacing

Backspacing

The distance from the axle mounting face to the tire mounting lip of the wheel is called the wheel "backspacing". The example wheel, a 16 x 10, has a 6-3/4" backspacing.

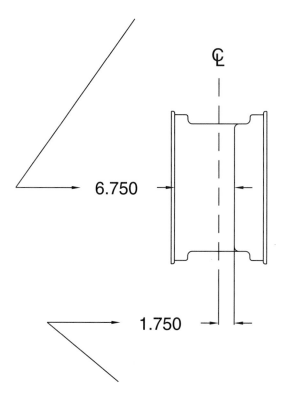

6.750

1.750

Offset

The distance from the axle mounting face to the centerline of the wheel is called the "wheel offset". The offset of the wheel is further defined by the direction of the offset. When the centerline of the wheel is offset toward the exterior of the car it is said to be "positive". Offsets toward the center of the car are called "negative". The example wheel has a 1-3/4" negative offset.

Fig. 9-2

redesign of the upper strut mounts or spindle to keep caster and camber within corporate design policies. Where this is leading to is the fact that the SVO wheel, with the 1" greater backspacing, provides adequate tire sidewall-to-strut clearance of about 1". Given that the SVO only uses a 7" wide wheel on a tire that has a section width of approximately 9", a much narrower space can be utilized with a wheel that is the maximum width recommended for the tire.

What does all this confusion mean? A basic rule of thumb is that if you are running a wheel that is more than 1/2" narrower than the tread width, start at 1/2" and add 1/2" of additional clearance for every inch less than the tread width, and adjust your offset accordingly. This is applicable to the lower profile tires like the 40 to 50 series. Section heights greater than 50% flex considerably more and require additional clearance of about 3/8" per inch undersize. For specific backspacing & offset recommendations, see the sidebar on p. 148.

How Modifications Affect Offset

Up to now the discussion of wheels has been centered around a stock LX Mustang. However, if you are a road racer or Conehead and have upgraded the brakes, then chances are the flange–to–flange distances have been changed. Therefore, the offsets must be increased to compensate for the changes.

Backspacing on a wheel is the distance from the axle mounting surface of the wheel to the outside lip. This SVO Mustang 16" x 7" wheel measures approximately 5.65" of backspacing.

Recommended Backspacing & Offsets

Front—Given the ideal tire section width of 255mm for the front of a stock Mustang , plan on a backspacing of:

> 5.75" on 10" wheel
>
> 5.50" on 9.5" wheel
>
> 5.25" on 9" wheel
>
> 4.75" on 8" wheel (minimum width)
>
> or
>
> an offset of 3/4" negative.

Experience developing the *Slot Car Mustang* has shown these combinations to work best on the front without modifying the fenders. Unfortunately the pre-'90 Mustangs have more narrow wheel openings on the front and may limit the tire diameter to 24-1/2". Generally a 245/45ZR16 on a 9" wheel is the limit on the front of these cars.

Rear—We previously determined that the maximum tire section width that could be utilized was 275mm. However, when fitting a tire this large to the *Slot Car Mustang,* the rear fenders and inside wheelwells had to be modified according to Step 13 in Chapter 3. Careful measurement of the wheelwells indicates the following backspacing:

> 5.25" on 10" wheel
>
> 5.50" on 9.5" wheel
>
> 5.75" on 9" wheel
>
> or
>
> an offset of .25" negative.

Although there is a recommended backspacing for using a 9" wheel on this tire, forget it. Even with a Panhard bar, experience has shown the tire will flex too much and rub severely. Stay with the largest width wheel you can get with the correct backspacing/offset.

Upgrading your brakes to the Ford Motorsport M2300–F 5–lug rear brakes includes axles that are 1-1/4" longer than the stock Mustang. This is done in the interest of cost savings, since most of the parts are from the T–Bird parts bins. Add to the longer axles the additional thickness of the rotors that fit on the outside of the axles and your rear flange-to-flange width increases about 2-3/4". As you can see, this kit requires you to add 1-3/8" negative to the rear wheel offsets to achieve the same centerline of wheel-to-body location as it was before installing the kit. With offsets this large, the wheels have to be very strong to withstand the additional stress. Even the front rotors in this kit have more outboard offset, requiring 5/8" additional backspacing. The front hub on Wilwood's racing brakes moves the wheel mounting flange 1" more outboard on the front with the rear rotor hat, adding 1/2" more in the rear than a stock LX/GT. Throw in a necessary set of Moser Engineering C–Clip Eliminators on the Wilwood rear brakes and you add another 3/8" to the outboard movement. No wonder it is so difficult to fit the proper wheels to the Mustang.

Solution—To save yourself a lot of grief, the best approach is to measure the distance your setup is from a standard location. On the front, measure from the frame, behind the strut, to the vertical wheel mounting flange on the rotor. This should be done with the weight of the car sitting on a jackstand placed under the control arm. Add the amount beyond 12" to the number from the sidebar nearby to determine your minimum backspacing requirement.

To determine the rear offset requirements, it will be necessary to measure from the brake backing plate's mounting flange on the axle housing, to the vertical surface of the wheel mounting flange, be it the axle or rotor hat. Start with the number from the sidebar that applies to you, and add the amount your

In order to reduce forward weight and rolling friction, a very narrow 3-1/2" wide wheel is used in drag racing. Generally this wheel will have a positive offset to provide the maximum reaction window at the lights.

measurement exceeds 2-1/2" to that number.

It is important to remember when selecting wheels to choose those that have the strength to withstand the loads they will be subjected to, especially when using large backspacing. Spend the extra bucks and get forged wheels. Cast ones are just too weak.

TIRE SELECTION

The selection of high–performance tires currently available is considerable. Goodyear GS–CS, BFGoodrich Comp T/A R1s, Yokohama A008Rs, Pirelli P Zeros, and Bridgestone RE71s are the current hot choices. All of these have outstanding handling characteristics and typical short tread life. However, they provide some righteous traction in the dry, especially the Goodyear GS–CS. This group of D.O.T.-approved tires are for corner racing but will also provide outstanding street traction for the occasional stoplight adventure.

Which tire you select is a matter of personal preference and is generally biased to who offers the best price. All of the aforementioned tires are outstanding, with the Yokohama A008Rs and Goodyear GS–CS more closely resembling racing slicks than street tires, especially the GS–CS with the holograms for tread. Each version of these tires comes in different compounds, with one better suited for autocrossing and the other for road racing or high–performance street. Generally, autocross compound tires are designed to come up to temperature very rapidly. Consequently, they will not hold up on a road course for more than a few laps, and they are completely unacceptable on the street. The best approach is to choose the tires that fit your application, mount them on a spare set of wheels with the correct widths and offsets, and use them only in competition.

This is the sign of a smart racer. It is very important in road racing or autocrossing to mark the tires for the corners they will be used on. Racing tires are generally unidirectional and can be destroyed if run in the wrong direction, not to mention the need for maintaining the correct tire stagger. Always label your tires in large letters.

The 28.5 x 10.5-15 is the largest slick that will fit under the Mustang without going to tubs. Significant big hammer massaging is necessary for these tires to clear. However, if your Mustang has the power to run 10-second quarters or less, then these tires are a must to get that power to the ground.

This is a narrow "front runner" tire used in drag racing. It provides low rolling friction and front drag. These tires come in all heights to accommodate your chassis setup. Properly matched to your car, these tires can save several hundredths off your launch time at the lights.

A dead giveaway to the traction capability of a tire is the treadwear rating. These tires have a 000 treadwear rating, which means they will come up to temperature quickly and offer excellent grip, but they will not last very long on the street.

D.O.T. Tires—There are a couple of important points to note about high–performance motoring or competing with D.O.T.-approved tires. First, always have them shaved for truing after they have been mounted on the wheel they will be run on. When a tire is out of round, even a small amount, it will bounce when the high side contacts the pavement. Reduced traction and possible flat spots can result when a tire is out of

round. I have yet to see a street tire that is perfectly round. If you are competing seriously then this procedure is a must.

Second, if your budget permits, always run fresh rubber with the tread shaved to between 2/32" and 4/32", especially for qualifying. I conducted tire tests with all of the major D.O.T. performance tires at Texas World Speedway on the *Slot Car Mustang,* and found lap times would increase 1/2 to 1-1/2 seconds a lap after

the tires had been heat cycled through 6 or 8 laps and allowed to cool. Obviously this can mean the difference between sitting on the front row or being just another car in the pack.

For the more serious street car used for drag racing, the D.O.T.-approved M&H Streetmaster 275/50B15 mounted on a 10" wide wheel with a 6" backspacing is the trick setup today. Some inner fender work with a large hammer will be

One of the most popular tires for the stoplight-to-stoplight crowd is the McCreary Road Star. They tires are D.O.T.-approved, have a treadwear rating of 000, are very reasonably priced and have enough tread to allow driving in wet conditions.

The Hoosier "Quick Time" tire has been used on some very fast quarter-mile cars. These tires are like a soft sponge when they are cold and they come with D.O.T. approval.

One of the best tire and wheel combinations for your '90 or newer Mustang with the wide fender openings is the Yokohama A008Rs mounted on the Mitsubishi 3000GT wheel. The "Yokes" are very popular with autocrossers and proved to be outstanding during the development and testing of *the Slot Car Mustang*.

The Goodyear GS-CS tires are some of the stickiest D.O.T. tires available for the road racing or autocross machine. The treads generally will last only one lap at the most before the tire becomes a racing slick.

necessary when utilizing this wheel and tire. Also, the dampeners and frame brackets are history.

If you are building a drag racing Mustang to run in the 10-second range, the largest tire you can fit in the rear fender well without tubs is the 28.5 x 10.5" slick mounted on a 10" wide wheel with a 6" backspacing. However, you'll have to do quite a bit of hammering to the inner fender panel as well as the fender lip. Currently the 9-second, Joe Rivera-prepared Mustang of Mario Meza runs this setup. It's a tight fit, but it works.

SUMMARY

If you are upgrading the wheels and tires on your Mustang, it is important to complete all the modifications to the chassis, suspension and brakes before placing an order. The selection of the correct wheel and tire combination should be addressed with methodical checking and double checking of all measurements. Know the rim width requirements of the tire you have selected and try to find a wheel that is at least as wide as the tread width. After you have bolted the wheels and tires to your car, check clearances closely. Cycle the steering lock to lock and watch for contact with the fenders. The best approach is to remove the springs and cycle the suspension from full droop to full bump and watch for interference, especially on the rear. When checking the rear, always cycle one side with the other side at normal ride height. Watch for contact with the inner fender radiuses and the fender lip. Finally, don't be stupid. If you don't have the correct width wheel for slick fat tires that look so cool on somebody else's car, don't succumb to brain melt and buy them anyway. Your car will perform many times better with a tire that is properly suited for the width of wheel you have, than it will with a bad combination. ∎

CHASSIS SETUP

10

Correct caster and camber settings are essential for good handling as well as fast quarter-mile E.T.s. Taking your car to an alignment shop each time you make a suspension change is expensive and time consuming. The trick setup is this slick Caster/Camber gauge from Longacre Racing Products. This gauge is accurate to within 1/4 degree and is very rugged. Don't leave home without it.

Once you have completed the modifications to your car it is important to dial in the chassis. You will need a three-ring binder with ruled paper for notes, and copies of the accompanying worksheets in the Appendix of this book to record your findings. I can not emphasize the importance of carefully recording everything about your car. Detailed records will make setup and tuning considerably easier when you can compare results with actual settings rather than "I think we did..."

To effectively set up your car you will need the items listed in the chart on the next page.

MEASURING & CHECKING

Step 1

Align the suspension, setting the caster and camber to racing specifications. Set the toe at 0^0. Adjust shocks and struts to full soft. See the accompanying chart on p. 152 for suggested settings. If you do not have a caster/camber gauge, then a visit to an alignment machine is next.

Step 2

With the driver sitting in the car, roll the car back and forth several feet on a level surface, jousting the suspension before reversing direction. Drop a plumb bob across the edge of each of the four fender openings where it will bisect the

BASIC SUSPENSION SETTINGS

	ASSEMBLY TESTING	STREET	DRAG RACING	AUTOCROSS	ROAD RACING
TOE	0"	1/16" IN	1/8" IN	1/4" OUT	1/32" IN
CAMBER	0°	1/2° NEG	0°	2-1/2° to 3-1/2° NEG	1-1/2° to 3° NEG
CASTER	0°	3° POS	3° to 5° POS	3° to 4° POS	2-1/2° to 3-1/2° POS

centerline of the rear axle or spindle. For reference, clearly mark this location on the lip of the fenders with a wax crayon. Measure the height at the four locations and note on the data sheet. Measure the ride height below the frame next to each of the lower trailing arm bolts and note on the data sheet. On the front, measure the ride height under the #2 crossmember below the forward control arm attachment bolts and record on the data sheet. Finally, measure the distance from the fender lip to the center of each axle or spindle and record on the chassis data sheet on p. 174 and 175. Be sure the wheels are facing straight ahead and the driver is sitting in the car when you take these measurements.

Step 3

Mount the car on jackstands placed under the rocker panels at the jacking notches. The car should have at least 18" of floor clearance. Remove the springs and rear swaybar. Disconnect the front swaybar. Reassemble the suspension without the springs and swaybars. Be sure to install the rear shocks and dampeners if used, as well as the wheels with racing tires mounted.

EQUIPMENT REQUIRED FOR CHASSIS SETUP

(4) car ramps of equal height

floor jack or equivalent jack

bump steer gauge (see Fig. 10-1, 10-2, 10-3)

toe gauge

camber gauge

(2) anti–friction plates for front wheels

(4) bathroom scales of identical manufacture and model number

(4) scale platforms (see Fig. 10-4, 10-5)

calculator

dial indicator and magnetic stand

Plumb Bob

wax crayon

Step 4: Measuring Rear Camber

Check the rear axle housing camber by placing an inclinometer on the vertical face of the axles. Check each side and record your findings. The 8.8 axle housing comes stock with 0° camber. However, one trip to an open track event or SCCA race and the housing bends permanently with negative camber. Virtually every V8 Mustang with more than 50,000 miles on it has some amount of negative camber in the rear housing. If you are racing on fat tires without maximum width rims, this can help your lap times. It has been my experience that you need about 1/2° negative camber on the Mustang housing, when running radial tires, to get the best handling. If your housing has more than 1° negative or any positive camber you probably should consider replacing the housing.

Obviously, if you are a drag racer, negative camber is unacceptable. Any negative camber and the slicks will ride on the inner edge of the tire only. This condition prevents the slicks from achieving 100% traction. You should check the slicks immediately after a burnout with a pyrometer. Check the inside, middle and outer edges. If the inside is hotter than the outside you have negative camber. Too hot in the middle and you're running too much air pressure.

Step 5: Checking Rear Clearance

In 1" increments, cycle the rear suspension from full droop to full bump with a jack and check for clearance. Test each side individually with the opposite side sitting at normal ride height, then 1, 2 and 3 inches down. Refer to the measurements you recorded in Step 2 to adjust the height on the opposite side. Pay particular attention to the front and rear inside radiuses. Be sure the brake lines or hoses do not get caught between the bump stops and the axle housing.

Watch for any unusual shifts in the axle housing that might indicate that something is binding up. If you have cut your bump stops down it is important to check the shocks with the rear end at full bump to ensure they are not bottoming out. Note any clearance problems and fix them before proceeding.

Step 6: Checking Front Clearance

In the front, cycle each side in 1" increments from full droop to full bump to check tire clearance. At each checkpoint, have someone slowly turn the steering from lock to lock and watch for interference, especially at the lower front fender edge. Like the rear, always check the struts to ensure they are not bottoming out. It is particularly important to watch the clearance on the brake hoses. These things twist around and can end up against a tire. Not good. Again, correct any problems before moving on.

Step 7

If you have not done so already, check

the runout on the rotors and correct as necessary. Runout of more than .005" will require machining.

Step 8: Wheel Bearings

Clean and repack the front wheel bearings. Check bearings and races closely for any discoloration or early signs of deterioration. Always replace the seals. Set the preload on the front wheel bearings by spinning the rotor with one hand and tightening the nut until the rotor begins to drag to seat the bearings, usually about 45 ft-lbs. Carefully turn the nut backward until you feel it release the bearings, then turn it clockwise until you feel it touch the bearing. This will provide the proper preload to the bearings for racing conditions.

Step 9: Checking Driveshaft

Mustangs that have been subjected to drag race-type launches or power shifts with stock or worn trailing arm bushings, especially upper bushings, have a tendency to bend the driveshaft.

Although it may be bent to the point of severe vibration, many times it is small enough to be ignored or blamed on something else. However, if your driveshaft is not true it will vibrate at high speed and trash the transmission output shaft bushing, as well as the pinion bearings. If it is significantly out of round, it could overstress a U-joint at speed and separate from the car. Driveshaft hoops are mandatory in most racing classes for a reason. Losing a driveshaft can really get your attention, so check this closely.

Mount a dial indicator with a magnetic base to the underside of the body, just above the driveshaft in front of the yoke. With the transmission in neutral, measure the runout on the driveshaft at this point, in the middle and just behind the front yoke. Jack the axle assembly up at the center section if necessary to access the driveshaft with the dial indicator. If the runout is greater than .035", replace the driveshaft. If your driveshaft is within tolerance, note the amount of runout. This will help isolate a vibration in the future by comparing measurements to the original data.

If you notice a wobble at the transmission end, check the side play on the output shaft housing bushing. Wobbles on the pinion end require you to check the radial runout on the yoke. If the yoke is more than .010" out, remove it and replace it 180° from its original location. Check the runout again. If it exceeds .010" replace it.

Step 10: Differential Breakaway Torque

For those cars running a limited slip type differential (Auburn, Ford Traction-Lok, etc.), it is important to check the breakaway torque. If your differential will not hold the manufacturer's minimum torque requirement then rebuild it. To check, reassemble one side of the rear suspension with the spring in place.

It is very important to check caliper deflection before each race to determine if the caliper is starting to break down. While you have the dial indicator out, be sure to check the runout of the rotors. Anything beyond .005" will require turning the rotors.

Mount the wheel and lower the car until the tire on the assembled side rests on the ground. Check the breakaway preload on the clutches in the differential with a large torque wrench. You will have to fabricate an adapter to bolt to the axle for the torque wrench. Typically you must have at least 100 ft-lbs. for the differential to function, with 175 to 300 ft-lbs. being best for racing.

If your Ford Traction–Lok is not holding sufficient breakaway torque, replace the clutches and preload the "S" spring. However, instead of following the Ford service procedure, replace one of the driven plates on each side with a drive plate. Sandwich the driven plates between the drive plates for better lock up.

Step 11

Install the final rear spring and set the car on jackstands placed under the axle tubes. Joust the rear suspension to settle the springs. With the help of a friend carefully bolt up the rear swaybar so it is even and unbiased.

Step 12: Bump Steer

Although you may have already checked and adjusted the bump steer, it is important to make a final check with all changes in place. If you do not own a bump steer gauge, one can be fabricated from plywood, a couple of bolts and hinges. I have provided drawings (see Figures 10-1, 10-2 and 10-3 on p. 160) on how to fabricate one of these. Basically you can make one from almost any material, just keep the proportions even.

To measure bump steer, you must remove the front springs (if installed) and reassemble the suspension, leaving the swaybar disconnected and the steering wheel locked. Chock the rear wheels tightly (fore and aft) on both sides and place a jack under the control arm for the side you will be testing. Jack the control arm up until the spindle is the exact distance from the fender lip previously

recorded in Step 2, p. 152. Attach the measurement plate to the rotor with a couple of lug nuts. Hold the measurement plate level and insert a wedge between the rotor and the caliper to prevent it from rotating. With the new bump steer gauge you have fabricated, secure its base to the floor with something heavy (battery, dead T–5, etc.) and adjust the height of the measurement stops so they rest against the measurement plate at its 0" position.

In 1/2" increments, jack the control arm up and down and plot the width of the gap that will appear on one of the bolts previously resting against the measurement plate, on your Bump/Roll Steer worksheet (located in the Appendix). For more accurate results, substitute a dial indicator for one of the bolts and record the changes. To determine consistency between left and right, test both sides. If there is more bump steer on one side than the other the rack housing probably needs to be shifted

left or right.

If you find the rack needs to be relocated then follow Step 6 in Chapter 4, p. 56 for the procedures.

The perfect suspension setup provides no change in toe through 100% of the wheel's travel, which is virtually impossible in a production car. Typically, the first 2" in either direction are the most important. You should do all you can to correct any bump steer within this range.

Step 13

Completely reassemble the front suspension, including wheels, except leave the swaybar disconnected on one end. Relocate jackstands under the control arms or better, place car ramps under the wheels (all four preferably). Joust the suspension to settle the springs. Assemble the remaining swaybar end link and slowly tighten the nut. Watch to see if the end link clamps squarely on the bar's eyelet. If the bar is drawn down as

For corner racing, minimizing bump steer is critical to optimum handling. Fabricate a bump steer gauge from the accompanying drawings or go whole hog and buy a first-class gauge from Longacre Racing Products. Check the bump steer in increments of 1" using the worksheet in the Appendix and make corrections by relocating the rack and pinion housing with offset bushings.

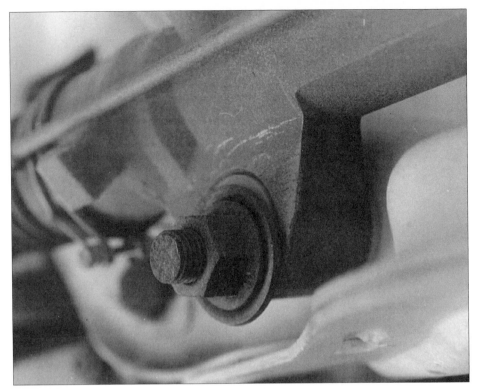

Correcting bump steer can be achieved simply by adding or subtracting positive caster, or by replacing your tie rods or relocating the rack and pinion housing. There are several companies that sell the offset rack bushings, however, the best approach is to follow the guidelines set out in Chapter 5 and make a set per the accompanying drawings.

Step 16: Weight Distribution

Next is measuring and correcting the weight distribution in your Mustang. This is a very important step for maximizing handling. Manipulating the center of gravity on your car can provide dramatic improvements. Where the weight is distributed defines the polar moment of inertia and how quickly and evenly the car changes directions. Achieving a good balance is a tedious process but well worth the effort. Take your time and carefully record the changes you make to the car.

Scales & Platforms—Finding the location of the center of gravity is not difficult and can in fact be accomplished with limited tools. Owning a set of the slick four-wheel electronic car scales would be real nice. However, if your budget is anything like mine, the closest you'll get to a set is watching Bob Glidden's crew use them on his car. Given the normal budgetary limitations you'll probably want to improvise by using standard bathroom scales and a few simple laws of physics. While it may not sound sophisticated, it works. (I even used it when I fabricated an aluminum

it tightens, insert washers between the sleeve and grommet washer to correct the length. If the link is too long, tighten it to a normal, snug fit and then adjust the other side with washers to achieve a correct fit. This procedure will ensure your front suspension is not biased by the swaybar. Record the thickness of the washers used to adjust the bar as well as the side they were fitted to.

Step 14: Toe

Set the toe–in to the correct specifications. See the accompanying chart on p. 153. If you do not have the basic tools to correctly align your suspension, then you will need a trip to an alignment shop.

Step 15: Final Checks

Before you finish with the underside of the car, grease all zerk fittings and check every single suspension, shock, strut, Panhard bar, swaybar, crossmember, driveshaft, exhaust, transmission and

engine mount bolt. It is amazing how often you will miss tightening a bolt when you assemble a car. Take your time, start at one end and work to the other.

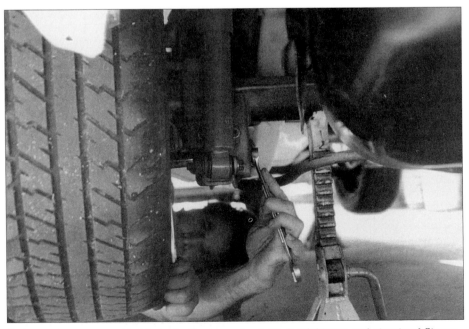

Before every race you should check all suspension bolts for tightness and structural fitness. Racing conditions put tremendous stress on fasteners, causing them to break or work loose, so do not skip this step.

Correcting weight distribution for optimum handling will require a minimum of two corner weighing mechanisms. For best results use weighing mechanisms on all four corners. Be sure to do your measurements on level ground with no wind present.

airplane and had to take it through the air worthiness certification.)

If you are a serious racer, especially a Conehead or road racer, you may want to fabricate a set of scale platforms. They are light and can be set up quickly at the track. I have included detailed drawings of the scale platforms that I used to weigh my airplane and race cars (see Figures 10-4, 10-5 on p. 161).

If you construct these platforms it is very important to be as accurate as possible when determining the locations for the end footings, tire centerline pad, and scale pad. Since you will be multiplying your scale readings by the lever length of the platform, any discrepancy will result in an error that could be four times what you perceive. Take your time and keep the measurements consistent for each set of platforms. Additionally, if you choose to fabricate a complete set of four platforms to weigh all four corners at once, buy four scales from the same manufacturer with the same model number. This will provide more reliable measurements.

WEIGHING & BALANCING

To measure your car's weight and the location of its center of gravity, you must first locate a concrete surface that is level in all directions where there is no wind present. The car must be in as-raced

condition, with driver in racing outfit (fire suit, helmet, boots and gloves), and a full tank of gas. Obviously this means you will need a friend to take the scale readings if you are the driver. Make a copy of the Center of Gravity Worksheet in the Appendix to record your findings and calculate the results. These measurements will be based on the assumption that the center of gravity of each wheel's unsprung weight is located at the centerline of each wheel assembly. This is, of course, ludicrous; however, for the relatively crude suspension of the Mustang, this will do.

Don't be fooled into thinking your garage meets the level requirements. Most garages are built with a slight slope to the slab for drainage purposes. However, the garage will work fine, as

long as you use a string level to adjust or shim the platforms so they are all level to one another. The readings will be much more reliable if you take the time to do this.

If you are using anything other than a four-scale system, it is important that the remaining wheels be placed on blocks that will match the exact level height of the weighing system you are using on the other wheel(s). I strongly recommend you use at least a two-scale system for weighing your car; however, to determine center of gravity height it will be necessary to use a four-scale system. The scale platforms must be set up under each tire with the center of the tire resting on the centerline drawn on the tire pad. Be sure the scale is located directly center of the platform's scale pad.

If you are using a two-scale system, then start with the rear tires on your Mustang. They are not subject to the side loading that the independent front suspension creates. Adjust the end pivot footings on the platforms to create a level surface for the tires to rest on. Write down the readings on your copy of the CG chart. The driver must be sitting in the car in driving position (doors closed) when the measurements are taken. This procedure must be adhered to for all readings.

Jack up the front of the car and remove the blocks you installed to match the

Shown here is a very simple lever and bathroom scale system for doing weights and balance. The accompanying drawings provide specifications to build similar mechanisms.

One of the best ways to manipulate corner weights is by relocating the battery to the rear of the car. Since the Mustang is nose-heavy, moving a heavy object will have a significant effect on the weight and balance.

scale platform height at the rear. Return to the rear of the car, jack the car up and remove the scale platforms and scales. Insert the blocks previously used in the front under the rear tires and move to the front.

Setup of the scale platforms in the front is complicated by the side loading created as the independent suspension compresses and moves the wheel outward. To prevent inaccurate readings, you must set the footings of the scale platform and the scales on a greased hard and smooth surface (two steel plates sandwiched together with grease between the plates, then placed under the scale and the footings, will generate the best results). This will allow the weighing system to move with the suspension so no side loading occurs. Follow this procedure and write down the readings on your CG chart.

With the four corner readings you can follow the formulas provided on the CG chart and calculate the weight, front to rear distribution percentages, diagonal ratios and two–dimensional center of gravity for your car. For the road racer, it is important to achieve close to a 50/50

relationship between the fore and aft weight distribution as well as the diagonal ratios. Typically you should relocate everything possible to the rear seat platform with things generally biased on the right side in a pure race car. This will reduce the polar moment of inertia while shifting the weight

rearward. However, it is extremely important to shift the weight around in your car to achieve as close as possible to a 50/50 diagonal balance, left front/right rear to right front/left rear. Obviously this is more easily achieved with a pure race car. Still, relocating the battery to the trunk and shifting it around can do wonders for the diagonal ratios.

Once you have shifted things about as much as possible, fine tune the weight distribution by raising and lowering different corners to shift the weight. It is best to start with a heavy corner and lower it slightly to reduce the weight on that wheel. Raising a light corner will increase the weight there. In practice it is best to spread the adjustments around between the light and heavy to achieve the best balance. If your car does not have adjustable spring seats, you can fabricate aluminum spacers to fit between the spring and the upper spring seats to adjust the corner heights. Re–weight the corners after every change and limit the changes to not more than 1/2". Anything more screws up the suspension geometry.

Generally, calculating the two-

In order to improve weight distribution while minimizing the polar moment of inertia, Doug Wille relocated his battery to the passenger side rear floorpan. Obviously, passengers are optional.

Do not forget to properly secure a relocated battery. A battery develops an extremely high mass as the cornering forces increase. Wimpy battery holddowns will break and battery acid redecorates the inside of your car and possibly yourself.

dimensional CG is sufficient for drag racers and will clearly demonstrate where the weight must be shifted. For road racers, the vertical CG, or center of gravity height, should also be calculated. Proceed with the following steps to get the data necessary to make this calculation. (A typical stock Mustang will have a vertical CG of about 16.5" to 17".)

Vertical CG—To find the vertical CG you must set the car up on four scale platforms as specified previously, taking care to eliminate side loading in the front. Air the tires up to 40 lbs. to eliminate tire deflection bias in the readings and set the shocks to maximum stiffness. The best results are found by substituting aluminum bars for the shocks and struts. However, this is difficult and impractical on a MacPherson strut-equipped production car. After you have recorded the readings with the car sitting level,

drop plumb bobs at the exact side centers of the front and rear wheels to accurately measure the wheelbase. Record your finding on the CG chart.

Next, jack up the rear of your Mustang at the center section high enough to insert

blocks under the tires that are at least 20" tall, with 24" being more ideal. The higher the rear end the more accurate the readings. Remeasure the wheelbase using the plumb bobs and record your findings on the CG chart along with the new weight readings from each of the four scales. Considerable care must be taken to prevent the car from rolling off the scales and platforms. You will be most unhappy if your Mustang decides to launch from the blocks—very messy.

The next step is to repeat the previous measuring procedures with the fuel tank empty. This will provide a good baseline for adjusting the suspension for specific track conditions and events.

When you have determined all the measurements, determine the additional weights as specified on the CG chart to calculate the tare weights that must be subtracted from your weight readings. Then, just follow the formulas on the CG chart and you will be able to determine a reasonably accurate three–dimensional CG location.

This completes the basic setup of your car for testing. Before attempting to do any racing you should follow the testing procedures in the last chapter of this book to dial in your car's suspension to suit specific track conditions and achieve optimum performance. ∎

When doing weight and balance testing, it is very important to have the driver in the car. Cars do not drive themselves, consequently weight and balance numbers without the driver are pretty useless.

Bump Steer Gauge

1

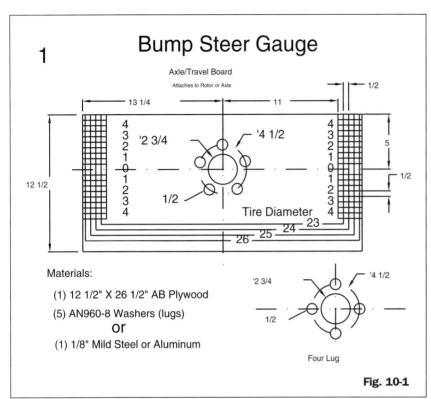

Axle/Travel Board

Attaches to Rotor or Axle

Tire Diameter

Four Lug

Materials:

(1) 12 1/2" X 26 1/2" AB Plywood

(5) AN960-8 Washers (lugs)
or
(1) 1/8" Mild Steel or Aluminum

Fig. 10-1

Bump Steer Gauge
Measurement Lever

2

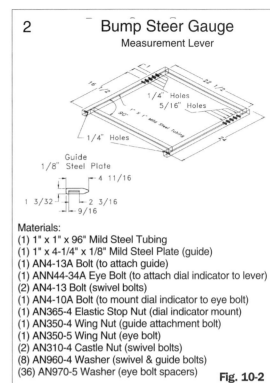

Guide
1/8" Steel Plate

Materials:
(1) 1" x 1" x 96" Mild Steel Tubing
(1) 1" x 4-1/4" x 1/8" Mild Steel Plate (guide)
(1) AN4-13A Bolt (to attach guide)
(1) ANN44-34A Eye Bolt (to attach dial indicator to lever)
(2) AN4-13 Bolt (swivel bolts)
(1) AN4-10A Bolt (to mount dial indicator to eye bolt)
(1) AN365-4 Elastic Stop Nut (dial indicator mount)
(1) AN350-4 Wing Nut (guide attachment bolt)
(1) AN350-5 Wing Nut (eye bolt)
(2) AN310-4 Castle Nut (swivel bolts)
(8) AN960-4 Washer (swivel & guide bolts)
(36) AN970-5 Washer (eye bolt spacers)

Fig. 10-2

Bump Steer Gauge
Swivel Base

3

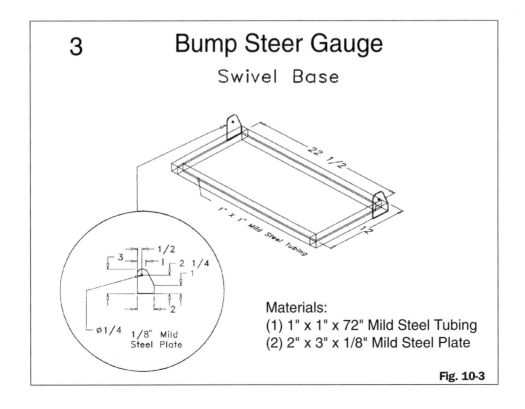

1/8" Mild Steel Plate

Materials:
(1) 1" x 1" x 72" Mild Steel Tubing
(2) 2" x 3" x 1/8" Mild Steel Plate

Fig. 10-3

1 Scale Platform
For Testing Corner Weights
4:1 Ratio

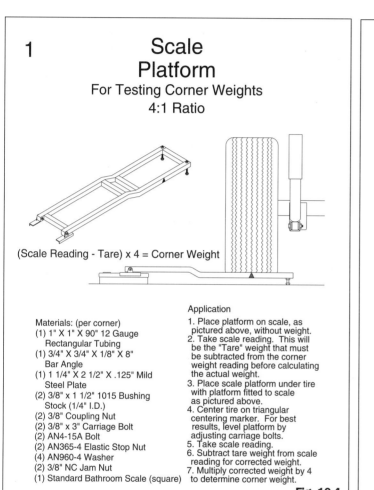

(Scale Reading - Tare) x 4 = Corner Weight

Materials: (per corner)
(1) 1" X 1" X 90" 12 Gauge Rectangular Tubing
(1) 3/4" X 3/4" X 1/8" X 8" Bar Angle
(1) 1 1/4" X 2 1/2" X .125" Mild Steel Plate
(2) 3/8" x 1 1/2" 1015 Bushing Stock (1/4" I.D.)
(2) 3/8" Coupling Nut
(2) 3/8" x 3" Carriage Bolt
(2) AN4-15A Bolt
(2) AN365-4 Elastic Stop Nut
(4) AN960-4 Washer
(2) 3/8" NC Jam Nut
(1) Standard Bathroom Scale (square)

Application
1. Place platform on scale, as pictured above, without weight.
2. Take scale reading. This will be the "Tare" weight that must be subtracted from the corner weight reading before calculating the actual weight.
3. Place scale platform under tire with platform fitted to scale as pictured above.
4. Center tire on triangular centering marker. For best results, level platform by adjusting carriage bolts.
5. Take scale reading.
6. Subtract tare weight from scale reading for corrected weight.
7. Multiply corrected weight by 4 to determine corner weight.

Fig. 10-4

2 Scale Platform

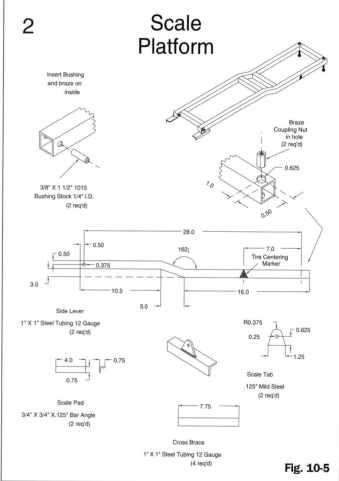

Insert Bushing and braze on inside

3/8" X 1 1/2" 1015 Bushing Stock 1/4" I.D. (2 req'd)

Braze Coupling Nut in hole (2 req'd)

0.625

1.0

0.50

28.0

0.50

0.50

0.375

162¡

3.0

10.5

3.0

7.0

Tire Centering Marker

16.0

Side Lever
1" X 1" Steel Tubing 12 Gauge (2 req'd)

4.0

0.75

0.75

Scale Pad
3/4" X 3/4" X.125" Bar Angle (2 req'd)

R0.375

0.625

0.25

1.25

Scale Tab
.125" Mild Steel (2 req'd)

7.75

Cross Brace
1" X 1" Steel Tubing 12 Gauge (4 req'd)

Fig. 10-5

TESTING & TUNING

11

Now the fun stuff begins! All those skinned knuckles and bruised body parts will be forgotten when you experience the quantum leap in the handling and performance of your Mustang. However, all is not complete. Before you get to smoke your buddies at the next event, it will be necessary to dial in the changes you have made to your car.

Every car must go through a specific pre–race inspection and servicing procedure to ensure it is safe and reliable. Testing new setups is no exception. Before you go to the track, always go through the Pre–Race Checklist in the Appendix.

Every racer knows to take the usual tool box full of tools, jack and jackstands. However, it is also very important to bring along specific extras to ensure a successful racing event. See pages 163 and 171 for a list of recommended tools, equipment and spare parts. The items in these charts are necessary for testing as well as for a racing event.

Obviously one can spend several suitcases full of $100 bills outfitting a racing team. However, if you are road racing, you should take along at least one of every spare part you have. Experience has clearly demonstrated that anything

Do not let this happen to you. Take the time to test and dial in your suspension before you suffer embarrassing moments such as this one.

TOOLS & EQUIPMENT FOR TESTING

Leather gloves

Tire pyrometer

Quality tire pressure gauge with air release valve

Air bottle, preferably 2, and small compressor driven off of cigarette lighter outlet

White shoe polish

Clipboard, notepad and several pens

Multi–function stopwatch; for road racing, 2 stopwatches

Camber measuring device

First Aid kit

Minimum 5 lb., preferably 10 lb., fire extinguisher

Hand cleaner and shop towels

Several towels to cool driver between sessions

Paper towels

Glass Cleaner

Brake–Kleen

Rain X

Duct tape

Safety wire and safety wire pliers

4–way lug wrench

Tow strap

Most air hoses will not reach from the local service station to your test track, so be sure to bring a good air tank. Testing different tire pressures is important to dialing in your suspension.

Accurate air gauges are a must in racing. If your budget allows, buy a liquid-filled gauge as they are generally more consistent and accurate.

TESTING FOR AUTOCROSS & ROAD RACING

Every successful racing team knows you must test before racing a car. Even if you are an amateur autocrosser or SCCA club racer, testing can provide valuable information about the limits of your chassis. The Mustang is a heavy, unsophisticated production car that will benefit significantly from a day or two on a skidpad. Don't underestimate the value of this type of testing. Sophisticated race cars need track time to dial in. However, they are designed past the skidpad level: The Mustang is not. Save your track time for fine tuning and do the preparation on the skidpad.

Finding a Skidpad

A skidpad is a flat area of pavement with a painted circle at least 200 to 300 ft. in diameter. It is used to measure a vehicle's grip and lateral acceleration. Basically, you drive your car around the circle as fast as possible without spinning out. The speed is measured, and the grip and lateral acceleration are calculated from the speed and size of the circle.

Some race tracks have a skidpad available for testing, at a price far less than the track rental price. Check the

road courses in your area to see if one is available. You can also call your local SCCA region and ask them. If there is a road racing team in your area, chances are they will know where one is, or they may know of a good place where they can make their own skidpad. Finally, check with a local sports car club, such as the Porsche or Ferrari club, to see if they have any suggestions.

If you cannot find a skidpad, check shopping centers, business offices or stadiums with large parking lots that are closed on Sundays or weekends. Talk to the property managers/owners about what you want to do. Explain about the safety equipment (helmets & fire extinguishers) you will be bringing and

You have to be able to change caster and camber accurately when testing suspension setups. The Longacre Racing Products gauge is the cat's meow.

you don't bring will be needed about 10 minutes before the race is to begin. Also, anything that is indestructible isn't, and will break on the first practice lap or run.

If you are going autocrossing you will not need a truckload of spares. However, it is a wise racer who asks a friend with a pickup to come along. Just in case something in the engine decides to go south, you can at least be towed home.

the low risk involved (slow speeds), and offer to draft and sign a disclaimer absolving the owner of all liability. If he or she is a car nut, offer to time their car to determine its cornering force. Above all, look neat, responsible and professional. If someone gives the okay, get permission in writing. Next, go to the police station that the test lot is patrolled by, and explain how and when you will be doing the testing. Take along a copy of the written permission to give to the police. Write on the back your name and phone number and those responsible for the parking lot. This will save potential hassles from the police who invariably show up wanting to know what the hell you're doing there.

As it is unlikely you will be running your engine at maximum horsepower, be sure you have mufflers on the car. Other businesses and homes generally don't approve of the noise. Do not leave a mess. Clean up your area and leave it in better condition than you found it. Finally, send a personal thank you note to the person giving you permission to use the lot. Do this within three days after your testing. You may want to do this again.

Laying Out the Pad—When using a parking lot, look for the most level place without obstructions at least 100 ft. away from the outside radius of the circle. You will need a 150-ft. tape to mark the circle (a rope previously marked at 100 ft. and 150 ft. will work). Have someone hold the tape at the desired center location while someone else walks the circle spraying a continuous line at 100 ft. and at 150 ft. Use a water soluble non–permanent aerosol paint. The parking lot owner may not appreciate something that cannot be removed with ordinary water. Or, you can use a series of bright orange plastic bowls taped (duct tape) to the pavement upside down. You will need about 30 cups for the 200-ft. test and 50 for the 300-ft. test. Lay these out about every 20

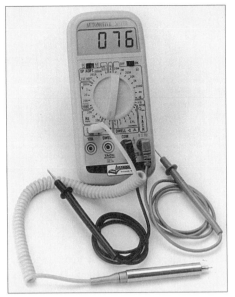

Like an accurate tire gauge, an accurate and reliable pyrometer is crucial to optimum suspension testing and setup. Photographed is a large display digital pyrometer/VTOM meter manufactured by Longacre Racing Products.

ft. on the circle. Mark a standard starting and stopping point with an easily recognizable object, such as a large cone or drinking cup.

Once you have the skidpad marked, sweep an area starting 10 ft. inside the test circle out to 10 ft. beyond it. This is important, as the wind generated by the

car will draw sand and debris onto the test circle. Your test will be less accurate if you have to run on sand and other bits of trash.

If you are the test driver, then select someone who is detail oriented to perform the actual tire temperature testing and operate the stopwatch (preferably a separate person for each task). If possible, have someone else record the times. Always have the same person take all readings and operate the stopwatch for consistency. Always record tire temps in a consistent manner, immediately after the car stops, starting with the same tire every time, and recording the outside, middle and inside temps in the same order. This will save time calling out which tire and which spot so quicker and more accurate readings can be taken. On a skidpad the temperatures of the tires on the outside of the turn are most important. Have these people stand inside the circle, where it is actually safer. If the car spins it will be thrown away from the center. Having said this, place a person on the outside of the turn, at a safe distance away, and have them take a picture of the car head

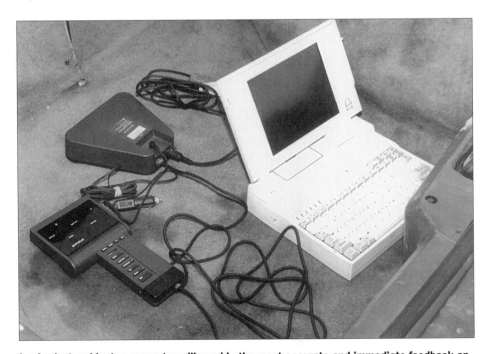

A *g*-Analyst and laptop computer will provide the most accurate and immediate feedback on how your suspension settings are working. If your budget can handle it, the *g*-Analyst is well worth the bucks. It will save you a lot of time and effort setting up your car.

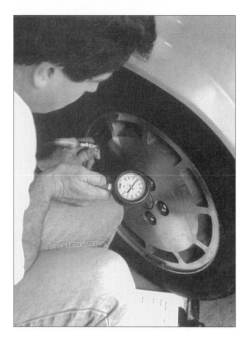

Before you begin your test session, inflate your tires to the estimated testing pressure. Do not overinflate them. Overinflating tires stretches them and permanently changes their circumference. Since no two tires stretch exactly the same, the stagger will be affected and handling will suffer.

Head-on Polaroid photos of your car as it travels around a skidpad will help explain why and how your car is handling the way it is. Studying the photos during cool-down periods can provide important information on such things as the adequacy of roll stiffness, camber angles and tire pressures.

on as it comes around the turn, with a Polaroid camera. This will be used to evaluate body roll. However, make sure this person is well away from the circle, with plenty of maneuvering room to get out of the way should the car spin.

Performing a Test

Essentially the purpose of the testing is to determine the optimum settings for each given combination of springs, swaybars, and tires used. Obviously, the speed of the laps defines how well things are working. If you make a change and the car goes slower, go back to the pre–change settings and take a different tack. The test sheets in the Appendix provide the formula for determining

"g's" for comparison to other recognized levels of performance. A typical 3,000-lb. Mustang sporting the modifications noted in Chapter 5 should be able to pull 1.2 g's on the Yokohama A008Rs or the Goodyear GS–CS tires.

If you can get access to a *g*–Analyst or one of the new Vericom computers, your testing will go must faster with accurate and immediate information. These things are well worth the investment and

Initial skidpad testing invariably finds the limits of the suspension and tires. Turning right to go left, the driver of this Bob Bondurant Mustang has found and exceeded the limits of adhesion. (Photo courtesy The Bob Bondurant School of High Performance Driving)

Study the outside wheel in this photo and the high placement of the body on the inside of the turn. Inadequate roll stiffness, a high mass centroid axis and lack of camber on the outside wheel limit the ability of this Mustang to reach maximum cornering speeds. (Photo by John Hafemeister)

should be high on the list of acquisitions for a road racing team. The following is a typical corner racer test plan.

1. Check all suspension settings and note on test sheet.

2. Set tires to the base cold testing temperatures. Probably 28 to 32 in the rear and 32 to 36 in the front. Note settings on test sheet.

3. Test the surface temperature of the pavement and note on test sheet.

4. Record the ambient temperature and humidity if possible.

5. Fire the engine and let idle until all fluids are within operating temperature.

6. Make at least two plug readings to dial–in the fuel pressure and ignition timing to current conditions.

7. Station the stopwatch operator and recorder inside the circle where they are facing the standard starting and stopping marker. The pyrometer should be out and ready for immediate use.

8. Have the driver put some heat in the tires by driving across the lot weaving back and forth.

9. Start the driver circling around the track as close to the line or cups as possible without running over them.

10. After two passes around the circle, start timing the laps. At this point the driver should slowly start accelerating until he can no longer hold the line. No speedway type sliding. This does not provide useful data.

11. Run two laps at the maximum, carefully noting the lap times. Be sure to watch for the steering angle of the front wheels to determine how much understeer and tire scrub is taking place.

12. Flag the driver to a stop and read the tire temperatures on the outside tires.

13. Test and record all tire pressures.

Inadequate roll stiffness has pushed the tires to their limit in this photograph. Compare the outside rear tire to the inside tire. The tire on the outside has rolled over and is collapsing, while the inside tire has almost lost contact with the track. Higher rate rear springs (probably 50 lbs-in more) should greatly improve this problem.

14. Allow the tires to cool below 180°, then run the test in the opposite direction. Follow testing procedures 9 through 13.

15. Recheck your suspension settings (camber, caster, toe) to determine if anything has changed from the original settings. If there are changes, trace the problem and fix it. Then, scrap your first tests and start over.

16. Evaluate the tire temperature readings (See chart on next page).

17. Make adjustments to camber as necessary to optimize tire contact patch. Don't forget to reset toe–in to the original baseline settings. Do not make more than one change at a time. It can be very frustrating to isolate the problem without having to go back to square one. Also, if the camber has to be set more than 2-1/2° negative you must add some roll stiffness to the car. Most tires cannot roll under quick enough in a turn to plant the tread flat when camber is set beyond 3°. Consequently, tuning your suspension to work at this setting on a skidpad may generate some impressive "g" calculations, however, you will be very disappointed with the performance on the track.

18. After tires have cooled below 180°, run tests again.

19. Again evaluate tire temperatures and adjust the camber to optimize the tire contact patch. If temperatures are balanced inside–to–outside on the tires, adjust tire pressure to balance temperature across entire tread.

20. When you have adjusted the camber and tire pressure temperatures for best results, take a break and allow the tires to cool completely to determine optimum cold pressure. Record the numbers.

In this photo the driver has pushed the car to the limits of adhesion as the tires are just on the brink of rolling under and breaking loose. This car is equipped with a Griggs torque arm rear suspension and exhibits the characteristic lack of rear roll stiffness common to these installations. Seeing air under the inside tire is not uncommon on this setup. Stiffer rear springs would probably improve this car's cornering speeds.

Although the camber angle on this car appears to be adequate in relation to the car's frame, a high roll center and inadequate rear roll stiffness have caused the tire to roll under and limit the cornering speed. A stiffer rear swaybar and more negative camber are neccessary to correct this situation.

During the cool-down periods, be sure to study the edges of the tires. You will be checking to see how far the tire has rolled over. Excessive tire rolling can mean too low an air pressure, inadequate negative camber, the wheel is too narrow for the tire, or the roll stiffness is inadequate, as well as several other problems. Test and change the settings until you have the proper setup.

TIRE TEMPERATURES

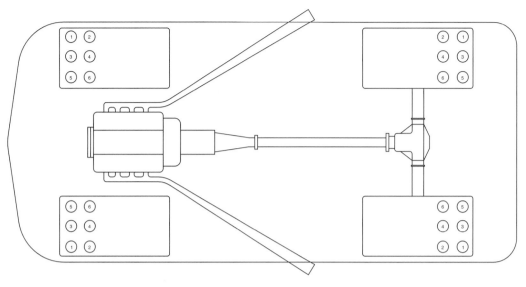

1. TAKE TEMPERATURE READINGS USING A PYROMETER. PUSH PYROMETER PROBE INTO TIRE SURFACE AT LEAST 1/16" FOR ACCURATE READINGS.

2. READ TEMPERATURES AT THE (6) SIX LOCATIONS INDICATED ABOVE AND AVERAGE THE READINGS AT THE OUTSIDE, MIDDLE AND INSIDE FOR EACH TIRE. RECORD YOUR FINDINGS ON A COPY OF THE CHASSIS & TIRE TESTING SHEETS AT THE BACK OF THIS BOOK.

3. COMPARE THE AVERAGE TEMPERATURE READINGS ON EACH TIRE INDIVIDUALLY. THE TEMPERATURES SHOULD BE WITHIN 5^0 OF EACH OTHER.

INDICATION	SUGGESTION	AVERAGE TEMPERATURE READING		
		5 / 6	3 / 4	1 / 2
WELL-BALANCED SETUP	ADD HORSEPOWER	184	185	185
TIRE IS LOADED EXCESSIVELY ON OUTSIDE INDICATING LACK OF NEGATIVE CAMBER, INADEQUATE ROLL STIFFNESS OR EXCESSIVE TOE IN.	CHECK TOE, INCREASE NEGATIVE CAMBER, ROLLBAR SIZE OR SPRING RATE	164	187	211
TIRE IS LOADED EXCESSIVELY ON INSIDE INDICATING EXCESSIVE NEGATIVE CAMBER, TOO MUCH ROLL STIFFNESS OR EXCESSIVE TOE OUT.	CHECK TOE, DECREASE NEGATIVE CAMBER, ROLLBAR SIZE OR SPRING RATE	188	165	145
TIRE IS LOADED EXCESSIVELY ON MIDDLE INDICATING OVER-INFLATION OR IMPROPER RIM WIDTH/TIRE SECTION WIDTH RELATIONSHIP (RIM TOO NARROW FOR TIRE).	DECREASE AIR PRESSURE, GO TO WIDER RIM OR SMALLER SECTION WIDTH TIRE.	178	210	176
TIRE IS LOADED EXCESSIVELY ON EDGES INDICATING UNDER-INFLATION OR IMPROPER RIM WIDTH/TIRE SECTION WIDTH RELATIONSHIP (RIM TOO WIDE FOR TIRE).	INCREASE AIR PRESSURE 5 p.si., GO TO NEXT SMALLER RIM WIDTH OR WIDER SECTION WIDTH TIRE.	205	186	204
TIRE IS LOADED EXCESSIVELY ON MIDDLE AND OUTSIDE EDGE INDICATING A COMBINATION OF OVER-INFLATION OR IMPROPER RIM/TIRE WIDTH RELATIONSHIP OR LACK OF ROLL STIFFNESS OR NEGATIVE CAMBER.	DECREASE AIR PRESSURE OR GO TO WIDER RIM OR SMALLER SECTION WIDTH TIRE, AND INCREASE ROLL STIFFNESS OR ADD NEGATIVE CAMBER.	148	185	189
TIRE IS LOADED EXCESSIVELY ON MIDDLE AND INSIDE EDGE INDICATING A COMBINATION OF OVER-INFLATION OR IMPROPER RIM/TIRE WIDTH RELATIONSHIP AND TOO MUCH ROLL STIFFNESS OR NEGATIVE CAMBER.	DECREASE AIR PRESSURE OR GO TO WIDER RIM OR SMALLER SECTION WIDTH TIRE, AND DECREASE ROLL STIFFNESS OR REDUCE NEGATIVE CAMBER.	210	207	163
TIRE IS LOADED EXCESSIVELY ON OUTSIDE EDGE INDICATING A COMBINATION OF UNDER-INFLATION OR IMPROPER RIM/TIRE WIDTH RELATIONSHIP AND LACK OF ROLL STIFFNESS OR NEGATIVE CAMBER.	INCREASE AIR PRESSURE OR GO TO NEXT SMALLER RIM OR SMALLER SECTION WIDTH TIRE, AND INCREASE ROLL STIFFNESS OR ADD NEGATIVE CAMBER.	148	147	204
TIRE IS LOADED EXCESSIVELY ON INSIDE EDGE INDICATING A COMBINATION OF UNDER-INFLATION OR IMPROPER RIM/TIRE WIDTH RELATIONSHIP AND TOO MUCH ROLL STIFFNESS OR NEGATIVE CAMBER.	INCREASE AIR PRESSURE OR GO TO NEXT SMALLER RIM OR SMALLER SECTION WIDTH TIRE, AND DECREASE ROLL STIFFNESS OR REDUCE NEGATIVE CAMBER.	210	161	163
TIRE IS OVER HEATED AND PROBABLY BEYOND BEST OPERATING RANGE	GO TO HARDER COMPOUND TIRE OR WIDER RIM AND TIRE SETUP	251	253	257
TIRE IS BELOW OPTIMUM OPERATING TEMPERATURE	GO TO SOFTER COMPOUND TIRE OR SMALLER RIM AND TIRE COMBINATION	146	144	145

Be sure to check tire pressures and temperatures immediately after a test. This is to determine how well the changes are working. When you have found the optimum hot tire pressure, take a tire pressure reading after the tires have cooled completely to give you a cold setting, and make a note in your test binder for future reference.

Set Brake Bias—Once you have accumulated the data from the combinations set out in your original plan, you must set the brake bias and determine the shock settings necessary for sudden transition changes. This is best done immediately after the car makes two laps left and two laps right on the 200-ft. circle to ensure the tires are up to temperature. Have the driver do the maximum stopping efforts, adjusting the brake proportioning a half round at a time until all four wheels are on the verge of lockup at the same time.

TESTING FOR DRAG RACING

Setting up a production Mustang for drag racing is considerably simpler than corner racing. Unfortunately, it is difficult to find a place to do the testing without going to a drag strip. Even then, access to the track can be limited due to the large number of cars that may be competing or testing. You may have to

21. During the break evaluate the handling with the driver. Determine if the car is pushing the front end (understeer) at maximum circling speed or if the rear end is loose and the car is trying to spin (oversteer).

22. Based on the information determined in the previous step, make your first change. Note exactly what change you made on a new test sheet. Before making a component change, you should evaluate the Polaroid picture to determine if the body roll is excessive. A change to spring rates may be necessary before addressing roll stiffness. At this point it becomes important to understand what causes a car to understeer or oversteer.

23. Follow steps 8 through 21 and run a second set of tests. Continue the testing, experimenting with different spring rates and roll bars. Don't forget to keep accurate records of every change you make.

24. When you have completed testing at the 200-ft. circle, take your best settings and try them at the 300-ft. line.

By the way, if you race in the rain, skidpad testing in the wet will give you a tremendous advantage over the competition the next time you have to run in the rain.

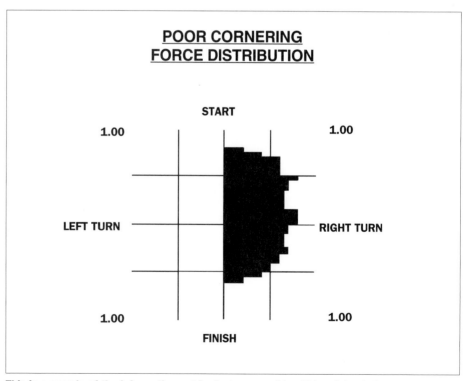

This is a sample of the information a g-Analyst can provide. This print-out shows poor cornering force distribution. The uneven lines show that either the car or driver (or both) are having trouble maintaining full cornering power throughout the corner. The g-Analyst can also record and display acceleration, deceleration (braking) and quarter-mile E.T. If you're serious about competition and superior handling, this is a worthwhile purchase.

Between test rounds download the information from your g-Analyst and compare the results to previous tests.

Performing a Test

Unlike road racing, it is considerably more difficult to measure launch without a Vericom or *g*–Analyst. With one of these computers you perform all testing quickly with accurate results. If you don't have access to one, you will need to set up a launch track 10-ft. wide and 100 ft. long for comparative time measurement. Although current launch rates are typically discussed in terms of 60-ft. times, 60 ft. is pretty short, making it difficult for someone to accurately time the launch in that distance, especially if the car is fast. Without a Vericom or *g*–Analyst, the longer track will give more accurate test results. Bright orange or red plastic 16-oz. drinking cups taped to the pavement 20 ft. apart will provide boundaries for the 100-ft. launch section. Align the car with the front wheels at the starting line. Tape a large brightly colored drinking cup to the ground just outside the driver's door that can be used as a reference for easy staging during the testing.

Before testing, make sure the driver and stopwatch operator (timer) understand the test procedures and hand signals you have designated. The timer should have the stopwatch mounted to a clipboard next to the data sheet. When the testing starts, the timer should be standing 20 ft. to the side of the 100-ft. markers. To avoid biasing the launch time based on the sound, the timer should wear pistol shooter's type ear protectors. With his ears covered, the timer will have to rely on his eyes to see the movement of the car to start the stopwatch. The following is a typical drag racing test:

1. Check the alignment settings on the front end and set to maximum caster, 0° camber and 1/8" toe–in, with the front end jacked up about 2" from the at-rest ride height.

2. Adjust the shocks to full soft.

3. Set the initial air pressure in your slicks at about 15 to 18 lbs.

4. Air the front tires to 40 lbs.

5. Inflate the Air Lift bags in the rear springs to 15 lbs. left and 20 lbs. right.

6. Warm the engine to bring the oil up to operating temperature.

7. If you are running slicks, pour two puddles of water at least 30 ft. away from the starting line and directly behind it. Back the car into the water where the slicks rest directly in the middle. Hold the line–lok or front brakes (assumes you have adjusted the rear drums to reduce contact) and do a burn-out in the water to heat the tires. Release the line–lok and let the car spin out of the water to dry the tires. Do not do this if you are running treaded tires. The water will remain in the treads and trash your launch.

8. Immediately following the water burn-out, move up to the line and do a dry hop, which is essentially a false start.

9. Stage your car using the bright drinking cup you set up for a staging reference.

10. Test the launch, varying the engine speed 500 rpm at a time, until the slicks can no longer hold. Then, back down the rpm 100 at a time until the bite returns. Have the timer record the time and engine rpm for every launch.

11. Have someone with a Polaroid camera take pictures of your launch when you have reached the optimum acceleration rate. He or she should take pictures of the rear slicks and the front end.

12. When you have reached the

optimum launch rate with the current settings, take a break and evaluate the data. Pay close attention to the squat in the rear and the rise of the front end in the pictures. If you are having to launch below the maximum torque point of the engine you need additional traction. Drop the air pressure 2 lbs. in the slicks and reduce the Air Lift bag inflation 2 lbs. each side. If your testing indicates you are having to launch well above the maximum torque point of the engine, you will need to reduce the bite. Increase the rebound rate on the front struts to slow the transfer rate. Decreasing the air pressure in the front tires 5 lbs. each and increasing the air pressure in the slicks can also be used to fine tune. If the car bites too hard and hops, increase the Air Lift bag inflation rate to 24 to 28 lbs., depending on how severe the hop is.

13. Make one change at a time and run three launches to evaluate the change. If there is no improvement, revert to the original setting and try a different approach.

Repeat these tests until you have the car launching at maximum rate with the fastest 100 ft. times. Don't be afraid to try different combinations. There is no magic to this, just methodical testing. As with every form of motor racing, the more accurate and consistent you make your testing, the faster you will be able to go. Again take your time and keep good records.

SUMMARY

The data gathered during skidpad or launch testing will provide more insight into how to set up your car than can be accomplished in many weekends of racing. How careful and consistent you take the measurements will determine the quality and reliability of your data. Take your time and record every condition and change associated with the testing. This means track temperature, humidity, surface temperature and condition as well as driver attitude. Don't forget to record the engine settings, timing, fuel pressure, and ignition retard, if applicable, as well as the axle ratio you are running. The changes you make may be simple and add only small amounts to the perfor-mance of your car. However, it is only through testing that you can maximize what you have. Again, all things being equal, it is the little things that win races. ■

Good luck and always remember...
Keep the rubber side down!

SPARE PARTS FOR RACING

	Autocross	Road Racing	Drag Racing
Radiator cap		X	X
Radiator hoses & bypass hose	X	X	X
Radiator hose clamps	X	X	X
Serpentine belt	X	X	X
Oil	X	X	X
Oil filter		X	X
Spark plugs		X	X
Plug wires		X	X
Cap & rotor		X	X
Coil		X	X
ECU Computer		X	
Freeze plugs		X	
Rear axle grease		X	
Transmission grease		X	
Power steering fluid	X	X	
2 qt. Ford HD Brake Fluid	X	X	
Swaybars	X	X	
Springs		X	
Shock & strut		X	X
Brake pads	X	X	
Brake hoses		X	

	Autocross	Road Racing	Drag Racing
Lug nuts	X	X	X
Swaybar end links		X	
Control arms		X	
Control arm bolts		X	
Trailing arms		X	
Trailing arm bolts		X	
Spindles		X	
Rotors		X	
Axle		X	
Gearbox		X	X
Differential/clutches		X	
Fuel line coupling lock	X	X	X
Thermostat discs 1/2" – 1-1/4"		X	
Gasket:			
Heads	X	X	
Header	X	X	
Intake	X	X	
Valve cover	X	X	
Oil pan	X	X	
Timing cover	X	X	
Head bolts	X	X	
Rod bearings	X	X	
Main bearings	X	X	
Oil pump	X	X	
Oil pump shaft	X	X	
Water pump	X		
Alternator	X		
Throttle cable	X		
Clutch cable	X		
Pressure plate, disc & TO bearing	X	X	
Motor mounts	X	X	
U–joints/spare driveshaft	X	X	

Nice Optionals:

  Vericom or g–Analyst

  Gasoline air compressor

  Generator

  10 Ton Port–a–Power

  Ford 9000 Tractor w/ completely outfitted trailer

  Paid Pit Crew

APPENDIX

Chassis
Data Sheet

1

Car

Setup by: _____

Date _____

Springs Front: Manufacturer _____ Part No. _____

Height _____ " Rate _____ lbs./in.

Rear: Manufacturer _____ Part No. _____

Height _____ " Rate _____ lbs./in.

Swaybars Front: Manufacturer _____ Part No. _____

Size _____ " Rate _____ lbs./in.

Rear: Manufacturer _____ Part No. _____

Size _____ " Rate _____ lbs./in.

End Links Manufacturer _____ Part No. _____

Length _____ " Bias Correction Left _____" Right _____"

Struts Manufacturer _____ Part No. _____

Length _____ "

Shocks Rear: Manufacturer _____ Part No. _____

Length _____ "

Brake Pads

Front: Manufacturer _____ Part No. _____

Compound _____

Rear: Manufacturer _____ Part No. _____

Compound _____

Corner Weights LF_____ lbs. RF_____ lbs. F/R _____ %

LR_____ lbs. RR_____ lbs. LF/RR _____ % RF/LR _____ %

Chassis
Data Sheet

Car

Testing Setup: Track: _____

Springs   Height Adjustment   LF _____ "   RF _____ "

LR _____ "   RR _____ "

Struts   Settings:

LF: Compression _____ Turns   Rebound _____ Turns

RF: Compression _____ Turns   Rebound _____ Turns

Shocks   Settings:

LR: Compression _____ Turns   Rebound _____ Turns

RR: Compression _____ Turns   Rebound _____ Turns

Air Lift   Air Pressure: LR _____ P.S.I.   RR _____ P.S.I.

Upper Trailing Arms   Preload Bias: LR _____ Turns   RR _____ Turns

Brake Bias   Rear _____ %   Setting _____ Turns

Tires   Air Pressure: LF _____ P.S.I.   RF _____ P.S.I.

LR _____ P.S.I.   RR _____ P.S.I.

Rotor Thickness   LF _____ "   RF _____ "

LR _____ "   RR _____ "

Camber   LF _____ °   RF _____ °

Caster   LF _____ °   RF _____ °

Toe   _____ "

Bump/Roll Steer
Worksheet

Car

Test by: _____

Date _____

Test

	1	2	3	4	5
4					
3.5					
3					
2.5					
2					
1.5					
1					
.5					
0					
-.5					
-1.5					
-2					
-2.5					
-3					
-3.5					
-4					

Adjustments

TEST	Left Tie-rod Shim	Rack Elevation Change	Right Tie-rod Shim
1			
2			
3			
4			
5			

Notes: _____

_____

_____

_____

_____

_____

_____

Test:

Center of Gravity
Worksheet

Date: _____

Car: _____

Fuel Wt.: _____ lbs.

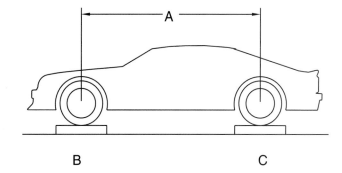

B   C

Measure:

Level Attitude

(A) Wheelbase
(B_L) Left Front Wheel Weight
(B_R) Right Front Wheel Weight
(C_L) Left Rear Wheel Weight
(C_R) Right Rear Wheel Weight

Elevated Rear Attitude

(D) Wheelbase
(E) Vertical Axle Height(at least 24")
(F_L) Left Front Wheel Weight
(F_R) Right Front Wheel Weight
(G) Front Track Width

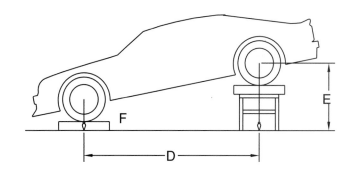

$$\text{Front-to-Rear CG} = A \times \left(\frac{C_L + C_R}{B_L + B_R + C_R + C_L} \right)$$

$$\text{Lateral CG} = -G \times \frac{G}{2} \left[\left(\frac{B_L + C_L}{B_L + B_R + C_R + C_L} \right) \right]$$

Negative
Left CG

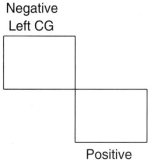

Positive
Right CG

$$\text{Vertical CG} = \frac{A \times D \times (F_L + [F_L) - (B_L + B_R)_R]}{E \times (B_L + B_L + C_R + C_R)}$$

Corner

Test No. ☐

Date _____

Car _____

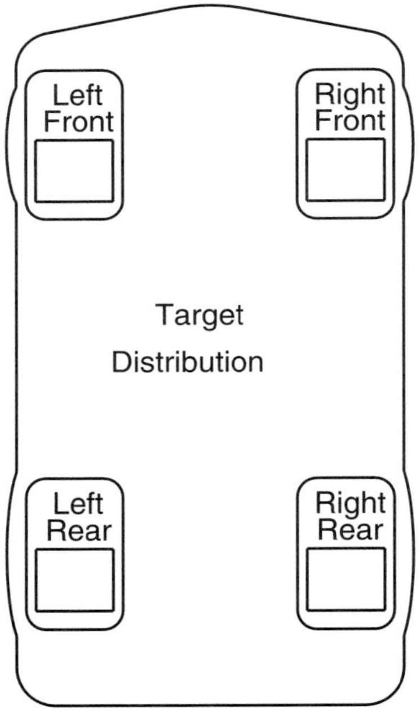

Fuel Wt. _____ lbs.

With Driver ☐   Without Driver ☐

Weights

	Left Side	Right Side
Ride Weight: Front	☐	☐
Height: Front		
Weight: Rear	☐	☐
Ride Height: Rear		

Total Weight ☐

Side Weight ☐
Side % ☐

Front Weight | Rear Weight | Front-to-Rear %

LF/RR Weight | LF/RR % | RF/LR Weight | RF/LR %

Target Distribution

Right Front ☐   Right Rear ☐

Left Front ☐   Left Rear ☐

Location

Front-to-Rear CG ☐

Lateral CG ☐

Comments: _____

Track Results: _____

Lateral Acceleration Testing

Date _____

Car _____

Tires _____

Skidpad Diameter _____ ft.

Ambient Temperature _____ °

Surface Temperature _____ °

r

Skidpad

r = radius of skidpad

t = lap time in seconds

$$g = \frac{1.225 \times r}{t^2}$$

	Outside Tire	Suspension Settings			Results	
	Air PSI	Camber	Caster	Toe	Lap E.T.	g
CCW Test 1						
CCW Test 2						
CCW Test 3						
CW Test 1						
CW Test 2						
CW Test 3						
CCW Test 1 Front						
CCW Test 2 Rear						
CCW Test 3						
CW Test 1						
CW Test 2						
CW Test 3						

1. Lap skidpad circumference at moderate pace to bring tires up to operating temperatures.
2. Slowly accelerate car to the maximum speed it can run and still stay on the circle.
3. With stopwatch, measure lap times in hundreths of a second.
4. Change directions and test times in opposite rotation.
5. Use "g" formula to calculate lateral acceleration.
6. Make small singular changes to suspension and start over.

Comments: _____

_____

_____

_____

Chassis & Tire Testing

Date ______________________

Car ______________________

Tires ______________________

Driver ______________________

Track ______________________

Ambient Temperature ______°

Surface Temperature ______°

	Air Pressure: Air PSI	Tire Temperature: Average	Tire Temperature: Outside	Tire Temperature: Middle	Tire Temperature: Inside
Base					
Test 1					
Test 2					
Test 3					
Test 4					
Base					
Test 1					
Test 2					
Test 3					
Test 4					

Final Cold Temp
Final Cold Temp
Toe
Camber
Caster
Final Cold Temp
Final Cold Temp

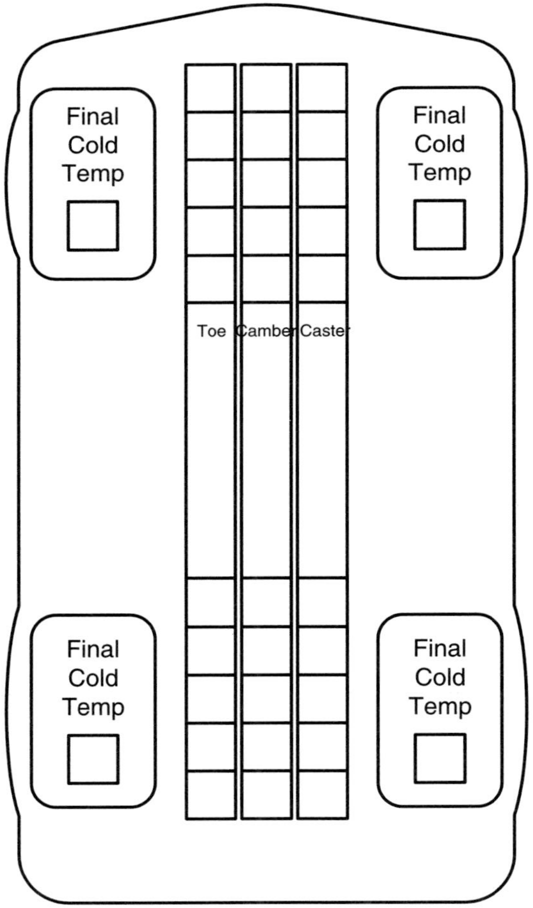

Tire Temperature: Inside	Tire Temperature: Middle	Tire Temperature: Outside	Tire Temperature: Average	Air Pressure: Air PSI	Results: E.T. M.P.H.

Comments: ______________________

Mathis

Pre-Race Checklist

Date _____

Car _____

POWERTRAIN

❑ Engine oil changed since last race, drain and replace it with a synthetic oil. Also replace the filter with a high–performance piece.

❑ Check the valve covers and oil pan bolts. Look for any leaks.

❑ On a race car, drain the transmission fluid and replace with fresh synthetic oil. For a street-driven autocross car this should be changed at least every third event.

❑ Check the input and output shaft seals for leaks. On T–5 gearboxes, the input shaft seals are notorious for leaking and require constant attention. If yours leaks it will pour hot transmission fluid on the clutch every time you stand on the brakes.

❑ On a race car, drain and replace the rear axle gear with a synthetic gear oil.

❑ Check axle seals for leaks, especially if you are running the Moser C–Clip eliminators. These have a history of leaking when subjected to severe corner duty.

❑ Check the driveshaft bolts and condition of U–joints.

❑ Drain the engine, transmission and rear axle catch tanks if applicable. Examine catch tank hoses and clamps for cracking and tightness of fit.

❑ Check the condition of all radiator hoses, paying particular attention to the bypass hose. If they are soft, swollen or showing surface cracks, replace them. Nothing is more irritating than to sit out a race because of a blown hose.

❑ Check the weep hole on the bottom of the water pump. Any signs of water leaking, replace the pump.

❑ Check the radiator water condition and top off. This fluid should be changed at least every third event. Add 4 cans of Redline Water Wetter to keep things cool.

❑ Check the condition of the radiator cap seal. Replace if cracked or brittle.

❑ Remove and examine the serpentine belt. If it has cracks, replace it and save as an emergency spare.

❑ Check the throttle cable for fraying at the throttle body and at the accelerator pedal. Replace if broken strains are showing.

❑ Go over all accessory bracket bolts, checking for ones that may have worked loose. Check the fan clutch bolts also.

❑ Tighten all exhaust manifold or header bolts and replace any missing ones.

❑ On a race car, drain and replace the power steering fluid with fresh synthetic fluid. Street cars being autocrossed should replace this fluid every season. If you have gotten the fluid hot enough to boil, replace it with fresh synthetic fluid.

❑ Change the fuel filter.

❑ Clean or replace the air filter.

❑ Check & top off the water level in the battery with distilled water.

❑ Check battery tie–down bolt(s).

❑ Check the timing.

❑ Check the fuel pressure.

❑ Check and adjust the ignition timing retard if applicable.

❑ Install fresh spark plugs.

❑ Adjust valves, if applicable.

❑ Check all wiring connectors for secure fit.

❑ Check fuel log and fuel lines for leaks .

❑ Check the alternator for signs of bearing failure.

INTERIOR

❑ Check the shifter handle bolts.

❑ Check the brake pedal pad. If it is loose, SuperGlue it down.

❑ Examine the seat belts and safety harnesses. Make sure the latch works correctly.

❑ Examine all roll bar/cage padding. Repair or replace any torn or damaged pieces.

❏ Check the seat mounting brackets and floorpan around the attaching bolts for cracks. Repair as necessary.

❏ Check pressure on Halon fire bottle if applicable.

❏ Vacuum the interior thoroughly. Sand and other small particles fly around inside the car and can get in the driver's eyes, which will break his concentration or force a stop to remedy.

❏ Clean the windows and apply Rain-X to windshield.

❏ Check the rear view mirror for tightness.

❏ Check the clutch pedal action for early signs of imminent failure.

❏ For autocrossing street car, remove old tennis shoes, magazines, golf bags, speaker boxes and all non–racing related paraphernalia from car. This includes the usual junk floating around in the trunk.

CHASSIS

❏ Check camber, caster and toe settings and record in setup diary.

❏ Measure thickness of rotors with calipers or micrometer and compare to factory minimum requirement. Note measurements on data sheet.

❏ Measure thickness of rotor pads and note on data sheet. Examine for unusual wear that might indicate a caliper might be dragging or cocking sideways in guides.

❏ Check all caliper mounting and bracket bolts for tightness. Safety wire as needed.

❏ Examine brake hoses for leaks and signs of wear.

❏ Check wheel bearings and reset bearing preload.

❏ Bleed and flush the brakes with Ford Heavy Duty Brake fluid. This is very important on all cars. Even a street car that is autocrossed needs to have the brake fluid replaced before an event. If you boil the fluid during an event you must bleed and flush the system completely.

❏ Check the #2 crossmember for signs of movement.

❏ Examine the right engine mount for cracks.

❏ Survey all suspension bushings for wear. If you are running rubber bushings in the trailing arms, it is very important to check the upper trailing arm bushings at the frame end.

❏ Check the Panhard bar and bracket for cracks, especially around areas that are welded.

❏ With the car on jackstands under the rocker panels and a handful of wrenches, go over every suspension and exhaust nut and bolt.

❏ Examine the struts and shocks for signs of fluid loss.

❏ Reset struts and shocks and note settings on data sheet.

❏ Check the fuel lines at the tank and safety wire the couplings together.

❏ Slowly examine the entire underside of the car for anything odd.

❏ Torque the lug nuts. Very important.

❏ Inflate the tires to cold racing pressures and note settings on data sheet. Do not overinflate. Excessive tire pressures will stretch the tires and change the stagger. Handling may be affected.

INDEX

ABOUT THE AUTHOR

William "Butch" Mathis was still in high school in 1965 when he first became hooked on Fords. It happened one night when a Weber-carbureted GT-350 rumbled into the local Dairy Queen. Since then, he has been building and racing Shelbys, Boss 302s, SVOs and 5.0 Mustangs. Although a noted CPA and federal tax authority, he is a self-taught engineer who utilizes sophisticated computer programming to design, test and evaluate new ideas. Except for a few years spent building championship-winning Kawasaki road racing motorcycles and high-performance airplanes, he has accumulated thousands of hours designing and testing engine, suspension and chassis components for the Fox Mustang. The popular *Slot Car Mustang* was one of the many test mules he has designed and built for various product evaluations. His company, High-G Performance, specializes in handling and Ford engine performance. He lives in south Texas.

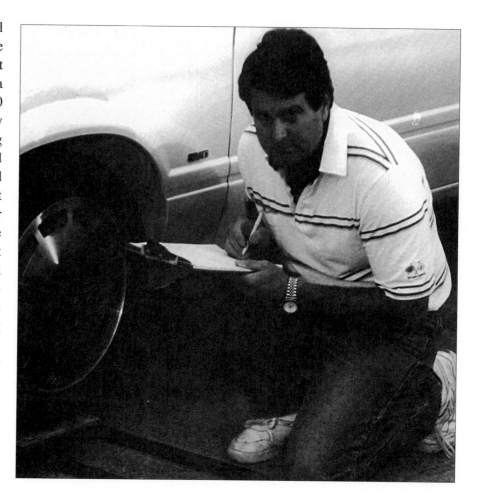

HANDBOOKS

Auto Electrical Handbook: 0-89586-238-7

Auto Upholstery & Interiors: 1-55788-265-7

Brake Handbook: 0-89586-232-8

Car Builder's Handbook: 1-55788-278-9

Street Rodder's Handbook: 0-89586-369-3

Turbo Hydra-matic 350 Handbook: 0-89586-051-1

Welder's Handbook: 1-55788-264-9

BODYWORK & PAINTING

Automotive Detailing: 1-55788-288-6

Automotive Paint Handbook: 1-55788-291-6

Fiberglass & Composite Materials: 1-55788-239-8

Metal Fabricator's Handbook: 0-89586-870-9

Paint & Body Handbook: 1-55788-082-4

Sheet Metal Handbook: 0-89586-757-5

INDUCTION

Holley 4150: 0-89586-047-3

Holley Carburetors, Manifolds & Fuel Injection: 1-55788-052-2

Rochester Carburetors: 0-89586-301-4

Turbochargers: 0-89586-135-6

Weber Carburetors: 0-89586-377-4

PERFORMANCE

Aerodynamics For Racing & Performance Cars: 1-55788-267-3

Baja Bugs & Buggies: 0-89586-186-0

Big-Block Chevy Performance: 1-55788-216-9

Big Block Mopar Performance: 1-55788-302-5

Bracket Racing: 1-55788-266-5

Brake Systems: 1-55788-281-9

Camaro Performance: 1-55788-057-3

Chassis Engineering: 1-55788-055-7

Chevrolet Power: 1-55788-087-5

Ford Windsor Small-Block Performance: 1-55788-323-8

Honda/Acura Performance: 1-55788-324-6

High Performance Hardware: 1-55788-304-1

How to Build Tri-Five Chevy Trucks ('55-'57): 1-55788-285-1

How to Hot Rod Big-Block Chevys:0-912656-04-2

How to Hot Rod Small-Block Chevys:0-912656-06-9

How to Hot Rod Small-Block Mopar Engines: 0-89586-479-7

How to Hot Rod VW Engines:0-912656-03-4

How to Make Your Car Handle:0-912656-46-8

John Lingenfelter: Modifying Small-Block Chevy: 1-55788-238-X

Mustang 5.0 Projects: 1-55788-275-4

Mustang Performance ('79–'93): 1-55788-193-6

Mustang Performance 2 ('79–'93): 1-55788-202-9

1001 High Performance Tech Tips: 1-55788-199-5

Performance Ignition Systems: 1-55788-306-8

Performance Wheels & Tires: 1-55788-286-X

Race Car Engineering & Mechanics: 1-55788-064-6

Small-Block Chevy Performance: 1-55788-253-3

ENGINE REBUILDING

Engine Builder's Handbook: 1-55788-245-2

Rebuild Air-Cooled VW Engines: 0-89586-225-5

Rebuild Big-Block Chevy Engines: 0-89586-175-5

Rebuild Big-Block Ford Engines: 0-89586-070-8

Rebuild Big-Block Mopar Engines: 1-55788-190-1

Rebuild Ford V-8 Engines: 0-89586-036-8

Rebuild Small-Block Chevy Engines: 1-55788-029-8

Rebuild Small-Block Ford Engines:0-912656-89-1

Rebuild Small-Block Mopar Engines: 0-89586-128-3

RESTORATION, MAINTENANCE, REPAIR

Camaro Owner's Handbook ('67–'81): 1-55788-301-7

Camaro Restoration Handbook ('67–'81): 0-89586-375-8

Classic Car Restorer's Handbook: 1-55788-194-4

Corvette Weekend Projects ('68–'82): 1-55788-218-5

Mustang Restoration Handbook('64 1/2–'70): 0-89586-402-9

Mustang Weekend Projects ('64–'67): 1-55788-230-4

Mustang Weekend Projects 2 ('68–'70): 1-55788-256-8

Tri-Five Chevy Owner's ('55–'57): 1-55788-285-1

GENERAL REFERENCE

Auto Math:1-55788-020-4

Fabulous Funny Cars: 1-55788-069-7

Guide to GM Muscle Cars: 1-55788-003-4

Stock Cars!: 1-55788-308-4

MARINE

Big-Block Chevy Marine Performance: 1-55788-297-5